DIAMOND HANDBOOK

Above: Joseph Asscher cleaving the famous Cullinan diamond, which at 3,105 carats was the world's largest diamond (February 10th, 1908). It was found in the Premier Mine in South Africa and cut into nine principal diamonds. Cullinan I, the largest diamond, is mounted in the British Royal Sceptre and weighs 530.20 carats. *Photo from the Royal Asscher Diamond Company.*

Right, Title Page: 13.24 carat emerald-cut D-color VVS2 diamond lady's platinum ring, which sold for $960,000 in May 2007. *Ring from Joseph DuMouchelle International Auctioneers; photo by David Behl.*

DIAMOND HANDBOOK

A Practical Guide to Diamond Evaluation

2nd Edition

Renée Newman

I·J·P
International Jewelry Publications
Los Angeles

First Edition 2005
Second Edition 2008
Updated 2010

International Jewelry Publications
P.O. Box 13384
Los Angeles, CA 90013-0384 USA

(Inquiries should be accompanied by a self-addressed, stamped envelope.)

Printed in Singapore

Library of Congress Cataloging-in-Publication Data

Newman, Renée.
Diamond handbook : A practical guide to diamond evaluation / Renée Newman. - - 2nd ed.
p. cm. - - (Newman gem & jewelry series)
Includes bibliographical references and index.
ISBN 978-0-929975-39-9 (alk. paper)
1. Diamonds - - Purchasing - - Handbooks, manuals, etc. I. Title.
TS753.N44 2008
736'.23 - - dc22 2007026749

Front cover photo:
Platinum ring featuring a 1.15 carat Fancy gray-blue diamond flanked by two Fancy Deep pink round brilliants and accented by 2.66 carats of baguettes and princess cuts. *Ring from J. Landau Diamonds; photo by Leonard Derse.*

Back cover photo:
Three-stone Fancy Light blue, Fancy Vivid yellow and Fancy Intense pink diamond ring by J. Landau Diamonds. *Photo by Leonard Derse.*

Contents

Acknowledgments

I would like to express my appreciation to the following people and companies for their contribution to the *Diamond Handbook*:

Ernie and Regina Goldberger of the Josam Diamond Trading Corporation. This book could never have been written without the experience and knowledge I gained from working with them. Many of the loose diamonds pictured in this book are or were part of their collection.

Eve Alfillé, David Atlas, C.R. Beesley, Charles Carmona, Jim Caudill, Paul Cassarino, Adam Daniels, Branko Deljanin, Nick DelRe, Jerry Ehrenwald, Pete & Bobbi Flusser, Al Gilbertson, Michael Goldstein, Alan Hodgkinson, Mickey Ishida, Wolf Kuehn, Joshua Lamothe, Gail Levine, Dr. Daniel Nyfeler, Lynn Ramsey, Barry Rogoff, Howard Rubin, Debra Sawatsky, Michael Schachter, Sindi Schloss, Tom Tashey, Jennifer Thornton Davis, John S. White, Sharrie Woodring, Peter Yantzer, and Gary Zimmerman. They have made valuable suggestions, corrections and comments regarding the portions of the book they examined. They are not responsible for any possible errors, nor do they necessarily endorse the material contained in this book.

The teachers at the GIA. They helped me obtain the technical background needed to write a book such as this.

Ebert & Co., Mark Gronlund, J. Landau, Inc., Lisa Poff Cox and D & E Singer. Their stones or jewelry have been used for some of the photographs.

A & Z Pearls, Abe Mor Diamond Cutters, American Gem Society, Amgad, Inc, Avi Paz Group, Baroka Creations, Bez Ambar Diamonds, Inc., Britestar Diamond Co., Paul Cassarino, Dali Diamond Co., Diamco, Joseph Dumouchelle Intl. Auctioneers, EGL-USA, Exroyal Co., Finesse Diamonds, Pete Flusser. Gem International, Gemological Institute of America, Gemstone Designs, William Goldberg Corp, Yuval Harary Diamonds, Alan Hodgkinson, HRD, Doron Isaac, Scott Keating, Korloff, J. Landau, Inc., Arthur & Natacha Langerman, Lili Diamonds, Gail Levine, Douglas Mays, Moussaieff Jewellers, National Diamond Syndicate, Bertrand Pizzin, RCDC Corp., Todd Reed, Royal Asscher Diamond Co., Mark Silverstein, Ernest Slotar, Inc., Suberi Bros, Trillion Diamond Co, Tycoon Jewelry, Michael Werdiger Inc., Harry Winston, Inc., Robert Weldon, Sharrie Woodring. Photos and/or diagrams from them have been reproduced in this book.

Don Nelson, Joyce Ng and Frank Chen. They've provided technical assistance.

Louise Harris Berlin. She's spent hours carefully editing the *Diamond Handbook*. Thanks to her, this book is much easier to read and understand.

My sincere thanks to all of these contributors for their kindness and help.

Preface

When my first book, the *Diamond Ring Buying Guide,* was published in 1989, it was designed as a basic guide to evaluating diamonds and ring mountings. Over the years, I've updated it and added many color photos and new information. However, in order to maintain a competitive price, I've had to limit the total number of pages for that book.

Still, readers requested information on diamond grading reports, appraisals, antique jewelry, recutting, and branded diamonds—topics not included in the *Diamond Ring Buying Guide.* They also wanted me to expand on subjects that I'd already covered, such as fluorescence, synthetic diamonds, and fancy shapes. The logical solution was to write a new book on diamonds, called the *Diamond Handbook,* which was published in 2005. Details on judging diamond quality were also included in that book, but were presented differently.

Major changes have occurred during the past three years. New diamond reports have been introduced with cut grades that take into account optical brilliance. More sophisticated diamond treatments have been introduced. The supply of man-made diamonds has increased. Fancy color diamonds are more available. As a result, I've added to this new edition of the *Diamond Handbook:*

- ♦ A chapter on fancy-color diamonds and how they're evaluated
- ♦ A chapter on diamond treatments and how to detect them
- ♦ A chapter on evaluating light performance in diamonds
- ♦ Additional information on man-made (synthetic) diamonds

I've updated the entire book and changed several antique jewelry photos and replaced many of the black and white photos with color photos.

The *Diamond Handbook* is designed to be a complement to the *Diamond Ring Buying Guide.* If you are looking for information on gold, platinum, settings styles, ring mountings, diamond care, and detecting diamond imitations, you should purchase the *Diamond Ring Buying Guide.* If you want a more advanced, in-depth guide to diamond evaluation, cutting styles, cut grading, lab reports, antique jewelry and detecting lab-grown diamonds and treatments, then this new edition of the *Diamond Handbook* is for you.

Both books share a common goal—to help you visually evaluate diamonds. Grading reports don't tell you everything you should know about a diamond, and they are too expensive to be a worthwhile option when purchasing small diamonds. Therefore to be a savvy buyer and seller, you should learn how to make visual judgments about their quality. If you're able to do this, you'll not only be able to get better buys, you'll be able to help your customers have a greater appreciation for the diamonds they select. The *Diamond Handbook* will help you in that endeavor.

1

Basic Facts about Diamonds

Compared to many other gems, diamonds are relatively abundant. Why then, are they so prized? Marketing campaigns, of course, have spurred a demand for diamonds. However, the diamond mystique emerged long before television and De Beers (PR firms) ever existed.

Because of its outstanding durability, the diamond was revered as far back as 800 B.C. in India, the first major source of diamond. In fact, it owes its name to its unparalleled hardness. "Diamond" is derived from the ancient Greek word *Adamas*, which means "unconquerable." Uncut diamonds were worn as talismans that could protect soldiers in battle and ward off illness, snakes, thieves, floods, and evil spirits. Eventually the diamond became coveted for its extraordinary cutting power.

The diamond's distinctive clarity and luster added to its intrigue and accorded it the virtues of purification and enlightenment. In 1681, the famous gem dealer Jean Baptiste Tavernier wrote, "The diamond is the most precious of all stones, and it is the article of trade to which I am most devoted." (Book II, Chapter 15 of *Voyages des Indes* [*Travels in India*]. The diamond became the "king of gems" because of its intrinsic properties and the resulting supernatural powers associated with it. Advances in diamond cutting brought out its beauty as a center stone and also made it the perfect complement to other gemstones.

What is Diamond?

Diamond is a mineral that is a crystalline form of carbon, the element C. Like graphite, diamond's chemical formula is C. However, the carbon atoms in graphite are arranged in layers and have weak bonds between the layers, making it soft and slippery. The carbon atoms in diamond are arranged in tight three-dimensional patterns with strong bonds in all directions, which makes diamond the hardest natural substance and an ideal gem for everyday wear.

How are Diamonds Formed?

Diamonds form between 90 and 120 miles (about 140 and 190 kilometers) under the surface of the earth, deep beneath the continents. This is where ideal conditions for natural diamond formation can exist—a temperature range of 1652°F to 2372°F (900°F to 1300°F) and pressures between 45,000 and 60,000 times the normal sea-level pressure (45 to 60 kilobars). Diamonds form there in two types of rock called peridotite and eclogite. They may remain below the earth for millions and even billions of years until conditions within the earth's mantle lead to violent eruptions that blast the already-formed diamonds and magma rapidly to the surface of the earth, leaving carrot-shaped conduits, called **pipes**. Then the diamonds that are not blasted onto the surface may stay in the pipes for millions of more years before somcone discovers them. The host rock of the diamonds in the pipe is kimberlite or lamproite. (Source: GIA *Diamonds & Diamond Grading* Course 2002, #4 pp 7–9)

Often erosion occurs, carrying the diamonds into neighboring rivers and streams, and even into the ocean. Since diamonds are heavy, they sink to the bottom when caught in small whirlpools. Deposits in rivers and streams are called **alluvial deposits** and often contain higher quality diamonds than primary deposits within a diamond pipe because the better ones are more likely to survive the water's tumbling action against rocks. If the diamonds reach the ocean, they are called **marine deposits**.

Where are Diamonds Found?

For centuries, diamonds were only found in India. Then in the 1700's, just as production began to wane in India, diamonds were discovered in Brazil, and it became the world's major supplier. Both countries were overshadowed by South Africa's huge deposits, which appeared in the late 1800's. Since then, Russia, Botswana, Australia, Congo, Canada, Angola, the Republic of Congo and Namibia have become major diamond sources. Diamonds have also been mined in China, Sierra Leone, Ivory Coast, Venezuela, Ghana, Liberia, Sierra Leone, Guyana Tanzania, Indonesia, Guinea, Arkansas and Colorado.

Country	% World Prod 2001–2005	% World Value 2001–2005
USSR/Russia	23	21
Australia	20	5
Botswana	19	26
Congo/Zaire/ DRC	15	5
South Africa	9	13
Canada	6	11
Angola	4	10
Namibia	1	5
Ghana	1	–

From *Gems & Gemology*, Summer 2007, pp 114, 115

A Closer Look at Diamond's Remarkable Properties

Hardness

Diamond's atoms have a strong interlocking atomic structure and are exceptionally close together. As a result, diamond is the hardest natural substance; in other words, it's more resistant to scratching and abrasion.

Diamond has a value of 10 on the Mohs scale of hardness, which rates hardness from 1 to 10, with 10 being the hardest. The intervals between the numbers on the scale are not equal, especially between 9 and 10. For example, diamond is more than 100 times harder than ruby, which has a Mohs hardness value of 9. Because of diamond's superior hardness, it's an invaluable industrial material for cutting, grinding, polishing and drilling.

Even though diamond is exceptionally resistant to scratches and abrasions, it is not immune to breakage and chipping. In some directions of the diamonds, there are planes where the bond is weaker than in other directions because in these directions there are fewer bonds per unit area. If a diamond is hit in the right spot with the right force, it can split in these directions. The tendency for a mineral to split along specific crystal planes is called **cleavage.** In their *Gem Reference Guide*, the Gemological Institute of America (GIA) describes the diamond's toughness (resistance to breakage) as good in cleavage directions and exceptional in other directions. By contrast, the GIA describes the toughness of tanzanite as fair to poor.

Brightness

The GIA and American Gem Society (AGS) define **brightness** as the amount of white light returned to the observer. Brightness is often called **brilliance** in the trade. However, brilliance can also have a broader meaning. For example, in her book *Diamond Grading ABC,* Pagel-Theisen states that the term "brilliance" involves several distinct optical processes in a diamond— internal brilliance, external brilliance (luster), dispersive brilliance (fire), and scintillation brilliance (sparkle) (pp 176-177). The AGS defines brilliance as "brightness plus positive contrast." In other words, besides appearing bright, a brilliant diamond has an attractive distribution of contrasting dark and bright areas.

For the sake of precision, this book uses the term "brightness" to specifically refer to the intensity of internal and external light return. Diamond has a greater potential for brightness than any other natural gemstone. This is because of diamond's extreme hardness, adamantine luster, lack of color, and high refractive index (the degree to which light is bent as it passes through a stone). The proportions, polish, transparency, color and clarity of the diamond all affect its brightness.

To fully understand why diamonds can be so bright, you need some basic information about light. When a ray of light strikes a diamond at an angle, it is split into two rays. One part of the ray is reflected off the surface of the stone and the other part enters the diamond as in figure 1.1.

Notice the perpendicular dotted line in the diagram that goes through the crown of the stone and that is labeled "normal." The **normal** is an imaginary line at a 90-degree angle to the point where light hits the surface of the diamond. It's used to measure the angle where light meets the surface (**angle of incidence)** and the angle at which light bounces off (**angle of reflection**).

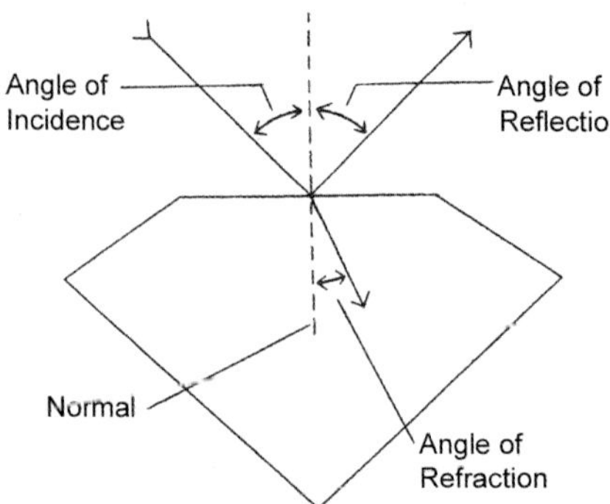

Fig. 1.1 Angles of refraction and reflection

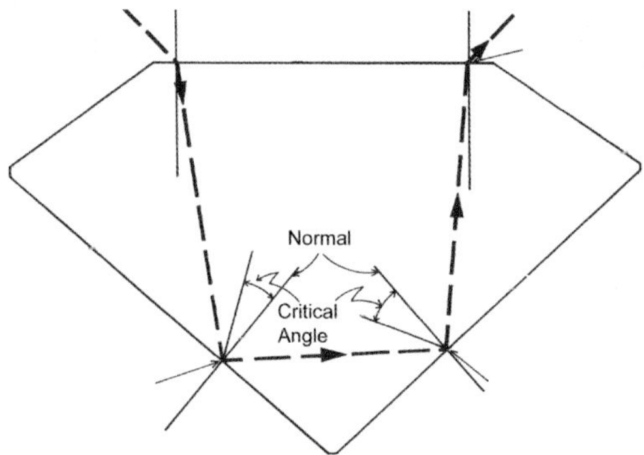

Fig. 1.2 Critical angle and normal

The greater the angle of incidence the more light is reflected from the surface. (The angle of incidence and the angle of reflection are always the same.) Maximum light reflection occurs when rays strike almost parallel to the surface of a diamond. Maximum penetration into the stone occurs when a ray strikes the diamond perpendicular to the surface; the ray is transmitted through the diamond without changing direction. The carbon atoms, however, slow its speed.

When a light ray passes through the surface of a diamond at an angle, the velocity of that light not only decreases, the ray bends and changes direction and bends. This change in speed and direction is called **refraction**. The ratio of the speed of light in air to its speed in a gemstone is called the **refractive index (RI)**. If all other factors are equal, the higher the refractive index of a gem, the greater its brilliance. The refractive index of diamond is 2.417, which is higher than that of other transparent, natural gemstones that are typically mounted in jewelry. Synthetic moissanite (silicon carbide), a diamond imitation, does have a higher RI—about 2.670.

The angle inside the diamond between the normal and a light ray that has entered the stone and been bent (refracted) is called the **angle of refraction** (see figure 1.1). After the ray enters the stone, it may exit out the pavilion if, for example, the diamond's pavilion is too deep. This creates **unplanned light leakage**. If a diamond is properly proportioned, the light ray can be reflected against inner surfaces of the diamond and reflected back out the crown of the diamond causing **planned light leakage**. This reflection of light out the crown without loss of any of the light is called **total internal reflection**.

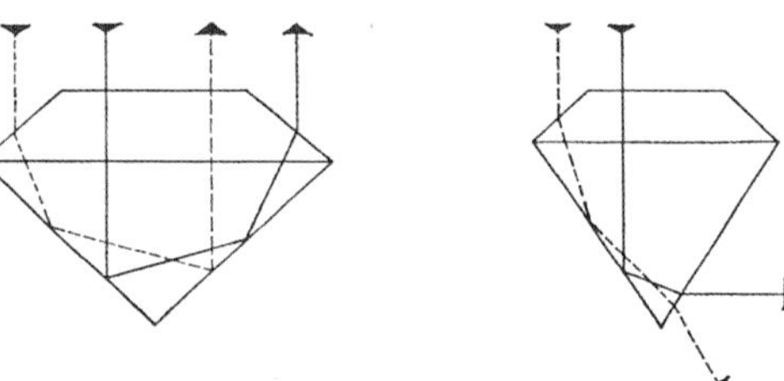

Fig. 1.3 Left: planned light leakage and total internal reflection, right: unplanned light leakage.

Notice the angles labeled **critical angle** in figure 1.2. This is the largest angle from the normal at which light rays can escape from the interior of the diamond. If light strikes an inner surface at an angle greater than the critical angle it will be internally reflected. The critical angle is directly related to the refractive index (RI). The higher the RI, the smaller the critical angle. The critical angle of diamond is 24°26' (about 24.5 degrees). Since most diamond simulants (imitations) such as cubic zirconia, glass, and colorless sapphire have a larger critical angle, it is easier for light to pass through them when they're faceted. As a result, the simulants have a lower brightness and are more likely to display a see-through effect, which allows you to read print through the stone. This is one means of distinguishing diamond from many imitations.

FIRE

If you look at a diamond under a light bulb or spotlight, you can usually see flashes of rainbow colors like those seen through a prism. This attractive phenomenon is called **dispersion** by mineralogists and **fire** by diamond dealers and jewelers.

White light is comprised of many different components (the spectral colors) and each has a different wavelength which means that a diamond (or a glass prism) bends each color at a different angle, thus splitting white light up into its spectral colors, creating "fire." The angle of refraction for red, for example, is different from the angle of refraction for violet.

Diamond's dispersion of light is among the highest of any natural transparent gem (0.044—the difference in refractive index between a red ray and violet ray passing through the gem). Even though every diamond has the same dispersion value, the amount of fire varies depending on how the diamond is cut. Chapter 4 explains how the cut affects diamond fire.

THERMAL CONDUCTIVITY

A material's ability to transfer heat is called its **thermal conductivity**. Diamond's thermal conductivity is higher than that of any other material, which is why diamonds feel cool to the touch. This property makes diamond invaluable as heat sinks for electronics, space exploration and industrial usage.

RESISTANCE TO CHEMICALS

Untreated diamond is resistant to all chemicals. Good-quality, untreated diamonds can be boiled in acid and then steam cleaned. Don't do this to other gems. It's easier to clean dirty diamonds safely than any other gem, which is why diamonds are ideal for everyday wear.

Considering all the unique features of diamonds and the fact that they look good with any outfit and any gem, it's no wonder that diamond has become the most important and sought after gem in the world.

What Type of Magnification is Used to View Diamonds?

Diamond dealers typically view diamonds with a 10-power (10X) triplet loupe (figure 1.4). A triplet loupe has three lenses that are held in place by a metal ring. One lens is the magnifier, one lens corrects color distortions and another corrects linear distortions. The advantages of the loupe are that it is portable, affordable and faster to use than a microscope.

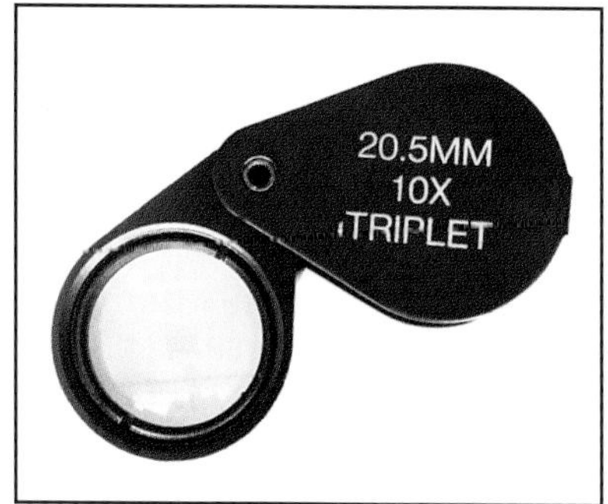

Fig. 1.4 A 10-power triplet loupe

You can find loupes at jewelry supply stores, rock shops and public gem shows. They normally cost at least $25 if they are of good quality. Before you use the loupe to look at diamonds, you may wish to try focusing it on your fingernail. You'll have to hold the loupe about ¾ of an inch (a little less than 2 centimeters) from the fingernail. If you hold the loupe close to your eye, you'll have a broader range of view than when you hold it further away from the eye. The distance of your fingernail, however, must remain at the same close distance from the loupe in order for it to remain in focus.

Gemologists and gem laboratories use a microscope for most of the diamond grading process. In his book *Photo Masters for Diamond Grading* (pg.4), Gary Roskin states that gem labs use a higher magnification than 10-power to help speed up the grading process. By starting with higher power, it's easier for lab graders to locate small inclusions. To make the final judgment, the microscope is reduced to 10-power; graders then view the diamond with a 10-power loupe to decide the final grade.

Both dealers and gemologists microscopes to help them detect treated diamonds and synthetic diamonds. Microscopes permit them to view diamonds at higher powers with a greater variety of lighting.

Which Type of Lighting is Best for Viewing Diamonds?

The most accepted lighting for grading the color of diamonds is balanced, daylight-equivalent fluorescent light According to the GIA, the overhead light on many gemological microscopes provides this kind of light. In her book *Diamond Grading ABC* (p.80), Verena Pagel-Theisen recommends that the color temperature of the light have a value of 5500° Kelvin for diamonds in the blue-white range and 6500° Kelvin for colored diamonds.

Diamond dealers also use fluorescent lights when evaluating diamond quality. Fluorescents provide an even, diffused light, which is ideal for judging the brightness of the diamond. (Diffused light is spread over a wide area instead of concentrated on one spot. Translucent white plastic can diffuse the concentrated light of a clear light bulb or halogen spotlight.)

Incandescent bulbs have a metal wire that glows white-hot when an electric current is passed through it, e.g., halogen bulbs and normal household light bulbs. These bulbs, pen lights and candlelight tend to highlight a diamond's sparkle and fire (spectral colors). They may also make diamonds appear a bit more yellowish than they would look in daylight or under a fluorescent light. As a result, these light sources are not recommended for grading color or brightness. However, they are useful for evaluating a diamond's fire.

The surrounding environment also affects the light quality. Ideally, diamonds should be graded in a standardized environment with a neutral background—dull white or gray. The GIA sells a viewing box called the Diamond Dock™, which provides a consistent viewing environment for diamonds. It has fluorescent lighting for evaluating brightness and incandescent lighting for viewing fire.

When the GIA gem trade lab grades the clarity of a diamond it uses **darkfield illumination**, which lights the stone from the side against a black, non-reflective background and causes the tiny inclusions and even dust particles to stand out in high relief. This can make the clarity of the diamond appear worse than it would if the light were above the stone. Besides being used for clarity grading, darkfield illumination is invaluable for detecting treatments and diamond imitations.

When looking at jewelry with the unaided eye, you normally view it with **overhead lighting**. This lighting is above the stone (not literally over a person's head). Overhead lighting is reflected off the facets, whereas darkfield lighting is transmitted through the stone. Curiously, when salespeople show diamonds under a microscope, they seldom use its overhead lamp. Instead they may only show the stone under darkfield illumination. The inclusions will look more prominent than under overhead lights. To give customers a balanced perspective of a stone's clarity through a microscope, salespeople should also show the diamond illuminated with the microscope's overhead lamp.

Besides making flaws more prominent, darkfield illumination hides brightness. To accurately assess the beauty and brilliance of a diamond, you should view it with overhead lighting. The quickest and easiest way to see a diamond's beauty magnified is with a good 10-power loupe.

The best gemstones look good under all types of light. In fact one dealer told me that the beauty of his diamonds is particularly noticeable under candlelight where they shimmer and sparkle much more than ordinary diamonds. It's a good idea to view diamonds under a variety of lighting conditions, especially those in which they will normally be worn.

Other Tips on Viewing Diamonds

It's best to evaluate diamonds when they are loose (not mounted) because settings can hide flaws and the metal reflects into the stone, affecting its apparent color. The tips below are valid whether you are viewing a loose or mounted diamond.

- **Clean the stone with a soft cloth before viewing**. Dirt and fingerprints hide color and brightness. Dust can also be mistaken as inclusions.
- **Look at the diamond first without magnification** to determine your initial overall impression of it.
- **When evaluating *color*, view the diamond against a non-reflective white background**. For example, you can fold a white business card in half and lay the diamond in the crease, or you can place the diamond in a white grading tray. View it from the side and face up. See the section on diamond color in the next chapter for more information and photos.
- **When evaluating *brightness*, view the diamond against a gray background**; a white background can make a diamond look brighter by masking areas of light leakage, and a black background can make the diamond look unnaturally dark.
- **Examine the stone under direct light and away from it.** Diamonds won't always be spotlighted when worn. If it's of good quality, the diamond will still look good out of direct light.
- **Rotate the diamond and examine it from a variety of angles** with and without magnification. The next four chapters will provide more information on what to look for.
- **Pick up the stone more than once with the tweezers** to view it under magnification and under a fluorescent light. The tweezers can hide a chip or a flaw on the **girdle** (outer edge around the circumference of the diamond). In addition, the diamond looks different depending on where along the girdle it is held.
- **Compare the stone side by side with other diamonds**. Nuances in color, transparency and brightness will be more apparent. (**Transparency** refers to how clear, hazy, cloudy or opaque a gemstone is.)
- **Every now and then, look away from the diamond** at other objects to give your eyes a rest. When you focus too long on a stone, your perception of it may become distorted.
- **Make sure you're alert and feel good when you examine diamonds.** If you're tired, sick or under the influence of alcohol or drugs, your perception of color and brightness will be impaired.

2

Diamond Price Factors

There are seven basic price factors for diamonds:

♦ **Color**

♦ **Carat weight**

♦ **Cut quality** (Proportions and finish)

♦ **Cutting style & stone shape**

♦ **Clarity** (Degree to which a stone is free from flaws)

♦ **Transparency** (Degree to which a stone is clear, hazy, or cloudy)

♦ **Treatment status** (Untreated or treated? What type of treatment?)

Why the 4 C's is No Longer an Adequate Pricing System

The 4 C's of color, clarity, cut and carat weight of explaining diamond pricing was developed by the GIA (Gemological Institute of America) in the 1950's. At that time, cloudy diamonds were considered industrial grade stones and were not set in jewelry, so transparency was not an issue. Neither was the treatment status because almost all diamonds were untreated. There were fewer faceting styles in the 1950's and no separate price lists for rounds and other shapes; therefore it didn't matter that "cut" referred to both shape and the quality of the cut.

Times have changed. Cloudy and hazy diamonds are now used in jewelry, more and more diamonds are being treated to improve their color and clarity grades, and shape is a distinct price factor from cut quality.

The 4 C's system of valuing gems is a clever, convenient way to explain gem pricing, which is why it's still the most frequently used pricing system. The problem is that it causes consumers and even some trade members to overlook the importance of transparency, treatment status and cut quality.

This problem is evident when customers look at mini-certs (certificates) that list the color, clarity, weight, and cut. After "cut," the cert may state, "round brilliant cut," without indicating proportion measurements. A lay person would therefore assume that the term "cut" just means shape and cutting style. But even though the quality of the cut is not indicated, it *is* a price factor; and it's separate from shape.

Likewise, transparency is separate from clarity. A diamond can be hazy or slightly cloudy and still get a high clarity grade of VS, yet it is less valuable and desirable than a highly transparent diamond. On the other hand, a diamond can have an imperfect clarity grade and be transparent. Clarity and transparency are somewhat interconnected in the lowest clarity grades of I_2 and I_3 because the large

Fig. 2.1 GIA Resident masterstones ranging from E to O colors. Do not use this photo to grade the color of diamonds. The printing and developing processes and paper color usually alter the true color of gems in photographs. *Photo © Gemological Institute of America; photo by Tino Hammid.*

number of inclusions present in these grades can sometimes block the passage of light and prevent the diamond from appearing clear.

The seven price factors I've listed are explained in the rest of this chapter. To remember what they are, just call them the 5 C's and 2 T's.

Price Factors Explained

Color

Basically the less color, the higher the price (except for fancy colors). D is the highest and most rare colorless grade. As the grades descend towards Z, color increases and the price decreases. See the GIA (Gemological Institute of America) color grading scale below, which was developed in the 1950's.

D E F*	G H I J	K L M	N to R	S to Z	Z+
colorless	near colorless	faint yellow	very light yellow	light yellow	fancy yellow

(*Colorless for 0.50 ct or less, near colorless for heavier stones)

Each letter on the scale represents a narrow color range, not a specific point. In their diamond grading course, the GIA states that each of their masterstones "marks the highest point—or least amount of color—in that range. A diamond with slightly less color than the H masterstone is considered G-color, and so on." A GIA G-H split-grade masterstone represents the middle of the G grade. It doesn't have as much color as an H, but has more color than a straight G grade. A few other color grading systems besides the GIA's are also used. They are compared in Table 2.1.

A diamond is not bad quality because it's yellowish. It's simply worth less because there's a higher demand and lower supply of natural colorless diamonds.

Brown and gray diamonds are graded on the same scale, but with some modifications. GIA graders describe brown diamonds darker than K with the letter grade and an accompanying colored diamond grade: e.g. Faint brown for K to M, Very Light brown for N to R, and Light brown for S to Z. So an L–grade brown diamond would be graded as L-Faint brown. The GIA does this to distinguish brown stones darker than K in the normal range from yellow stones in that range. Light brown diamonds typically sell for less than light yellow diamonds.

Table 2.1 Color grading systems compared

	GIA	CIBJO / IDC	Scan. D. N.	AGS	GIA
	D	Exceptional White +	River	0	D
	E	Exceptional White		1	E
	F	Rare White +	Top Wesselton	2	F
near colorless	G	Rear White		3	G
	H	White	Wesselton	4	H
	I	Slightly Tinted White	Top Crystal	5	I
	J		Crystal	6	J
faint yellow	K	Tinted White	Top Cape		K
	L			7	L
	M	Tinted Color	Cape		M
very light yellow	N				N
	O		Light Yellow	8	O
	P				P
	Q				Q
	R		Yellow	9	R
light yellow	S				S
	T				T
	U			10	U
	V				V
	W				W
	X				X
	Y				Y
	Z				Z

The data in this table is based mainly on information in *Diamonds* by Eric Bruton and *Diamond Grading ABC* by Verena Pagel-Theisen.

The GIA grades gray diamonds with more color than the J masterstone using their fancy-color system. "So a K-color gray diamond would be graded simply as Faint gray without a letter grade." (From the GIA *Diamonds & Diamond Grading Course*, 2002.)

Diamonds with a natural body color other than light yellow, light brown or light gray are called **fancy color diamonds**. These colored diamonds may cost a lot more than those that are colorless. For example, a one-carat natural pink diamond could sell for five to fifteen times more than a D color diamond of the same size and quality.

Fancy color diamonds are graded with the diamond in the face-up position because their cut can influence the apparent color and because their price is based on the face-up color. The more intense the color, the higher the price.

Diamonds in the colorless to light yellow range are color graded with the diamonds face down because their price is based on the absence of color and because subtle nuances of color are more visible through the bottom of the diamond. You don't need a plastic grading tray for color viewing; just fold a white business card in half and place the diamonds in the crease on the backside.

Occasionally, diamonds in the face-up position may appear lighter or darker than their color grades. Therefore it's good to compare them face up as well as face-down. What the diamonds look like when mounted is more important than their color grade on a diamond report.

Be careful not to mistakenly downgrade larger diamonds. They often appear darker than small masterstones of the same color grade because the color appears to deepen when it is viewed through a larger medium. Also, keep in mind that precise color grading can only be done with loose diamonds. The color of the metal surrounding diamonds set in jewelry influences the appearance of the diamonds. Consequently, their color can only be estimated.

CARAT WEIGHT

In most cases, the higher the carat weight category, the greater the per-carat price of the diamond. A carat is a unit of weight equaling 1/5 of a gram. The weight of small diamonds is frequently expressed in points, with one point equaling 0.01 ct (carat). In diamond districts, you may hear the term **grainer**. This is a word that is used to describe the weights of diamond in multiples of 0.25 ct (one grain). A four grainer is a 1 ct diamond.

If a diamond is advertised as weighing ".25 points," this can be misread as being .25 ct in weight when in fact .25 points is equal to 1/400 of a carat instead of " 1/4 carat." Make sure that your customers understand the correct weight of the diamonds in the jewelry that you sell. Otherwise you could be accused of misleading them.

Consumers may also misread the labels **1 ct TW** (one carat total weight) and **1 ct** (the weight of one stone). A ring with a **1 ct** top quality diamond can be worth more than 10 times as much as a ring with 1 ct TW of diamonds of the same quality.

When you price diamonds, think in terms of the per-carat cost. To calculate the total cost of a diamond, use the equation: **Total cost of a stone = carat weight x per-carat cost**

Diamonds can be divided into weight categories. These categories often vary from one dealer to another but may be outlined as follows:

Table 2.2

Weight Categories for Diamonds		
0.01 – 0.03 ct	0.30 – 0.37 ct	0.96 – 0.99 ct
0.04 – 0.07 ct	0.38 – 0.45 ct	1.00 – 1.49 ct
0.08 – 0.14 ct	0.46 – 0.49 ct	1.50 – 1.99 ct
0.15 – 0.17 ct	0.50 – 0.69 ct	2.00 – 2.49 ct
0.18 – 0.22 ct	0.70 – 0.89 ct	2.50 – 2.99 ct
0.23 – 0.29 ct	0.90 – 0.95 ct	3.00 – 3.99 ct

The above weight categories are based mainly on those listed in the *Rapaport Diamond Report*. As diamonds move up from one weight category to another, their prices may increase from about 5% to 50%. So if you buy, for example, a 0.97 ct diamond instead of a 1 ct, you'll normally pay less per carat, even though the stone will resemble a one-carat diamond. Low-quality diamonds tend to show less of a price differential between categories than those of high quality, especially at the jump from just less than 1 ct to 1 ct or more.

Usually the greater the weight, the greater the rarity, which is one reason for price jumps when diamonds move from one weight category to another. But demand also plays a role. One caraters and half caraters are in high demand so there can be a considerable price jump when diamonds move to these categories. In the 1980's when tennis bracelets were unusually popular, three pointers (0.03-carat diamonds) actually cost more per carat than five pointers because the three pointers were more in demand.

Cut Quality

Cut quality, also called **make**, refers to the proportions and finish of a stone. This is a crucial factor, which can affect prices by as much as 50%. Two of the main considerations of cut are:

1. **Do you see brilliance all across the stone when you look at the diamond face up?** (figs. 2.2 & 2.3) Diamond brilliance should not be interrupted by large dark areas (fig. 2.4).
2. **Are you paying for excess weight?** (fig. 2.5)

Fig. 2.2 Emerald cut with good brilliance

Fig. 2.3 Radiant cut with good brilliance

Fig. 2.4 Diamond with a dark center

Fig. 2.5 Diamond with excess weight

Photos above and below by author

Judge cut with the unaided eye and a 10-power magnifier. Chapters 3 and 4 explain cut evaluation in detail.

Cutting Style & Stone Shape

Currently rounds cost more than pear and marquise shapes and emerald cuts. The effect of shape on price varies depending on the stone size, demand and available supply. For example, there have been periods in the past where marquise shapes have sold for more than rounds.

Normally square shapes can cost as much as 15–30% less than rounds because there is less weight loss from the rough when cutting squares and there is usually less of a demand for squares. However, depending on demand, princess cuts (square shapes) have occasionally sold for more than rounds in certain areas of the world.

Four common diamond shapes are shown below and on the next page.

Fig. 2.6 Marquise (brilliant cut)

Fig. 2.7 Princess cut (square brilliant)

Fig. 2.8 Pear shape (brilliant cut)

Fig. 2.9 Oval (brilliant cut)

The preceding shapes can be cut with various faceting styles. The GIA has simplified the description of these cutting styles by limiting them to three basic types—step cut, brilliant cut and mixed cut.

Step Cut: Has rows of facets that are usually four-sided and elongated and parallel to the girdle (fig. 2.10). If step-cuts have clipped-off corners, they're called **emerald cuts** because emeralds are often cut this way (fig. 2.2). This protects the corners and provides places where prongs can secure the stone. Emerald cuts are in essence step-cut, octagonal rectangles. They tend to have more facets than baguettes. Emerald-cut diamonds are usually rectangular or square, but they can also be triangular (fig. 2.11).

Fig. 2.10 Step-cut rectangle

Fig 2.11 Step-cut triangle

Fig. 2.12 Trilliant (brilliant cut)

All photos above by author

Brilliant Cut: Has triangular-, kite-, or lozenge-shaped facets that radiate outward around the stone. Figures 2.6 to 2.9 and 2.12 are examples of brilliant cuts. The jewelry trade generally refers to round diamonds with 58 facets as **full cuts** or traditional **round brilliants**.

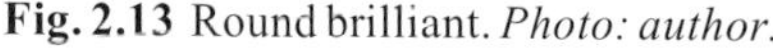

Fig. 2.13 Round brilliant. *Photo: author.*

Fig. 2.14 Mixed cut Lucere® diamond from Ernest Slotar, Inc.

Mixed Cut: Has both step- and brilliant-cut facets. The pavilion, for example, can be step cut and the crown can be brilliant cut, but the step- and brilliant-cut facets can also be scattered over the diamond. This cut is used a lot more on transparent colored stones than on diamonds, but some of the new branded diamonds are mixed cuts.

Brilliant-cut square diamonds (princess cuts) may cost slightly more than step-cut squares, depending on size. They have the same shape but different faceting styles. Patented and trademarked cutting styles typically sell for more than generic cuts of the same shape.

The most dramatic impact of stone shape and cutting style on price is with fancy color diamonds because their face-up color can be intensified by the shape and faceting style, and because the rough is so expensive. For example, a 1-carat, intense-yellow round diamond can cost from 10% to over 100% more than a radiant with the same weight and color grade, depending on the stones and the dealer selling them. This is because the rough of the round diamond must be darker than that of the radiant to achieve the same intense yellow face-up color; cutters can't play as much with the angles and shape of rounds to maximize their color. The stronger the color of the rough, the higher the price of the rough. The final price of the diamond is based largely on the cost of the rough.

CLARITY

Clarity is defined as the degree to which a stone is free from external marks called **blemishes** and internal features called **inclusions**. There are eleven GIA clarity grades, which are defined in the chart on the next page. Photo examples of eight clarity grades are shown in Chapter 5 of this book and in Chapter 7 of the *Diamond Ring Buying Guide.*

Lay people often refer to inclusions as "flaws" and "imperfections." Gemologists usually prefer not to use these terms because of their negative connotations. This book sometimes uses the term "flaw" because it's a short word that includes both inclusions and blemishes. The fewer, smaller and less noticeable the flaws, the better the clarity and the higher the price of the stone. Inclusions that are found in diamonds are described on the next page.

GIA CLARITY GRADES* * For trained graders using 10-power magnification and proper lighting	
Fl	**Flawless**, no blemishes or inclusions.
IF	**Internally flawless**, no inclusions and only insignificant blemishes.
VVS_1 & VVS_2	**Very, very slightly included**, minute inclusions that are difficult to see.
VS_1 & VS_2	**Very slightly included**, minor inclusions ranging from difficult to somewhat easy to see.
SI_1 & SI_2	**Slightly included**, noticeable inclusions that are easy (SI_1) or very easy (SI_2) to see.
I_1, I_2, & I_3 In Europe: **P_1, P_2 & P_3**	**Imperfect**, obvious inclusions that usually are eye-visible face up; in I_3, distinctions are based on the combined effect on durability, transparency, and brilliance.

Diamond Inclusions

- **Crystals** of all sorts of interesting shapes and sizes are commonly seen in diamonds (figures 2.15 and 2.16). Over 24 different minerals have been identified as crystal inclusions in diamonds, but the most frequent type crystal seen is another diamond. Minute crystals that look like small specks under 10-power magnification are called **pinpoints**. Crystals can lower the clarity grade of your diamond, but they can also turn it into a collector's item if they are unusual and attractive. The larger and more obvious crystals are, the more they impact the clarity grade.

- **Cracks** of various sizes are also common in diamonds. They may also be called **fissures** or **breaks**. When they follow the grain of the diamond, they are called **cleavages,** and appear straight and flat. Cracks that are not cleavages are called **fractures**.

  On lab reports, cracks are usually identified as feathers. In their diamond grading course, the GIA states that "a **feather** is a general term for any break in a diamond" (pg 18, lesson 10, 2002 course). Diamonds with insignificant feathers can receive VS clarity grades.

  The girdle (outer edge) of diamonds often has tiny hairline cleavages, which are called **bearding** (fig. 2.26). Light bearding does not prevent a diamond from receiving a clarity grade of VVS (very very slightly included). Tiny cracks are normal diamond features.

  Larger cracks like the one in figure 2.19 have a more serious effect on the clarity grade because they are more noticeable and they can sometimes threaten the stone's durability.

Fig. 2.15 Red crystal inclusion. *Diamond from Overland Gems; photo Pete Flusser.*

Fig. 2.16 Black and clear crystals and feathers. *Photo by author.*

Fig. 2.17 A minor cleavage (feather). *Photo by author.*

Fig. 2.18 Same cleavage from another angle. *Photo by author.*

Fig. 2.19 A serious crack (feather). *Photo by author.*

Fig. 2.20 Pinpoints and a cloud. *Photo: author.*

- **Clouds** are hazy or milky areas in a diamond (fig. 2.20). Most clouds are made up of crystals too tiny to see individually under 10-power magnification. Clouds may be hard to find in diamonds with high clarity grades. When clouds are large and dense, they diminish transparency and make diamonds look undesirably white.
- **Growth or grain lines** are fine lines or ripples caused by irregular crystallization (fig. 2.21). They're also referred to as twinning lines or simply graining. Sometimes diamonds look hazy or oily when many of these lines are present. White, colored or reflective graining can affect the clarity grade. Colorless graining does not normally lower the clarity grade but it can sometimes affect the transparency and brilliance of a diamond.
- **Cavities** are spaces left when a surface-reaching crystal comes out during polishing or when part of a feather breaks away and leaves a deep, angular opening. **Chips** often occur along the girdle (fig. 2,22).
- **Knots** are included diamond crystals that are left exposed on the surface by polishing. They may look like raised areas on the diamond, and there may be a difference in polish quality between the knot and the surrounding areas when examined with reflected light.
- **Laser drill holes** are tiny holes drilled into the diamond with a laser beam, allowing black spots to be dissolved or bleached out with chemicals (fig. 2.23). This treatment normally improves the appearance. There are times, however, when the diamond looks worse after drilling due to the resulting long white drill holes. To see laser holes you usually have to tilt the diamond or view it from the side. Some of the newer lasering techniques can be difficult to detect.

Surface Blemishes

- **Scratches, nicks, pits and abraded facet edges** are not considered as serious as inclusions because they can often be polished away.
- **Extra facets** are additions to the normal number of facets (flat, geometric diamond surfaces) (fig. 2.25). They are usually added to polish away a flaw. This helps retain weight by avoiding the alternative of repolishing the regular facet.. They don't affect the clarity grade of a diamond if they are on the pavilion and can't be seen face up at 10-power magnification.
- **Naturals** are part of the original surface of the diamond crystal left unpolished (fig. 2.26). Sometimes they have step-like ridges or triangular forms (called **trigons**) on them that help indicate your stone is truly a diamond. Naturals don't affect the clarity grade if they're confined to the girdle and don't distort the girdle outline.

Some people wonder if laser inscriptions on the girdle (rim around the stone) are inclusions. They're not, and they do not affect the clarity grade or damage the diamond. The inscriptions, which may consist of numbers, logo, pictures, and/or words, are confined to the girdle and are so small that you normally have

Fig. 2.21 Graining in a pink diamond from Overland Gems. *Photo by Pete Flusser.*

Fig. 2.22 Large chip. *Photo by author.*

Fig. 2.23 Laser drill holes. *Photo by author.*

Fig. 2.24 Abraded facet edges and pits. *Photo by author.*

Fig. 2.25 Extra facets. *Photo by author.*

Fig. 2.26 Natural and bearding. *Photo by author.*

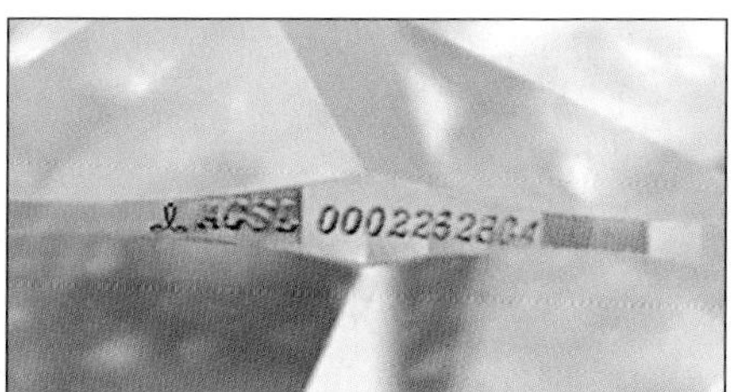

Fig. 2.27 Laser inscription. *Diamond from J Landau, photo by Derse Studio.*

Fig. 2.28 Same inscription at lower magnification. *From Landau, photo: Derse Studio.*

to view them at 25-power magnification in order to read them. A 10-power loupe is not strong enough. The inscriptions are engraved on the diamond with a laser.

Figure 2.27 shows the highly magnified (at least 25-power) numbers that correspond to an AGSL (American Gem Society Laboratory) diamond report. To give you a better idea of how small the numbers are, they are shown in figure 2.28 at a lower magnification. Laser inscriptions are also used for personal message such as "I love you."

Consumers are sometimes afraid of leaving their diamonds for repair for fear of having the diamonds switched. Thanks to laser inscriptions they can have peace of mind. The jeweler can show them the diamond under a microscope after the diamond comes back for repair and have the customer match the number on their lab report to the numbers on the diamond girdle. Another method is to compare the map of the inclusions on the diamond report to the inclusions in the diamond. It's possible to match the inclusions with a loupe, but it is easier with a microscope. Depending on how the diamond is mounted, it might also be possible to measure the diamond and compare its measurements to those on the diamond report.

Transparency

The GIA and the classic book *Gems* by Robert Webster define transparency as the degree to which a gemstone transmits light. They list five categories of transparency.

- **Transparent**—objects seen through the gemstone look clear and distinct.
- **Semi-transparent**—objects look slightly hazy or blurry through the stone.
- **Translucent**—objects are vague and hard to see. Imagining what it is like to read print through frosted glass will help you understand the concept of translucency.
- **Semi-translucent or semi-opaque**—only a small fraction of light passes through the stone, mainly around the edges.
- **Opaque**—virtually no light can pass through the gemstone.

Mineralogists use the term **diaphaneity**, but gemologists prefer the term "transparency" because it's easier for lay people to understand. Another word that

Transparency Examples

Fig. 2.29 Diamond with high transparency

Fig. 2.30 Sub-microscopic particles make this diamond look cloudy.

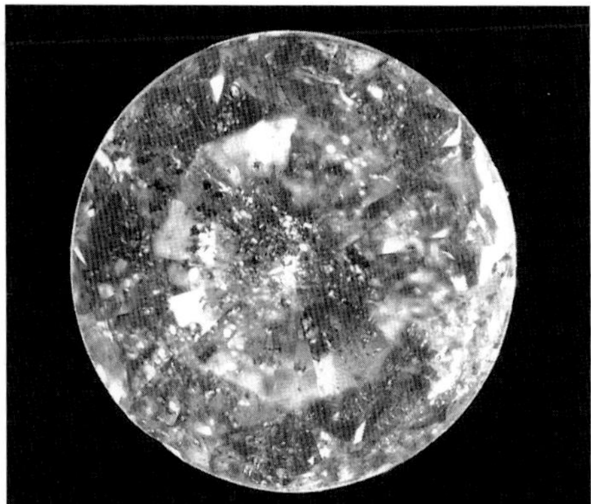

Fig. 2.31 Visible inclusions seriously affect the transparency of this I_3 diamond.

Fig. 2.32 Internal graining gives this diamond an oily appearance.

Fig. 2.33 This diamond only has a few pinpoint inclusions under 10x. However it's slightly cloudy, so it's not as valuable as a highly transparent diamond of the same clarity grade.

Fig. 2.34 A cloudy diamond with a cloud in the center

All photos on this page are by author

Fig. 2.35 Necklace featuring a 14.71 carat oval, "Golconda" quality, Type IIa diamond. *Necklace and photo from Alexandre Reza.*

refers to transparency is **texture.** AGL (American Gemological Laboratories) in New York applies this term to fine particles that interrupt the passage of light in a material. Jade dealers often use the term **translucency** and some other colored gem dealers use the term **crystal.**

I first became aware of the importance of transparency when a New York colored-gem dealer, Jack Abraham, mentioned that I had left the concept out of the first edition of my book *The Ruby & Sapphire Buying Guide.* Consequently, I added a section on transparency to all of my colored gem books and I eventually included the concept in the Sixth Edition of the *Diamond Ring Buying Guide.*

Transparency can play a major role in determining the value and desirability of a gemstone. In most cases, the higher the transparency the more valuable the gemstone.

Many of the large historical diamonds of exceptional transparency are known to have come from the Golconda mines in India. As a result, the term "Golconda" is occasionally used in the trade to describe a highly transparent diamond. The word "Golconda" is also used to describe highly transparent diamonds with other desirable attributes. For example, the Gübelin Gem Lab issues a Golconda appendix together with their diamond grading reports for diamonds that comply with a set of criteria, including D color, high transparency, Internally Flawless or improvable to IF, at least five carats in size, old cutting style and Type IIa (See Chapter 8 on synthetic diamonds for information about diamond types). The issuing of a Gübelin Golconda appendix is based on quality criteria known to be typical for the famous Golconda diamonds, and is not a determination of the geographic origin in the strict sense. It's important to note that a diamond with a Golconda appendix is not necessarily from Golconda, and conversely, diamonds originating from Golconda are not necessarily of high quality.

Clarity and transparency are interconnected, but they're different. If there's a cloudy spot in a transparent diamond, the cloud is a clarity feature. If the entire diamond is cloudy due to submicroscopic inclusions, then the cloudiness is a matter of transparency. If the diamond is very cloudy, this will normally affect the clarity grade. However, in most cases, clarity grades are not an indication of the degree of transparency of a diamond. This is because:

- Diamond grading labs don't normally take into account subtle differences in transparency. I've seen hazy and slightly cloudy diamonds with VS clarity grades.
- Diamonds with obvious transparency problems are seldom submitted to labs for grading. More often than not they're mounted in bargain-priced jewelry.

If you'd like to buy and sell brilliant diamonds, it's not sufficient to simply buy diamonds with high cut grades. The diamonds must also have good transparency. Ray-tracing software for grading cut does not factor in diamond transparency (Chapter 5 on light performance has further information). This is another reason why it's important to look at diamonds before selecting them.

To check for transparency, examine the diamond at different angles and check to see if it's as clear as crystal glass or pure water. Face-up, the diamond should be brilliant and there should be a strong contrast between the dark and bright areas. When judging transparency, make sure the diamond is clean; examine it both with your naked eye and a 10-power magnifier, and look at it under different lighting conditions (diffused fluorescent light, incandescent light, sunlight, and away from light). Keep in mind that white objects or walls can reflect into the diamond making it appear less transparent than it really is. It is helpful to have a highly transparent diamond sample for comparison. Nuances of transparency and haziness are more easily detected, and your evaluation will be more accurate.

You don't need a comparison stone or magnification to spot diamonds with serious transparency problems. You can see their cloudiness from several feet away. If diamonds don't sparkle or shine even under a store's special spotlights, there is definitely a problem. The diamonds will probably look worse away from the lights.

Diamonds with dirt and fingerprints may resemble low-grade milky diamonds. Therefore, it's important that estate and consignment jewelry be properly cleaned before displaying it.

Treatment Status

Unlike colored gems, most diamonds are untreated. However, that is changing quickly. Diamonds may undergo treatments such as fracture filling, laser drilling, coating, irradiation, heating, and HPHT (high pressure high temperature) treatment in order to improve their clarity, color, transparency, and marketability. Chapter 9 describes diamond treatments and gives some tips on detecting them. An important reason for getting diamond grading reports is to verify whether the color and clarity are natural or not.

Diamonds colored by irradiation or HPHT treatment are a fraction of the cost of natural fancy color diamonds. For example, a one-carat irradiated "fancy" green diamond of VS clarity may retail for $3000 to $4000 per carat. If the same diamond were of natural color, it would probably sell for over $100,000 per carat because natural green diamonds are unusually rare. In October 1999, a 0.90-carat vivid green diamond was auctioned for $736,111. Treated green diamonds are much easier to find and are often produced from low-priced diamonds that are brownish or below L color. In essence, the customer is paying for the cost of the low-priced diamond and the treatment process.

Some consumers buy diamonds with the intent of reselling them later. If this is their intent, you should sell them diamonds that are completely natural. Untreated diamonds are always in demand and can be resold in any type of market. Treated diamonds are hard to resell.

If a customer is buying a bridal diamond for an everyday ring, an untreated diamond is likely to be more durable and resistant to abrasions than fracture-filled diamonds or HPHT treated diamonds. High temperature heat treatment has made some colored gemstones more brittle and susceptible to chipping and abrasions. We don't know yet what effect it has on the durability of diamonds. Likewise, you can't be certain if fracture-filled diamonds are resistant to knocks, a normal occurrence when they're mounted in everyday rings. Diamonds with large fractures and cleavages, be they filled or unfilled, are not as durable as diamonds of good clarity. One of the main advantages of buying diamonds for bridal rings, instead of other gems is that untreated diamonds are more resistant to abrasions and damage. They have withstood the test of time.

Treated diamonds can be an affordable option to buying untreated ones. They can allow customers to get a big look or unusual colors at a low price. However, if there's not a significant price difference between the enhanced or unenhanced stones, they are better off buying untreated diamonds.

Most fracture filling, laser drilling and coatings can be detected by skilled jewelers and appraisers. Accurate detection of irradiation and high temperature heat treatment normally requires the special expertise and sophisticated equipment of a qualified independent gem laboratory. As mentioned earlier, an important reason for buying a diamond accompanied by a lab report is to verify that the diamond is untreated. Major labs are able to identify the vast majority of treated diamonds, otherwise they will state that the origin is undetermined.

With the proliferation of treatments and synthetic diamonds, it's a good idea for diamonds to be identified as untreated and natural on invoices, especially when dealing with new vendors. This can help protect jewelers from claims of possible misrepresentation if a diamond turns out to be treated. If a stone is identified as enhanced or processed, this means it is treated. Find out what the treatment is and explain it clearly to your customers before making the sale. Attractive untreated diamonds are still readily available and they pose the fewest potential problems for jewelers.

Other Sources of Photos and Information on Diamonds

This chapter is an overview of diamond grading and pricing factors. To get a better understanding, read the rest of this book and examine the photos. Additional photo examples will be helpful. You'll find them in the following publications, which are all excellent references.

American Cut: The First 100 Years by Al Gilbertson, GIA

Collecting & Classifying Coloured Diamonds by Stephen Hofer: Ashland Press.

Diamond Grading ABC by Verena Pagel-Theisen: Rubin & Son

Diamond Ring Buying Guide by Renée Newman: Intl. Jewelry Publications

Gems & Gemology in Review: Colored Diamonds, edited by John M. King, GIA

The MicroWorld of Diamonds by John Koivula: Gemworld International

Photo Masters For Diamond Grading by Gary Roskin: Gemworld International

Photos and information on the latest research about diamonds:

Australian Gemmologist. Gemmological Association of Australia, Brisbane

Canadian Gemmologist. North York, Ont: Canadian Gemmological Association

Gems & Gemology. Gemological Institute of America, Carlsbad, CA

IDEX. Magazine. Idex Online S.A., Ramat Gan, Israel

Journal of Gemmology. Gemmological Association and Gem Testing Laboratory of Great Britain, London

Rapaport Diamond Report, Rapaport USA Inc., Las Vegas, NV

3

Judging the Cut of Fancy Shapes

In the previous chapter, I stated that there are two fundamental considerations when assessing the cut quality of a diamond:

1. Do you see brilliance all across the diamond when it is face up?
2. Are you paying for excess weight?

This chapter will help you answer these two questions when examining a diamond. It will also help you present cut evaluation to customers in an easy-to-understand manner. The next chapter will explain how gem laboratories grade cut. Before learning the finer details of cut grading, you should understand the fundamentals presented in this chapter.

Here is some basic terminology:

Facets The flat, polished surfaces or planes on a diamond

Table The large, flat, top facet. It has an octagonal shape on a round brilliant diamond.

Culet The tiny facet on the pointed bottom of the pavilion, parallel to the table

Girdle The narrow rim around the diamond. The girdle plane is parallel to the table and is the largest diameter of any part of the stone.

Crown The upper part of the diamond above the girdle

Crown height The distance between the girdle and table planes

Pavilion The lower part of the diamond below the girdle. It's cone-shaped on a round diamond.

Pavilion depth The distance from the girdle plane to the culet

Brilliant cut The most common style of diamond cutting. The standard brilliant cut consists of 32 facets plus a table above the girdle and 24 facets plus a culet below the girdle. Other shapes besides round can be faceted as brilliant cuts.

Brightness The actual and/or perceived amount of light returned by a diamond

Brilliance Brightness with an attractive distribution of dark and bright areas that display good contrast. (This is based on the AGS definition of "brightness + positive contrast.")

Figure 3.1 illustrates a few of the preceding terms.

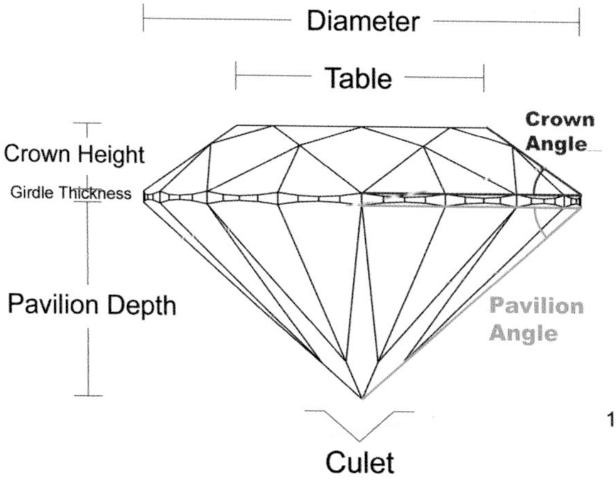

Diameter
Table
Crown Angle
Crown Height
Girdle Thickness
Pavilion Depth
Pavilion Angle
Culet

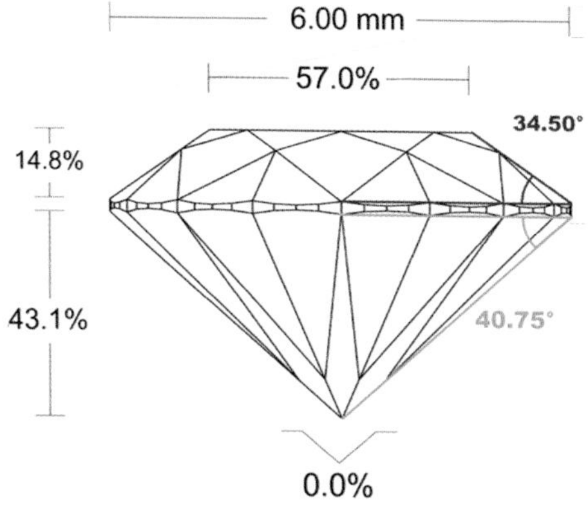

6.00 mm
57.0%
34.50°
14.8%
43.1%
40.75°
0.0%

Figs. 3.1a & 3.1b Profile views of well-cut round brilliant diamonds. The diamond on the right shows one set of proportions that can create an AGS Ideal™ cut diamond. *Diagrams from the American Gem Society Laboratory (AGSL).*

Judging Cut Quality

If a diamond displays high brilliance, then it is well cut and has good proportions. Therefore, brilliance should be your first consideration when judging cut. Ideally, diamonds should look bright and have an even distribution of bright and dark areas across the stone in the face-up view. It's easiest to achieve this with a round diamond.

Fig 3.2 Diamond with high brilliance. *Royal Brilliant® photo from Exroyal Co, Inc.*

The diamond in figure 3.2 is an example of a gemstone with even brilliance and good contrast. Notice the black triangular patterns interspersed throughout the diamond. Patterns similar to this are normal in well-cut diamonds providing the black areas are tiny, as in this diamond. In fact, their presence helps create a sparkle effect (technically called **scintillation)** because as the diamond or light moves, the dark areas shift from black to white making the brilliance appear to twinkle. The shape and size of the facets play a major role in determining the degree of scintillation.

Even though this diamond may not receive an "ideal cut"grade from a lab, its cut quality and brilliance are excellent. Diamonds do not have to be "ideal cuts" to be ideally cut.

It's more difficult to produce fancy shape diamonds with even brilliance than rounds. Each shape requires a different set of cutting angles to achieve maximum brilliance. Even though some dealers and appraisers have published recommended angles and proportions, there is no universal set of standards for cutting fancy shapes.

When evaluating the cut and brilliance of a fancy shape diamond, look for the following features, which are described afterwards in more detail:

- **Large dark black areas**, which are often in the shape of a bow tie, cross, or circle
- "**Windows** "—a clear or washed out area in the middle of the diamond that allows you to see right through the stone
- **Fisheye**—A white donut shaped girdle reflection

All three of these characteristics indicate diminished brilliance.

Bow Ties and Other Dark Patterns

If the pavilions (bottoms) of fancy shape diamonds are too deep or improperly proportioned, the stones may display a gray to black bow tie form across the width of the stone when viewed face up. Some squarish shapes may show a cross pattern and rounds can have a dark circular center. The larger and darker the bow tie, the less desirable the stone. Most fancy-shaped diamonds have at least a slight bow tie, but when it is so pronounced that it is distracting, the bow tie lowers the value of the stone.

Figures 3.3 to 3.14 show several examples of well-cut diamonds next to those with dark patterns. After you examine them, look at some fancy shaped diamonds in your inventory. Check if there is brilliance all across the stone or if it is interrupted with dark areas. Finding well-cut fancy shapes can be a challenge, but such stones are available. For easier comparison, the photos are in black and white. Color can affect perceived brilliance. The less color a diamond has, the brighter it may appear.

Fig. 3.3 Emerald cut with a large bow tie. *Photo by author.*

Fig. 3.4 Emerald cut with good brilliance. *Photo by author*

The manufacturer of the Cushette® in figure 3.6 told me that one of the distinguishing characteristics of their branded cuts is that they do not have bow ties.

Fig. 3.5 Cushion-shape diamond with a moderate bow tie. *Photo by author.*

Fig. 3.6 Diamond with good brilliance and no bow tie. *Cushette® photo from Diamco.*

Fig. 3.7 Brilliant-cut square (princess-cut) with some dark areas. *Photo by author.*

Fig. 3.8 A better brilliant-cut square. *Quadrillion® photo from Bez Ambar.*

Fig. 3.9 Tapered baguette with low brilliance. *Photo by author.*

Fig. 3.10 Diamond with higher brilliance. *Photo by author.*

Fig. 3.11 Pear shape with a bow tie. *Photo by author.*

Fig. 3.12 Pear shape with a minimal bow tie. *Photo by author.*

Fig. 3.13 A distracting black cross. Compare it to the more brilliant diamond in figure 3.14. *Photo by author.*

Fig. 3.14 Flanders Ideal Square Cut®. *Photo from National Diamond Syndicate.*

TEST: Which diamond below is better cut and displays more brilliance? Ask your customers this question. (See next page for answer.)

Fig. 3.15 Christmas tree diamond. *Photo by author.*

Fig. 3.16 Diamond star. *Photo by author.*

If your customers said that the diamond star is better cut and more brilliant than the Christmas tree, then you have proved that lay people are capable of making visual judgments about diamond cut. You don't need proportion measurements, a cut grade, or a lab document to determine that the large dark areas in the tree diamond reduce its brilliance. This can be determined with one's eyes. In this case, magnification isn't necessary, but a loupe or microscope can help magnify the beauty of a diamond and help detect finer nuances of brilliance. Comparison stones can also help.

Windows

When gemstones are improperly cut and are viewed face up, they may display a **window**— a clear or washed out area in the middle of the stone that allows you to see right through it. Windows (or windowing) can occur in any transparent, faceted stone no matter how light or dark it is and no matter how deep or shallow its pavilion. In general, the larger the window, the poorer the cut. Windowed stones are the attempt of the cutter to maximize weight at the expense of brilliance.

Windows are seldom seen in diamonds because of their high refractive index (the degree to which light is bent as it passes through the stone), but they are frequently seen in colored gemstones. When windows occur in diamonds, they are usually seen in emerald cuts and other step cuts (figure 3.17). Since diamonds are often mounted with colored gems, it's important to know how to evaluate them too, especially considering that few labs supply cut quality information on their colored gem reports. If you learn how to spot windows, this will help you select gems with good brilliance.

Fig. 3.17 A small window in an emerald-cut diamond through which print is visible. *Photo by author.*

Fig. 3.18 Similar shaped diamond with no window. *Lucére® Diamond; photo from Ernest Slotar, Inc.*

To look for windows, hold the stone about an inch or two (2 to 5 cm) above a contrasting background such as your hand or a piece of white paper. Then try to look straight through the top of the stone without tilting it, and check if you can see the background or a light window-like area in the center of it.

If the stone is light colored, you might try holding it above a printed page to see if the print shows through. If the center area of the stone is pale or lifeless compared to a darker faceted area surrounding the pale center, this is also a window effect. To better understand windowing, compare the two stones below to the ones in figure 3.21.

Fig. 3.19 Moderate window in a tanzanite. *Photo by author.*

Fig. 3.20 Very large window in an amethyst. *Photo by author.*

Fig. 3.21 Two citrines and an amethyst with no windowing and excellent light refraction. They were cut by Mark Gronlund. Even though their proportions may not meet traditional standards, they are well cut. *Photo by author.*

Fisheyes

Sometimes the face-up view of a diamond displays a white circle resembling a skinny donut (figs. 3.22 & 3.23). In the trade, this is called a **fisheye**. It's caused by the reflection of the girdle when the pavilion is too shallow. A large table (top center facet) can make a fisheye more noticeable. The thicker and more prominent the white circle, the poorer the cut. Besides looking bad, fisheye diamonds usually lack the brilliance of those that are well-cut.

Round brilliant fisheyes are more likely to be seen in stones under 0.20 carats, but they are found in larger sizes as well. Fisheyes can have a strong negative impact on diamond value. To detect fisheyes, look at the diamond face up with a loupe and tilt it slightly. Fine-cut diamonds do not display a fisheye effect, not even when slightly tilted.

Fig. 3.22 Narrow fisheve in a single cut (a cutting style with 16 facets and a table)

Fig. 3.23 Strong fisheye in a round brilliant cut diamond. *Photo by author.*

Excess Diamond Weight

If you are looking at two one-carat diamonds of similar quality and one of them has an extremely thick girdle (the rim around the edge of the diamond) and the other has a proper size medium girdle, the diamond with the extremely thick girdle will look noticeably smaller. The price of the diamond with the extremely thick girdle will probably be lower, but this does not mean it is a better buy. It costs less because it has a lot of unnecessary weight around the girdle area, which does not increase its brilliance and sparkle. In fact, the thicker girdle may even detract from its brilliance. The face-up size of a diamond is more important than its weight. Therefore in addition to checking for face-up brilliance, you should look at diamonds from the side to verify that they do not have a lot of unnecessary weight.

Fig. 3.24 Profile of a fancy-shape diamond with excess weight around the girdle area. Face up this diamond looks small for its weight. *Photo: author.*

Fig. 3.25 Profile of a well-cut round brilliant cut diamond. *Photo by author.*

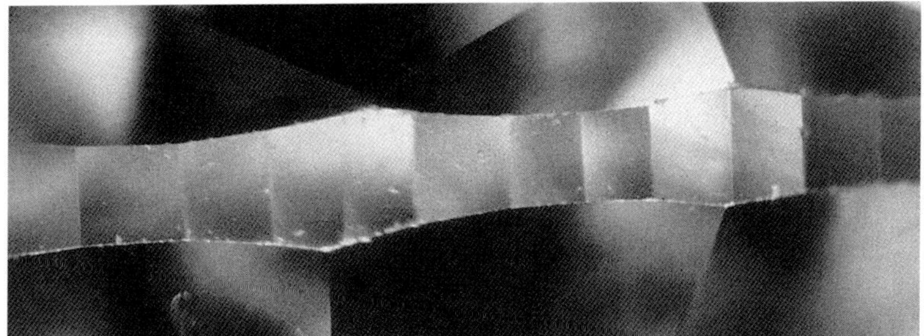

Fig. 3.26 A very thick faceted girdle. *Photo by author.*

Sometimes people mistakenly think a big spread is always desirable (**spread** is the face-up size compared to a gem's weight). Diamonds with windows and fish-eye effects typically have shallow pavilions, which makes them appear bigger than well-cut diamonds. However, if their goal is to purchase a beautiful diamond, they should buy one that was cut to maximize brilliance.

Fig. 3.27 Top heavy old mine cut. *Photo by author.*

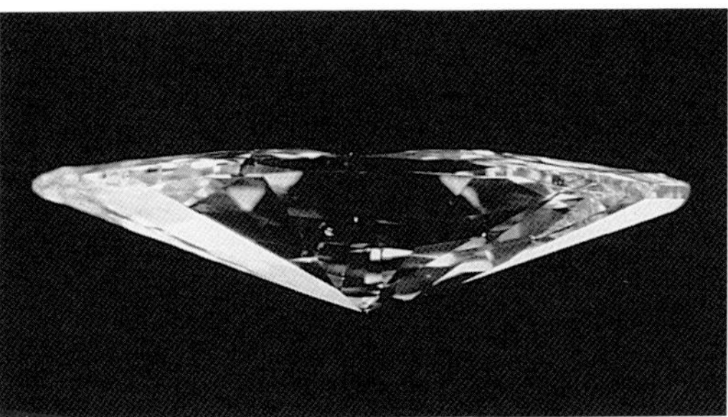

Fig. 3.28 Lengthwise view of a marquise with a profile that is too flat for adequate brilliance and a crown that is too thin to provide proper sparkle and fire. Face up the diamond looks big for its weight.

Thin crowns and large tables will also help increase the face-up size, but at the expense of sparkle and fire. See figure 3.28 for an example of a thin crown.

Figure 3.27 is an example of a diamond with a crown that is too high. Even though this is an old mine cut, which is explained in Chapter 9, modern-cut diamonds are sometimes cut with very high crowns in order to maximize weight retention of the rough.

Bulging pavilions are another sign of cutters placing more emphasis on weight retention than on beauty. When diamonds have thick girdles, high crowns or bulging pavilions, dealers call them heavy makes. Even though excess weight can often be detected from the face up view, it's easiest to see it in the profile view. It can play a major role in the price of a diamond. Both the GIA and AGS now factor in the weight versus diameter ratio into their new cut grading systems. For more information on these systems, read the next chapter.

I have not discussed shape outline and length to width ratios in this chapter because I believe that is largely a matter of personal choice. However, diamonds which conform to traditional shape outlines, such as the ones below, are often in higher demand and may therefore cost more.

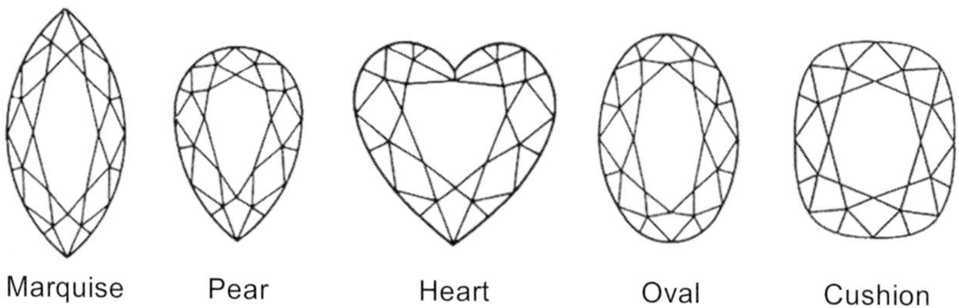

Fig. 3.29 *Diagrams courtesy of the Gemological Institute of America*

The next chapter will explain proportion measurements for round brilliants. Do not use those measurements to assess fancy shapes. They must be cut to different depths than rounds to prevent fisheyes and dark areas. For example, brilliant-cut triangles are normally cut more shallow than rounds, whereas squares are typically cut deeper.

Adam Daniels at Ernest Slotar, Inc. says that their Lucére Diamond (figure 3.18) must have a total depth averaging about 70% in order to maximize brilliance, unlike round brilliants which should have a total depth percentage closer to 60%.

The American Gem Society has done considerable research on evaluating cut of fancy shapes and they now offer cut grades of square princess and emerald cuts. Their cutting guidelines are available for trade members on their website www.agslab.com.

4

Judging Cut (Round Brilliants)

The previous chapter discussed two fundamental concepts of diamond cut evaluation: face-up brilliance and excess weight (e.g., thick girdles). This chapter provides additional information on assessing the following proportions of the 57- or 58-facet standard round brilliant style of cut:

- ♦ Pavilion
- ♦ Table
- ♦ Girdle
- ♦ Culet
- ♦ Crown
- ♦ Star facets
- ♦ Lower girdle facets

In addition, this chapter discusses **finish,** which consists of two subcategories:

- ♦ Symmetry
- ♦ Polish

In the previous 2005 edition of the *Diamond Handbook*, the guidelines presented in this chapter were primarily based on those of the American Gem Society Laboratory (AGS) and the HRD (abbreviation of the Flemish name Hoge Raad voor Diamant), a diamond laboratory in Antwerp, Belgium, which is better known in Europe, Africa and Asia, than in America.

The AGS no longer uses two-dimensional proportion measurements as the basis for their cut grade. Their new system is described in the next chapter. However, this chapter does briefly discuss the AGS cut factor of "tilt" and indicates their new ideal-cut table-percentage ranges.

In 2006, the GIA (Gemological Institute of America) published the cut grading guidelines for their new lab report cut grades in their *Diamond Grading Lab Manual* and in the "Diamond Essentials Supplement: Introduction to the GIA Diamond Cut-grading System." Most of the information in this chapter is based on the new GIA guidelines and those of the HRD.

Pavilion

The pavilion (bottom of the diamond) plays the most important role in determining brilliance—the amount of light reflected back to the eye. If the pavilion is too shallow, a fisheye effect (a reflection of the girdle, which looks like a white donut-shaped circle) will be visible (fig. 4.2) and there will be decreased brilliance. Some diamond dealers describe these diamonds as being "flat." The term "flat" is also associated with very thin crowns.

If the pavilion is too deep, the diamond will look dark in the center (fig. 4.3). Diamonds with black centers are called **nailheads**. On most diamond grading reports, a diagram usually indicates the **pavilion depth percentage**—the distance from the girdle plane to the culet, expressed as a percentage of the average girdle diameter. When the pavilion depth percentage falls below 41%,

TABLE
STAR FACET
BEZEL FACET
CROWN
UPPER-GIRDLE FACETS
CROWN
GIRDLE (enlarged)
PAVILION
SIDE VIEW
LOWER-GIRDLE FACETS
PAVILION
PAVILION FACET
CULET (enlarged)

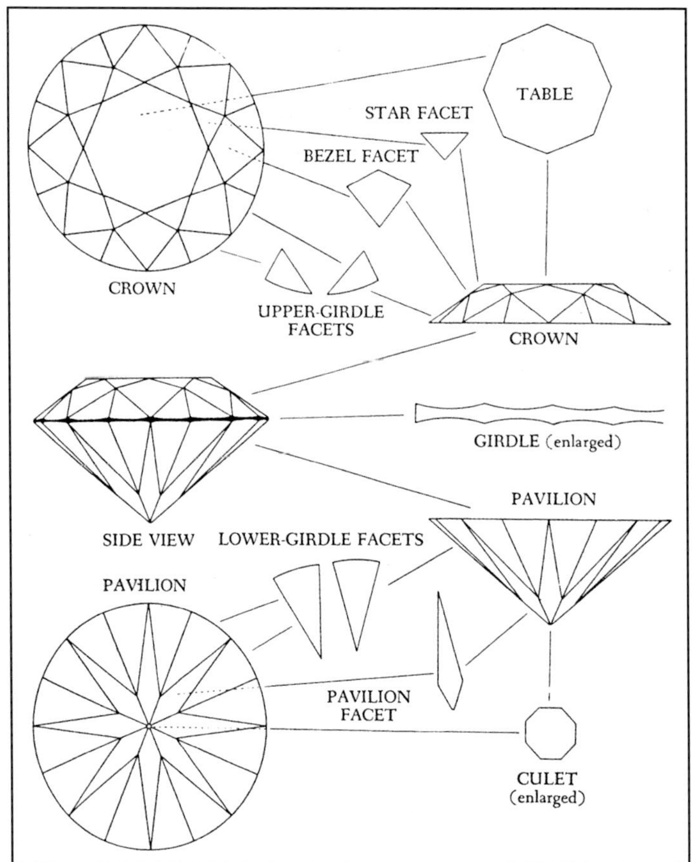

Fig. 4.1a Facet arrangement of a standard round brilliant cut. *Diagram reprinted with permission from the Gemological Institute of America.*

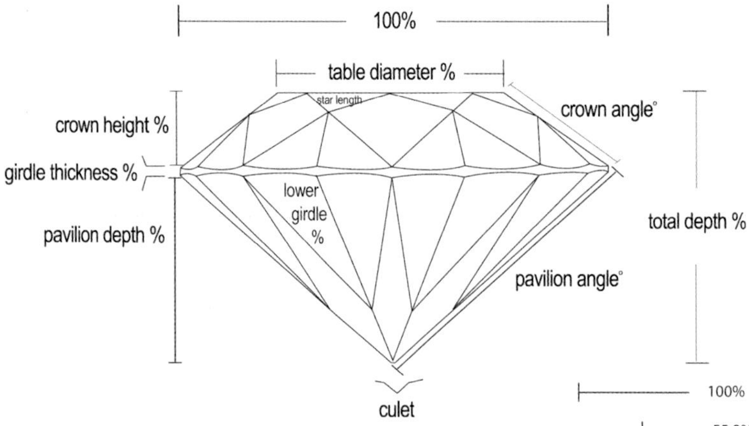

100%
table diameter %
star length
crown angle°
crown height %
girdle thickness %
lower girdle %
total depth %
pavilion depth %
pavilion angle°
culet

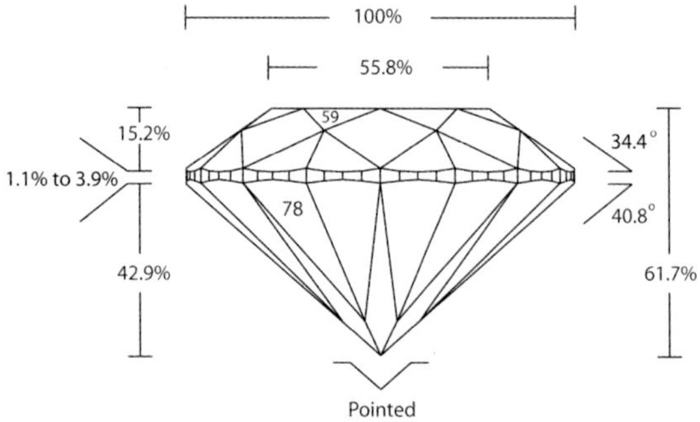

100%
55.8%
59
15.2%
34.4°
1.1% to 3.9%
78
40.8°
42.9%
61.7%
Pointed

Figs. 4.1b & 4.1c Profile views of a round brilliant cut diamond. The diagram on the right shows how the proportions are indicated on an AGS grading report. *Diagrams from the American Gem Society (AGS).*

Fig. 4.2 A fisheye in a round brilliant with a pavilion that is too shallow. *Photo by author.*

Fig. 4.3 Round brilliant with a dark center, a deep pavilion and very large table

a fisheye will start to form (with larger tables, the fisheye will be more prominent). The lower the percentage, the stronger the fisheye will be. In other words, the shallower the pavilion, the more visible the fisheye.

As the pavilion depth percentage rises above 48%, the diamond becomes darker in the center. The HRD lab (Hoge Raad vorr Diamant, Diamond High Council) in Antwerp, Belgium considers 41.5 to 45% to be a very good range for a round brilliant pavilion depth percentage. Any percentage below 40% or above 46.5% is classified as "not good" by the HRD.

Diamond cutters usually describe diamonds in terms of their angles instead of their depth percentages. The chart on the next page converts the pavilion depth percentage into the **pavilion angle**—the angle between the girdle plane and the pavilion main facets (the large pavilion facets extending from the girdle to the culet on a brilliant-cut; sometimes they are simply called pavilion facets, see fig. 4.1a).

Pavilion Depth % Approximately	**Pavilion Angle**
38.0%	37.4°
39.0%	38.0°
40.0%	38.8°
40.5%	39.0°
41.0%	39.4°
41.5%	39.8°
42.0%	40.0°
42.5%	40.4°
43.0%	40.7°
43.5%	41.0°
44.0%	41.4°
44.5%	41.8°
45.0%	42.0°
46.0%	42.8°
47.0%	43.4°
48.0%	44.0°

Data from GIA Diamond Grading Course

The GIA Cut Grade Reference Chart gives the following pavilion angle ranges required of a final GIA cut grade. (An overall grade of Excellent requires that all other proportions, finish and symmetry are also in the Excellent range. A final cut grade of Very Good would mean that no parameters are below Very Good, etc. This is true, too, of the other GIA proportion ranges listed in this chapter.)

Excellent 40.6° to 41.8°
Very good 39.8° to 42.4°
Good 38.8° to 43.0°
Fair 37.4° to 43.8°
Poor <37.4° to >43.8°

The diagram on lab reports normally includes the **total depth percentage**—the depth from the table to the culet, expressed as a percentage of the average girdle diameter in a round brilliant. According to the proportion standards of the HRD, very good round brilliants fall within a total depth percentage range of 55.5 to 63.9%. However, even if a diamond has an acceptable total depth, it could have a deep pavilion and low crown or vice versa. Consequently you can't determine if the pavilion of a diamond provides good light refraction just by reading a lab report that only lists the total depth percentage.

The total depth percentage is one of several factors used to determine the GIA cut grade. The GIA depth percentage ranges are:

Excellent	57.5% to 63.0%	Fair	51.1% to 70.2%
Very good	56.0% to 64.5%	Poor	<51.1% to > 70.2%
Good	53.2% to 66.5%		

Crown

The crown (top of the diamond) plays an important role in determining sparkle and fire.

If the crown is too thin or shallow, the diamond will have diminished sparkle and fire. When diamonds have the same table size, the shallower the crown, the smaller the **crown angle**—the angle between the girdle plane and the bezel facets (any of the four-sided, kite-shaped facets on the crown of a round brilliant-cut diamond, see fig 4.1a).

When the crown is too high, the upper girdle and bezel facet reflections will look crinkled. Flower-like patterns may be visible near the corners of the table (the large top facet) (fig. 4.8). Diamonds with very high crowns can have a lot of sparkle and fire; the problem is they tend to look small for their weight because too much weight is above the stone and not enough is spread across it.

A novice can normally tell from the side view when the crown of a diamond is very thin or very high. Experienced diamond professionals can also tell from the face-up view. Diamonds with shallow crowns can still have good brilliance, so crown height does not have as much of an impact on price as pavilion depth. In fact, many princess- and radiant-cut diamonds have thin crowns.

The crown angle is normally indicated on the lab report diagram. The HRD Lab considers 30.7° to 37.7° to be a very good crown angle range. The greater the angle, the higher the crown and vice versa. The GIA crown angle ranges are:

Excellent	31.5° to 36.5°	Fair	20.0° to 41.5°
Very good	26.5° to 38.5°	Poor	<20.0° to >41.5°
Good	22.0° to 40.0°		

Another measurement found on a diamond report's diagram is the **crown height percentage**—distance between the girdle and table planes expressed as a percentage of the average girdle diameter. A crown height percentage range of 11 to 16% is classified as very good by the HRD lab in Antwerp.

Fig. 4.4 A well-proportioned diamond

Fig. 4.5 Diamond with a shallow pavilion and low crown

Fig. 4.6 Diamond with too much weight above the pavilion

Fig. 4.7 Diamond with a very thin crown and a deep pavilion

Fig. 4.8 Face-up view of a diamond with a high crown

Fig. 4.9 Diamond with excess weight and an uneven and very thick bruted girdle

All photos on this page by author

The GIA crown height % ranges are:

Excellent	12.5% to 17.0%	Fair	7.0% to 21.0%
Very good	10.5% to 18.0%	Poor	< 7.0% to >21.0%
Good	9.0% to 19.5%		

Table

The size of the table (the large top facet) also plays a role in determining sparkle and fire. Table size is linked to the crown angle and crown height. When a diamond has a thin crown and steep crown angles, the table will be large.

The **table percentage**—a percentage of the average girdle diameter. For round brilliant cuts it is determined by dividing the largest table diameter by the average girdle diameter. For fancy shapes, it is calculated by dividing the width of the table by the width of the girdle.

When the American Gem Society (AGS) used a proportion-based cut grading system, the table size % range for their ideal cut grade was 52.4 to 57.5%. Most tables in this range can be spotted by the way their sides bow in (See fig. 4.10). (This bowing method only works with standard size star facets: a 57% table with 40% stars will bow out).Under the new AGS cut-grading system, diamonds with table percentages ranging from 47% to 61% can get a 0 ideal cut grade on their reports, providing the diamonds meet all the other required criteria. Both the new AGS and GIA Cut Grading Systems allow for some differences in personal taste.

For example, Europeans tend to like diamonds with table percentages a little larger than 57.5%. The Antwerp HRD lab considers 53 to 66% to be a very good table size range. Diamonds with small tables tend to emphasize fire whereas diamonds with larger tables highlight more the brilliance of the diamond. Opinions differ as to what is the best balance between fire and brilliance.

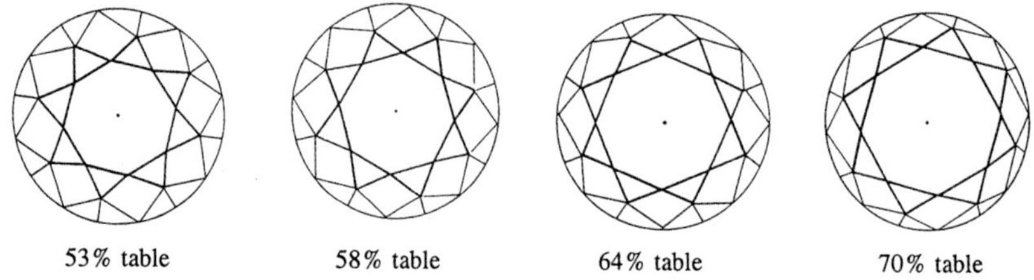

Fig. 4.10 Four table sizes ranging from 53% to 70% of the girdle width. The 70% table is too large for good sparkle and fire. *Diagrams courtesy Gemological Institute of America*

The GIA table percentage ranges for rounds are:

Excellent	52 to 62%	Fair	44% to 72.0%
Very good	50 to 66%	Poor	< 44% to >72%
Good	47 to 69%		

Another but less exact way to estimate and compare table size is by the flash method, a term used by the GIA. Gently tilt a diamond back and forth under an overhead light source and note the flash of white light that reflects off the table.

The larger the flash, the larger the table. Figure 4.11 shows this flash of white light on the six diamonds that are evaluated in the next chapter. The profile and normal face-up views are also shown.

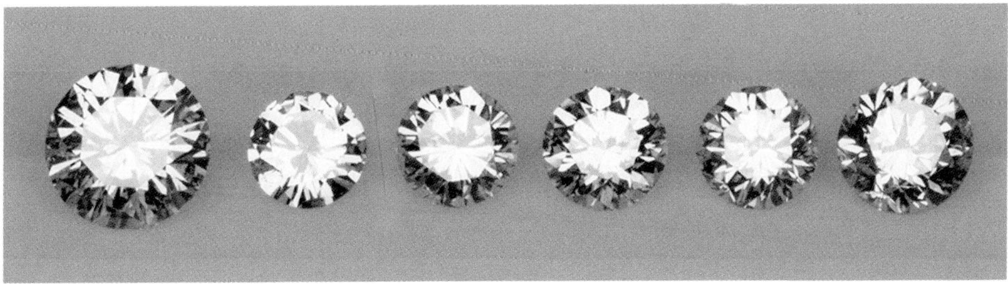

Fig. 4.11 A reflective flash off the tables of the six diamonds studied in the next chapter. The 1st and 4th diamonds from the left have a 58% table, the 5th diamond has a 59% table. The exact table sizes of the other diamonds is not known, but the tables of the 2nd and 3rd diamonds are the largest.

Fig. 4.12 Same diamonds in the face-up position under diffused lighting. From left to right: E I_1–2.20 cts ; G SI_2–0.70 cts; H VS_1–0.995 ct; I VS_2–1.00 ct; J SI_1–1.00 ct; L SI_3–1.41 cts

Fig. 4.13 The profile view helps explain why the "flat" second diamond is the least brilliant. The actual size of these diamonds in shown in the next chapter. *Photos 4.11 to 4.13 by author.*

Girdle

A certain minimal girdle thickness on a diamond protects it from chipping. If the girdle is too thick, it adds unnecessary weight to the stone and can sometimes detract from the appearance by causing a gray reflection in the stone. If the girdle is too thin (such as knife edged), it may chip during setting or during everyday wear.

The girdle thickness is judged in relation to the size of the diamond and has grades ranging from extremely thin (knife edged) too extremely thick (so thick that it is obvious to the unaided eye and may be difficult to set in jewelry).

The HRD lab in Antwerp classifies thin and medium girdles as very good. It is normal and desirable for fancy-shape diamonds to be thick at the points. This helps protect the points from chipping.

The GIA girdle thickness and girdle thickness percentage* ranges are:

Excellent	Thin to Slightly thick	2.5 to 4.5%
Very good	Extremely thin to Thick	2.0 to 5.5%
Good	Extremely Thin to Very Thick	0.0 to 7.5%
Fair	Extremely Thin to Extremely Thick	0.0 to 10.5%
Poor	Extremely Thin to Extremely Thick	0.0 to > 10.5%

*Girdle thickness % = total depth % - (crown height % + pavilion depth %). These percentages are true up to several carats. GIA also judges thickness by eye and uses comparative charts.

There are three types of girdles (or they could be a combination of these):

- **Faceted**: with small facets (fig. 4.14)
- **Bruted**: with a frosty, granular appearance (fig. 4.15)
- **Polished**: with no facets, looking like a smooth continuous rim of glass going around the diamond

Fig. 4.14 Faceted girdle. *Photo by author.*

Fig. 4.15 Bruted girdle. *Photo by author.*

Bruted girdles should be smooth and precision cut. If they are rough, they can trap dirt, giving the girdle a dark look, which in turn can slightly darken the face-up appearance of the diamond. Sometimes, girdles have fringes looking like whiskers and hairs extending into the diamond. They are appropriately called **bearded girdles** and can lower the clarity grade of diamonds, especially those of high clarity.

While GIA was doing their research on diamond cut, they discovered that sometimes the scalloping of the girdle can affect a diamond's face-up brightness and pattern of bright and dark areas. Figure 4.16 shows a normal girdle with even scalloping ("hills" and "valleys") all around the diamond. If a polisher wants to remove naturals or blemishes at the girdle, he may tilt the upper and lower girdle facets toward each other, creating a thinner girdle where these facets meet (fig. 4.17), which the GIA calls a **dug-out girdle**. Note how the girdle thickness at the points where the upper girdle facet junctions meet the lower girdle facet junctions is less than the girdle thickness at the points where the bezel facets meet the pavilion main facets.

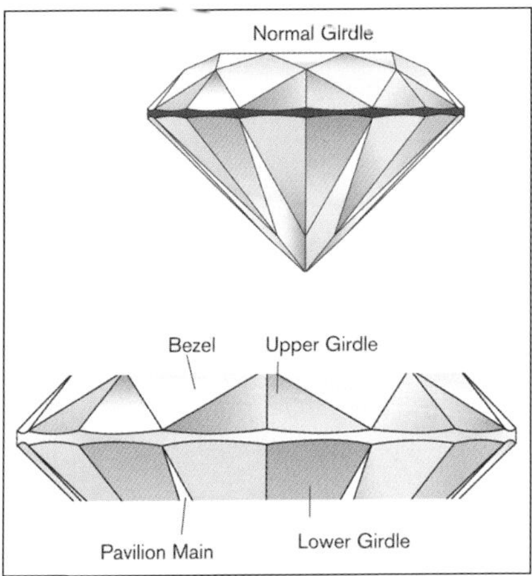

Fig. 4.16 Normal girdle with even scalloping. *Illustration by Peter Johnston/GIA,© Gemological Institute of America. Reprinted by permission.*

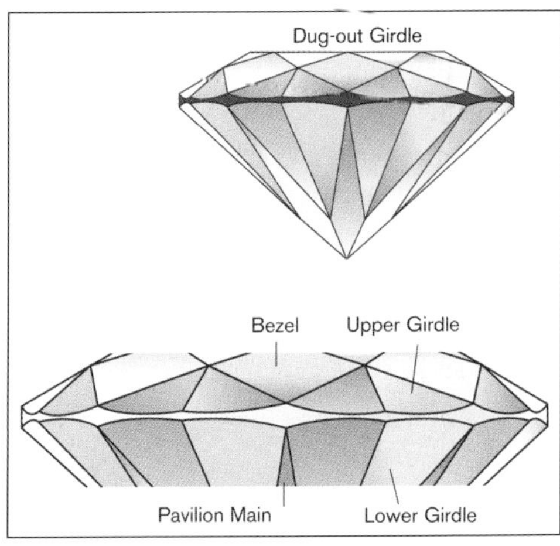

Fig. 4.17 Dug-out girdle. *Illustration by Peter Johnston/GIA,© Gemological Institute of America. Reprinted by permission.*

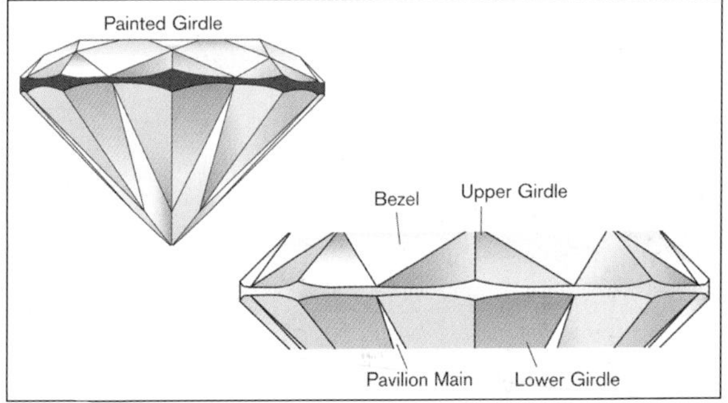

Fig. 4.18 Painted girdle. *Illustration by Peter Johnston/GIA, © Gemological Institute of America. Reprinted by permission.*

This type of scalloping may also be done to save weight. However, it can have the negative effect of making the stone look dark face up or appear smaller. The more strongly dug-out the diamond is, the more negative the appearance. This is because it creates a less desirable pattern of bright and dark areas face up.

Another type of uneven scalloping is called **painting** (fig. 4.18). It's the opposite of a dug-out girdle. The thickness at the points where the upper girdle facet junctions meet the lower girdle facet junctions is greater than the girdle thickness at the points where the bezel facets meet the pavilion main facets. This type of girdle can save weight, but in the case of severe painting, it can cause large areas of the diamond to flash all at once. This has a negative impact on sparkle and pattern. If there is significant to extreme painting or digging out, it can prevent a diamond from getting an excellent or very good cut grade. An excellent girdle has very little or no painting or digging out, and a very good girdle may only have moderate painting and digging out.

Culet

The culet is the last facet polished on the diamond. It is there mainly to protect the bottom of the diamond from abrading and chipping. Not all diamonds have culets; most stones below 0.25 carat have none. GIA culet ranges are:

Excellent	no culet to small	Fair	no culet to very large
Very good	no culet to medium	Poor	no culet to extremely large
Good	no culet to large		

Old cuts typically have very large to extremely large culets. These diamonds are in high demand by antique dealers and are not viewed as low quality because of their extremely large culets.

Star Facet Length %

The GIA has found that the size of the star facets can affect both brightness and fire, so they now include the star length as a cut grading factor. Star facet length is stated as a percentage of the total distance between the girdle edge and table edge (the red line across the yellow star facet extending to the girdle edge in figure 4.19.) The GIA star facet % ranges are:

Excellent	45 to 65%
Very good	40 to 70%
Good, Fair and Poor	any value

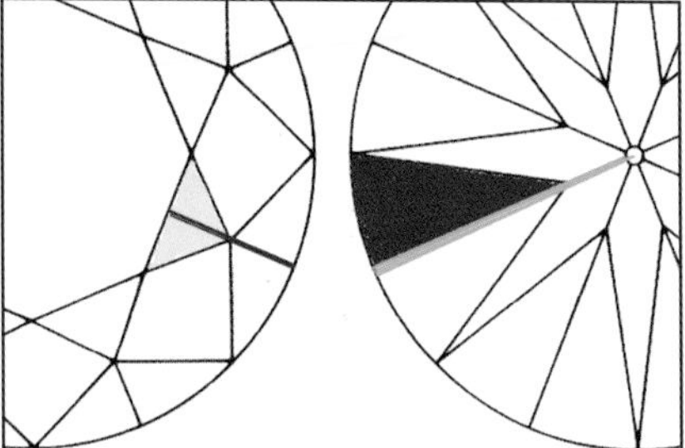

Fig. 4.19 The yellow star facet length is about 50% the length of the red line from the girdle edge to the table edge. The red lower girdle facet length is about 75% of the distance between the culet and the girdle (the green line).

Lower Girdle Facet Percentage

Another factor that the GIA has added to their cut grading system is the lower girdle facet percentage. The length of the lower girdle facets can affect the diamond's brilliance and face-up pattern of bright and dark areas. The lower girdle facet length is indicated as a percentage of the total distance between the girdle and the culet. The green line in figure 4.19 represents the total distance, along which the star facet length is measured. The star facet percentage is either estimated or calculated by dividing the total distance into the star facet length. If a diamond has a GIA or AGS report, the percentage will be noted on the diagram. For example, the diamond shown in figure 4.1c (an AGS diagram at the beginning of this chapter) has a lower girdle facet percentage of 78 and a star facet percentage of 59.

The GIA lower girdle facet percentage ranges are:

Excellent	70 to 85%
Very good	65 to 90%
Good, Fair and Poor	any value

Symmetry

Symmetry is a grading term for the exactness of shape and placement of facets. It is one of two subcategories of **finish**, which by GIA definition is the "quality of a diamond's polish, the condition of its girdle, and the precision of the cut." The other subcategory, polish, is discussed in the next section.

When gem laboratories assign a symmetry grade, they look for the following features:

- ♦ Out-of-round girdle outline
- ♦ Off-center culet
- ♦ Off-center table
- ♦ Tilted table, not parallel to the girdle plane
- ♦ Misshapen table that does not have sides of equal length and parallel opposing sides
- ♦ Wavy girdle that is not parallel to the table
- ♦ Girdle with unequal widths
- ♦ Pointing—facets fail to come to a point correctly.
- ♦ Misaligned crown and pavilion facets
- ♦ Similar facets of unequal size and shape
- ♦ Extra facets. (These only affect symmetry if they don't affect the clarity grade.)

In order to highlight the symmetry of their diamonds, some stores and dealers show their diamonds through a special viewer that displays an optical effect of hearts and arrows. When a round brilliant is perfectly symmetrical and well proportioned, distinct hearts and arrows patterns are visible in the viewer (fig. 4.20). The AGS Asset tool is a more sophisticated instrument that shows the optical symmetry characteristics of diamonds.

Fig 4.20 Hearts and arrows patterns. *Diamond, J Landau Inc; photo, Derse Studio.*

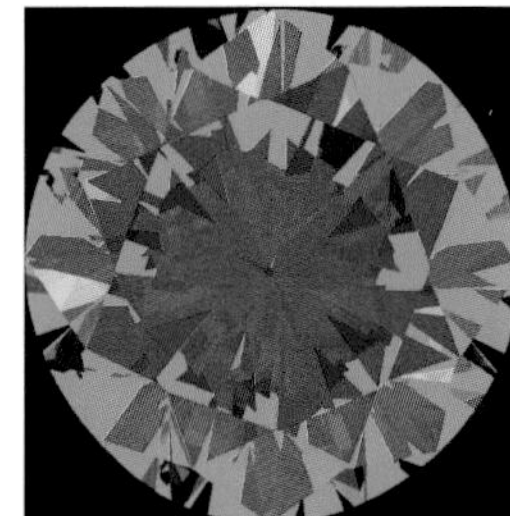

Figs. 4.21–4.23 Diamonds viewed through the AGS Angular Spectrum Evaluation (ASET) tool, an aid to assessing optical symmetry and light performance. Left: Ideal symmetry, center: average symmetry, right: poor symmetry. The red areas indicate the best use of light; the blue areas show contrast; and the green indicates less efficient use of light. *Photos from AGS.*

The GIA grades symmetry with the grades Excellent (E), Very Good (VG), Good (G), Fair (F), and Poor (P). Grades of Excellent are rare. Most diamonds have some minor symmetry problems, but this does not normally affect their beauty. You should be more concerned about the pavilion proportions and overall brilliance of the diamond than its symmetry grade.

Polish

Polish refers to the overall condition of the facet surfaces of a polished diamond. It is a subcategory of finish. When labs evaluate polish, they examine the diamond under 10X magnification and look for surface blemishes that do not affect the clarity grade. Some of these characteristics are listed below:

- ♦ Polish lines (PL): Fine, tiny, parallel grooves caused by faceting
- ♦ Burn marks: Hazy surface areas caused by excessive heat
- ♦ Rough girdle (RG): An irregular, granular or pitted girdle surface
- ♦ Scratches (S): Thin white lines
- ♦ Pits: Minute indentations that look like tiny white dots
- ♦ Abrasions (Abr): Scraped spots or areas along the facet junctions or edges that have a white or fuzzy appearance
- ♦ Lizard skin: A bumpy polished surface that looks like goose bumps. (The term was coined by John Koivula in the late 1970's.)

The GIA uses the same grades for polish that it uses for symmetry. Diamonds that are well polished will produce sharper light reflections and look brighter than stones with an inadequate polish.

"Ideal-Cut" Diamonds

The term "ideal cut" is a marketing term that has been used for excellent quality diamonds with proportions similar to those proposed by Marcel Tolkowsky, a mathematician and diamond cutter who is sometimes referred to as the "father" of the American brilliant cut. For a detailed and interesting history of the ideal cut, consult Al Gilbertson's *American Cut: The First 100 Years.*

The exact proportions of the "ideal-cut" vary depending on whom you talk to. However, since the American Gem Society (AGS) has established a reputable gem laboratory that offers ideal-cut diamond grading reports, more and more trade professionals are accepting their criteria for defining an "AGS Ideal™." (An example is shown in figures. 4.24 & 4.25.) If you have diamonds that AGS graded as a ideal before 2005, their proportions met the following criteria.

- ♦ Average pavilion depth percentage of 42.2 to 43.8%
- ♦ Average crown angle of 33.7° to 35.8°
- ♦ Average table diameter of 52.4 to 57.5%
- ♦ Average girdle thickness of very thin, thin, medium or slightly thick
- ♦ Culet size of pointed, very small, small or medium
- ♦ Symmetry and polish grades of AGS 0, which means the polish and symmetry characteristics are extremely difficult to locate under 10-power magnification. The 0 grades are the GIA equivalent of excellent.

Fig. 4.24 An AGS-quality "ideal cut" diamond from J. Landau. *Photo by author.*

Fig. 4.25 Profile of the same "ideal cut" *Photo by author.*

In 2005, AGS launched their Performance-Based Cut-Grading System. Instead of assigning cut grades based on two-dimensional proportion measurements, the AGS measures all facets of a diamond in three dimensions and includes factors such as brightness, fire and contrast.

Another new AGS cut-grading factor is **tilt**—the point at which the girdle of the diamond reflects under the table. A well-made round brilliant can have a greater amount of tilt before the girdle appears in the table of the stone than one which is not as well proportioned. Likewise the better cut a colored gemstone is, the more you can tilt it before a window (see-through effect) appears. Since gemstones are viewed from different directions when worn, rather than just exactly face up, the AGS believes that diamond cut should be evaluated from more than one angle.

The new AGS system is balanced with the biological capabilities of the human eye and human cognition, so the exacting symmetry seen with magnification is not necessary for a high grade. According to Jim Caudill, Director of Advanced Instruments of the American Gem Society, "A diamond with a degree of asymmetry (lack of exacting hearts and arrows) can perform as well as or better than those with clearly defined hearts and arrows. Optically, if the human eye and brain cannot resolve the detail, symmetrical or asymmetrical without magnification, there will be no deduction or penalty in our light performance metric. It's all about what we as humans can actually see in the most commonly encountered, stringent viewing conditions. Physical symmetry has a category of its own and assesses craftsmanship."

GIA and AGS Cut Grading Factors Compared

The GIA has also factored in brightness and fire into their new cut grading system. Both systems have three types of factors—light performance, proportion and finish. The GIA, however, does not use the term "light performance. A comparison of the GIA and AGS cut grading factors is shown on the next page.

GIA Cut Grade Factors	AGS Cut Grade Factors
Light Performance Factors	
Brightness	Brightness
Fire	Dispersion
Pattern	Leakage Contrast
Proportion Factors	
Girdle thickness Painting and digging effects	Girdle thickness
Culet Size	Culet size
Overweight percentage	Weight ratio
Total depth percentage Table percentage Crown angle Pavilion angle Crown height percentage Star facet length percentage Lower girdle facet percentage	Durability Tilt
Finish	
Polish	Polish
Symmetry	Symmetry

Even though diamond proportions such as the pavilion and crown angle are not used to calculate the new AGS cut grades, they are still indicated on the diamond diagram of the AGS report. Indirectly, the GIA proportion criteria are factored into the AGS grade because a diamond won't get a good light performance and tilt grade if the proportions are not good. Both systems allow for differences in personal taste. The way in which their grading factors interact is complex and is explained in their literature. It's more important for you to be able to make your own judgments about a diamond based on its appearance and the data on its report than to know how a lab calculates their overall cut grade

Other internationally known labs besides the AGS and GIA provide cut grades on their lab reports. The AGS and GIA were selected for this section because they have published more information on their cut grading systems than other labs. Even though cut grading is being approached in many ways, there is significant overlapping from one lab to another. Most labs provide more details about cut now than they used to. One of the biggest changes is the new emphasis on assessing diamond brilliance. That is the subject of the next chapter.

5

Judging Light Performance

Light Performance refers to the intensity, distribution, and type of light displayed by a diamond. Its definition may include any or all of the following, depending on who is using the term.

- **Brightness**: The actual and/or perceived amount of light returned by a diamond
- **Fire (dispersion):** The amount or display of spectral colors of light
- **Scintillation**: Flashes of light reflected from a faceted diamond seen when the stone, light source or observer moves. Some trade members say that "scintillation" is synonymous to "sparkle." Others say that scintillation has a broader meaning than "sparkle." For example, in its *Diamond Grading Lab Manual* (p. 11), the Gemological Institute of America (GIA) states that scintillation has two components: sparkle and pattern. David Atlas of Accredited Gem Appraisers (AGA) defines sparkle as "A static measure of the potential for scintillation."
- **Contrast**: A high contrast between bright and dark areas is desirable. A high-contrast diamond may appear brighter than a diamond that has low contrast but a higher light return. For more information on contrast, see the article by Michael Cowing, in the January/April 2005 issue of the *Journal of Gemmology* entitled "Describing Diamond Beauty."
- **Distribution, pattern, optical symmetry and light leakage**; These are terms used by different labs that refer to similar phenomena. In round brilliant diamonds, an even distribution of small patterns of light is usually more desirable than large, irregular areas that are bright or dark, which are usually the result of unplanned light leakage and cut problems.

The first lab report to show a diamond's light behavior was produced on July 1, 1996 by Diamond Profile Laboratory in Portland, Oregon. It was based on direct light performance reflector technology and was created by Craig Walters and Al Gilbertson. Even though the brilliance and life of a diamond has always been considered important, it's only been since about 2004 that internationally known gem labs have begun to offer diamond reports that describe or factor in brightness, fire and contrast on their reports.

Gem laboratories use a variety of systems to assess light performance and they may describe it in different ways. Not all labs evaluate light performance, however.

Methods for Judging Light Performance

Currently, four main methods are being used to measure or judge light performance:

- **Ray tracing or beam tracing** using a three-dimensional computer model
- **Lockup tables built using ray-tracing software, formulas for patterns, and observation testing with actual diamonds**
- **Direct light performance analysis**
- **Visual evaluation,** colloquially called the eyeball method

The ray or beam tracing method involves measuring a diamond using a non-contact measuring device, which creates a three-dimensional virtual diamond model. That information is then imported into the company's ray- or beam-tracing software and values for light performance are assigned. The values and categories of light performance vary depending on the company that produces the software. The software is based on a system that emulates how light interacts with a diamond from various viewing angles. Experienced diamond cutters, dealers, gemologists, and jewelers may have verified the software by ranking diamonds graded by the software. The resulting light performance values are either incorporated into the cut grade and/or listed separately on the diamond grading report. Three gem labs that have used ray or beam tracing to evaluate light performance in diamonds are the AGS (American Gem Society), GIL (Gemworld International Laboratories), and the GIA (Gemological Institute of America).

Proponents prefer three-dimensional ray or beam tracing over direct light measurement of a diamond in one face-up position because light performance can differ depending on the angle at which a stone is viewed. For example, the brightness of a diamond can change when you tilt it. Ray and beam tracing systems also have the advantage of being able to predict and grade diamond dispersion.

Opponents of ray tracing systems say that predictive tools should not be used in the world of science to set grades when a direct measurement exists.

The GIA has created **look-up tables** and a software program that were first based on ray tracing predications of brightness and fire. GIA researchers then tested these predictions by showing diamonds to trade professionals and laymen, asking them to rank the stones in terms of their brightness, fire and overall desirability. During this process they discovered that knowing the brightness and fire of a diamond was not sufficient for predicting its perceived beauty. Pattern (the size and arrangement of bright and dark areas) was also very important. Next the GIA team tried to find out the faceting and proportion characteristics of the best-liked and least-liked diamonds. They incorporated their findings into the final version of the GIA cut grading software and into tables that trade members and GIA students could use to assign GIA cut grades for diamonds.

The GIA believes that light performance systems must be validated by extensive observation testing of actual diamonds by experts and laymen because no method can reproduce or exactly measure what humans perceive when they look at diamonds. They also believe that it's desirable to have a cut grading system that allows for consistent grading with the human eye. The GIA found that most individuals could consistently discern five levels of diamond beauty, so they only have five cut grades. Other labs believe that small nuances of fine symmetry and light performance should be incorporated in a grading system. As a result, these labs may have up to 11 grades.

The direct light performance method uses advanced light measurement technology to demonstrate and measure the light behavior of an actual diamond rather than a model of the diamond. GCAL (Gem Certification and Assurance Lab) and AGA (Accredited Gem Appraisers) are two labs that use the direct light performance method. Direct measurement can take into account light-inhibiting inclusions, color, and transparency, which can all affect a diamond's light behavior. Therefore it can be used effectively with diamonds of all color and clarity grades. With ray and beam tracing and look-up tables, a subjective deduction may have to be made for diamonds of about SI2 and below and for other diamonds whose color and transparency may have a negative impact on their brilliance.

Another advantage of direct light performance technology is that it can readily be used with various shapes of diamonds. Ray and beam tracing models and the look-up table system are limited in the types of diamonds that they can grade for cut and light performance.

Visual evaluation is ultimately what buyers use to select the diamond they like best. Lab documents are useful selling tools because they offer the buyer an independent opinion of the diamond and guide buyers towards diamonds that are considered better looking diamonds by the trade. They're especially helpful for reporting small nuances of color, symmetry and clarity that affect price but that the eye may not be able to detect.

A lab report evaluation of light performance can offer added protection to buyers who wish to insure their diamond. Since American insurance companies typically offer replacement jewelry rather than cash for lost or stolen pieces, it's to the buyer's advantage to have a report and/or appraisal that offers as much information as possible. If someone pays a lot of money for a highly brilliant diamond, they naturally want an equally brilliant diamond replacement. But until recently, it wasn't possible to get reports describing light performance.

This doesn't mean that people no longer need to use their eyes to evaluate diamonds. No report can completely describe the actual appearance of a diamond. You still must look at the diamond to fully appreciate its brilliance, transparency, and color or lack of color. Both GIA and AGS would tell you that there are different appearances among their top grades, so you should look at the diamond to see which you prefer.

The light performance of mounted diamonds and small or low grade diamonds is just as important as those of high quality center stones. Yet it may not be practical or financially worthwhile to get lab reports for them. In these cases, it's even more important to know how to visually evaluate diamonds. The goal of this book is to help you make more accurate visual assessments. This will not only help you buy and sell diamonds, it will also help you understand the reports that accompany them. The last section of this chapter provides a few tips on evaluating light performance.

All of the preceding methods of assessing light performance have benefits and drawbacks. The best choices for your needs will depend on the size, quality and shape of the diamond(s) you wish to purchase or sell.

Gem Labs that Assess Light Performance

There are several reputable gem laboratories in the world. This section briefly analyzes the way that five of these labs factor in light performance on their reports. The selection of the labs was based on the following criteria:

- The amount of emphasis the lab has placed on describing cut and light performance
- How early the lab started to research light performance and use it on their diamond reports
- The amount of material the lab (or its affiliated organization) has published on light performance
- The diversity of reports, terminology and methodology among the labs

Gem labs use different terminology and factors for light performance, and sometimes the definition of terms differs from one lab to another. Therefore, the light performance factors evaluated by each of the five labs are indicated in the text and the categories are defined. When you discuss diamonds or read about them, don't assume that all trade members use terms such as "brilliance," "life," "sparkle" or "light performance" to mean the same thing that you do.

The text below also specifies which grades, method and type of software each lab uses to evaluate light performance. It shows sample reports and includes the website addresses where you can learn more on how each lab assesses light performance.

Accredited Gem Appraisers (AGA)

AGA uses ImaGem™ (www.imageminc.com) gem grading equipment to directly assess light behavior. It measures three factors:

Brilliance – the overall strength of light return

Sparkle – the amount and strength of spangle-like flashes of reflected and refracted light. A greater number and strength of flashes translates into a higher sparkle grade.

Intensity – the percentage of the whitest zones of light return within the diamond. Generally speaking, the greater the stone's symmetry, the higher its intensity will be.

AGA DIAMOND TRADE REPORT

Accredited Gem Appraisers

Div. of D. Atlas & Co., Inc. [est. 1898] Philadelphia, PA (215) 922-1926

Independent Diamond Quality Grading Certificate

Certificate Number: 7002126000 Client's ID#:

Client Name: To whom it concerns

Shape: Round

Weight: 1.54ct.

Dimensions: 7.44 x 7.42 x 4.56 mm

Total Depth: 61.4%

Table: 56.9%

100%
56.9%
15%
34.8°
Slightly thin to medium
40.8°
43%
61.4%
Closed culet

Negligible UV fluorescence
Slightly thin to medium faceted girdle
Closed culet
Laser inscribed girdle

Polish	**EX**	VG	GD	FR	PR
Symmetry	**EX**	VG	GD	FR	PR

LBI & DFS: EX+/0

Light Behavior	**Excellent**	Very Good	Good	Good to Fair	Fair	Commercial

Durability-Finish-Size	**0**	1	2	3	4

GIA COLOR: H

D	E	F	G	**H**	I	J	K	L	M	N	O	P	Q	R	S	T	U	V	W	X	Y	Z	Fancy Color
No color			Near colorless				Faint color			Light color					Obvious color								

GIA SI1

FL	IF	VVS1	VVS2	VS1	VS2	**SI1**	SI2	I1	I2	I3
No inclusions		Visible only under 10x magnification				May be visible to naked eye 1ct+		Eye visible		

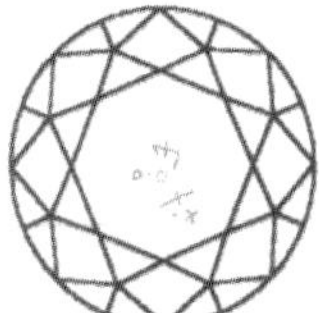

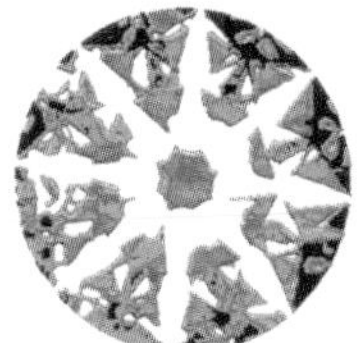

Comments:

Brilliance Image

ImaGem Measures

Brilliance: EX / 181

Sparkle: EX / 105

Intensity: EX / 359

David Atlas

Graduate Gemologist (GIA)
Senior Member, NAJA

Registered Trademark of ImaGem

While we use every reasonable effort to conform to GIA grading, we cannot guarantee our grading will be identical to the GIA. We do not represent our firm in any way connected with the GIA. No value is given on this form by Accredited Gem Appraisers.

Fig. 5.1 AGA (Accredited Gem Appraisers) sample Diamond Quality Grading Certificate

The grades of the AGA light behavior factors are shown separately on AGA diamond reports and are also combined into an overall Light Behavior Index (LBI), which has eight grades: excellent+, excellent, very good+, very good, good, good to fair, fair and commercial. The cut grade, which has five values from 0–4, is shown separately on the report. It has three components: durability, finish and size (DFS). The highest DFS grade is 0. You can get more information on the AGA grading report (fig. 5.1) at www.gemappraisers.com. Click on services and then reports.

American Gem Society (AGS)

AGS has created its own light performance software, the AGS Performance Grading Software® which is an actual ray-tracing engine. Each individual diamond is ray-traced using the actual geometry or surface map of the finished product. It can be purchased through the AGS Advanced Instruments Division at www.agsaid.com. The AGS Performance Grading Software® has also been embedded into the Sarin and OGI non-contact measuring devices.

The AGS Performance Grading Software® analyzes the following four factors to measure light performance.

Brightness – The amount of light returned to the observer that comes directly from the light source

Dispersion – The separation of white light, at the pupil, into spectral colors

Leakage – Areas that do not return light, which escapes through the pavilion and which is not returned when viewed either face up or when tilted.

Contrast – The darker areas caused by the observer obscuring a portion of the direct light. It can be positive or negative in its optical effect and ultimately contributes to the perception of brightness, scintillation and dispersion.

The AGS light performance grades for each factor are shown separately on its Diamond Quality Document and are also combined into an overall cut grade. Other components of the AGS cut grade are the finish factors of polish and symmetry and the proportion factors of girdle thickness, culet size, weight ratio, durability, and tilt (the point at which the girdle reflects under the table facet). There are 11 AGS grades ranging from 0 – 10 with 0 being the highest grade. Figure 5.2 is an example of the AGS Diamond Quality Document. More information is available at www.agslab.com.

Gem Certification & Assurance Lab (GCAL)

GCAL, a subsidiary of Collector's Universe, uses the Diamond Profile® optical light performance instruments and system for direct assessment analysis of diamonds. The Diamond Profile system analyzes the light returned through the crown into two light performance categories:

Optical brilliance – the overall return of light to the viewer

Optical symmetry – the alignment of facets and consistency of angles, a direct assessment of the precision of the cut and craftsmanship

A visual representation of both categories is shown on the GCAL Diamond Grading Certificate along with one of four grades: excellent, very good, good

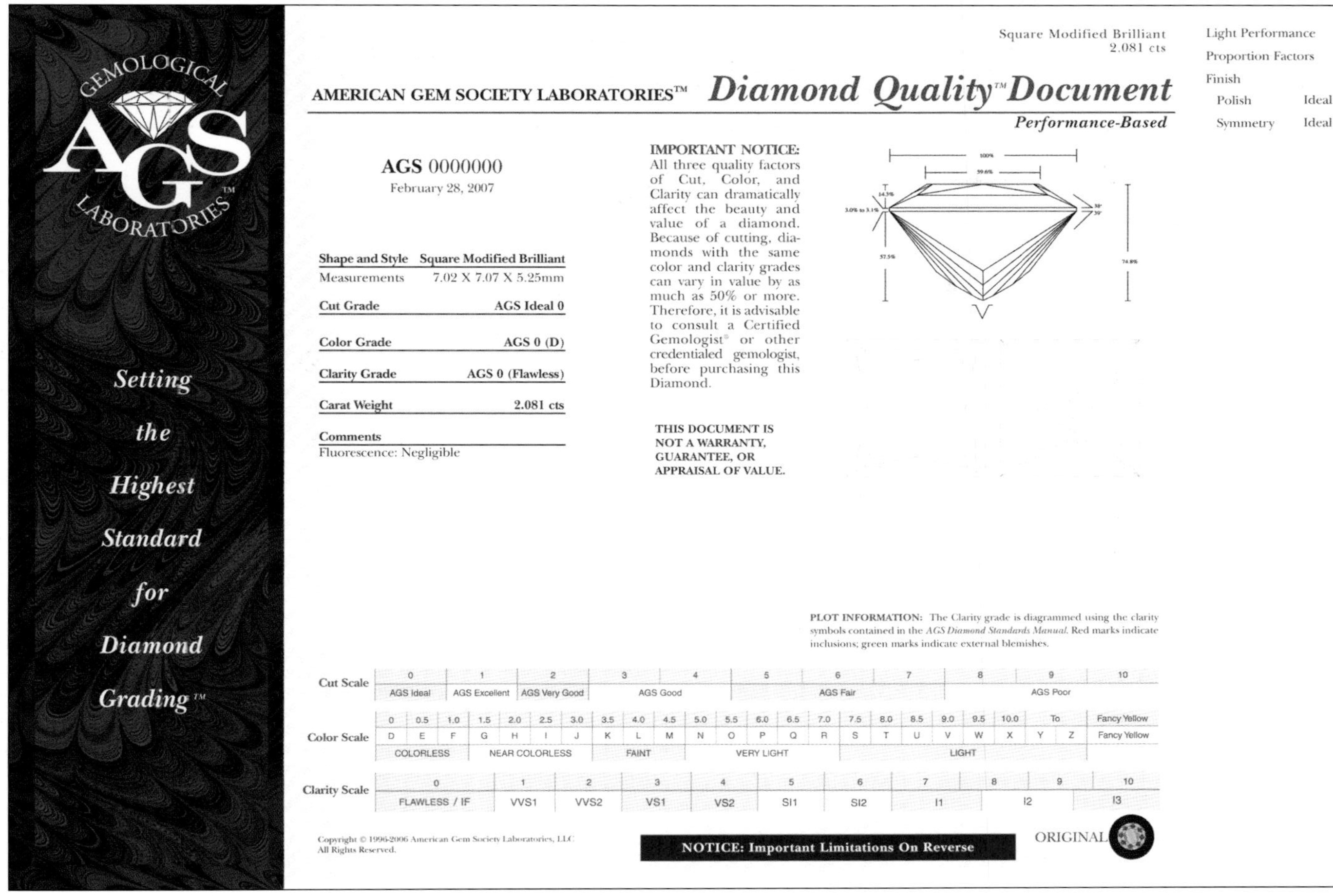

GEMOLOGICAL AGS LABORATORIES™

Setting the Highest Standard for Diamond Grading™

Square Modified Brilliant
2.081 cts

Light Performance
Proportion Factors
Finish
Polish Ideal
Symmetry Ideal

AMERICAN GEM SOCIETY LABORATORIES™ *Diamond Quality™ Document*

Performance-Based

AGS 0000000
February 28, 2007

Shape and Style	Square Modified Brilliant
Measurements	7.02 X 7.07 X 5.25mm
Cut Grade	AGS Ideal 0
Color Grade	AGS 0 (D)
Clarity Grade	AGS 0 (Flawless)
Carat Weight	2.081 cts

Comments
Fluorescence: Negligible

IMPORTANT NOTICE: All three quality factors of Cut, Color, and Clarity can dramatically affect the beauty and value of a diamond. Because of cutting, diamonds with the same color and clarity grades can vary in value by as much as 50% or more. Therefore, it is advisable to consult a Certified Gemologist® or other credentialed gemologist, before purchasing this Diamond.

THIS DOCUMENT IS NOT A WARRANTY, GUARANTEE, OR APPRAISAL OF VALUE.

PLOT INFORMATION: The Clarity grade is diagrammed using the clarity symbols contained in the *AGS Diamond Standards Manual*. Red marks indicate inclusions; green marks indicate external blemishes.

Cut Scale

0	1	2	3	4	5	6	7	8	9	10
AGS Ideal	AGS Excellent	AGS Very Good	AGS Good		AGS Fair			AGS Poor		

Color Scale

0	0.5	1.0	1.5	2.0	2.5	3.0	3.5	4.0	4.5	5.0	5.5	6.0	6.5	7.0	7.5	8.0	8.5	9.0	9.5	10.0	To		Fancy Yellow
D	E	F	G	H	I	J	K	L	M	N	O	P	Q	R	S	T	U	V	W	X	Y	Z	Fancy Yellow
COLORLESS			NEAR COLORLESS				FAINT			VERY LIGHT					LIGHT								

Clarity Scale

0	1	2	3	4	5	6	7	8	9	10
FLAWLESS / IF	VVS1	VVS2	VS1	VS2	SI1	SI2	I1		I2	I3

NOTICE: Important Limitations On Reverse

ORIGINAL

Fig. 5.2 AGS (American Gem Society) sample Diamond Quality Document

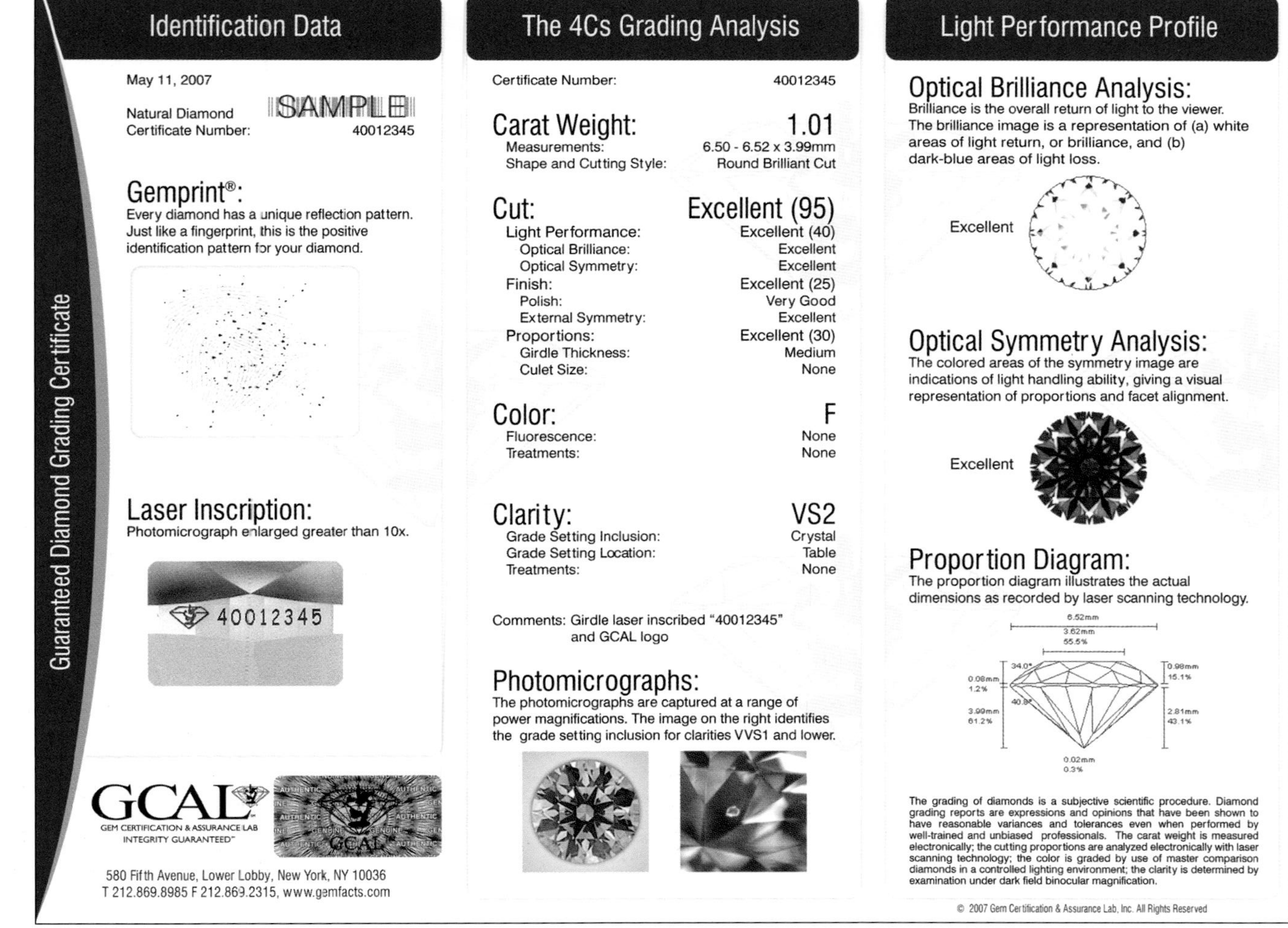

Guaranteed Diamond Grading Certificate

Identification Data

May 11, 2007

Natural Diamond
Certificate Number: 40012345

SAMPLE

Gemprint®:
Every diamond has a unique reflection pattern. Just like a fingerprint, this is the positive identification pattern for your diamond.

Laser Inscription:
Photomicrograph enlarged greater than 10x.

40012345

GCAL
GEM CERTIFICATION & ASSURANCE LAB
INTEGRITY GUARANTEED

580 Fifth Avenue, Lower Lobby, New York, NY 10036
T 212.869.8985 F 212.869.2315, www.gemfacts.com

The 4Cs Grading Analysis

Certificate Number:	40012345
Carat Weight:	**1.01**
Measurements:	6.50 - 6.52 x 3.99mm
Shape and Cutting Style:	Round Brilliant Cut
Cut:	**Excellent (95)**
Light Performance:	Excellent (40)
Optical Brilliance:	Excellent
Optical Symmetry:	Excellent
Finish:	Excellent (25)
Polish:	Very Good
External Symmetry:	Excellent
Proportions:	Excellent (30)
Girdle Thickness:	Medium
Culet Size:	None
Color:	**F**
Fluorescence:	None
Treatments:	None
Clarity:	**VS2**
Grade Setting Inclusion:	Crystal
Grade Setting Location:	Table
Treatments:	None

Comments: Girdle laser inscribed "40012345" and GCAL logo

Photomicrographs:
The photomicrographs are captured at a range of power magnifications. The image on the right identifies the grade setting inclusion for clarities VVS1 and lower.

Light Performance Profile

Optical Brilliance Analysis:
Brilliance is the overall return of light to the viewer. The brilliance image is a representation of (a) white areas of light return, or brilliance, and (b) dark-blue areas of light loss.

Excellent

Optical Symmetry Analysis:
The colored areas of the symmetry image are indications of light handling ability, giving a visual representation of proportions and facet alignment.

Excellent

Proportion Diagram:
The proportion diagram illustrates the actual dimensions as recorded by laser scanning technology.

The grading of diamonds is a subjective scientific procedure. Diamond grading reports are expressions and opinions that have been shown to have reasonable variances and tolerances even when performed by well-trained and unbiased professionals. The carat weight is measured electronically; the cutting proportions are analyzed electronically with laser scanning technology; the color is graded by use of master comparison diamonds in a controlled lighting environment; the clarity is determined by examination under dark field binocular magnification.

Fig. 5.3 GCAL (Gem Certification & Assurance Lab) sample Diamond Grading Certificate

and fair. Light performance along with finish and proportions are the three components of the GCAL cut grade and can earn up to 40, 30 and 30 points, respectively, for a total score of 100 points. GCAL has six total cut grades: ideal, excellent, very good, good, fair and poor. Figure 5.3 is an example of one of their reports. For more information, go to www.gemfacts.com.

Gemological Institute of America (GIA)

GIA used ray tracing software to develop a system that would predict brightness (the perception of white light return) and fire (the display of spectral colors created by the interaction of white light with a faceted diamond). The GIA found that a wide range of proportions could yield the same high light return. For example, a fisheye diamond, which is normally regarded as an inferior cut, could have a fairly high light return and be relatively bright. Likewise, a diamond with high fire might also have proportions that trade members consider inferior. This made GIA researchers realize that knowing the degree of brightness and fire does not necessarily indicate the desirability of a diamond.

In order to determine which diamonds are perceived as best, the GIA showed a wide variety of diamonds to dealers, jewelers, appraisers and even some lay people. Some tests were conducted in the dealers' offices or where the jewelers did their buying, and other tests were in controlled lighting environments arranged by the GIA. The researchers discovered that another seldom-mentioned element played an important role in determining a diamond's perceived desirability. It was pattern—the size and arrangement of bright and dark areas in a diamond. Then after careful analysis, the researchers found that the lengths of star and lower-girdle facets were critical to the cut assessment of round brilliants. They also found that in a few cases, variations in scalloping of the girdle gave diamonds an unattractive pattern or made it appear darker.

After 15 years of research, the GIA established a grading system for categorizing cut in standard round brilliants. The grades were based on the threshold at which the combination of brightness, fire and pattern would be distracting. Human observation was used to set the thresholds for their five grades—excellent, very good, good, fair and poor. Then the GIA created tables incorporating fifteen factors that they consider important in determining the beauty of a diamond—brightness, fire, pattern, total depth percentage, table percentage, crown angle, pavilion angle, crown height percentage, star facet length percentage, lower girdle facet percentage, girdle thickness, girdle thickness percentage, culet size, polish and symmetry. These factors were discussed in the previous chapter. The GIA Diamond Grading Course and Lab Manual explain the GIA system and diamond grading tables in more depth.

You can also determine how GIA would grade a diamond using a Sarin or OGI machine or the GIA Facet Scan device. However, as of the publication date of this book, these devices do not take into account the effect of the scalloping quality of the diamond's girdle. The GIA proprietary software used in their labs for grading does, however, consider the girdle scalloping quality. The GIA emphasizes that you should never rely solely on a grading report to make a buying decision. Cut grades are helpful in sorting out the better stones, but visual observation is what you should use to determine which diamond you like best.

When using facet scanning devices to assist in evaluating diamond cut, make sure the devices are calibrated regularly. You can get more information on GIA diamond grading reports by going to www.gia.edu and clicking on GIA Reports. A sample of the GIA diamond report is shown in the chapter on lab documents.

Gemworld International Laboratories (GIL)

The light performance software that GIL uses for their diamond reports is provided by Diamond Technologies, Inc. (DTI) (www.dtidiamondcut.com). It's based on advanced beam tracing research verified by the Optical Sciences Center at the University of Arizona upon referral from the Massachusetts Institute of Technology (MIT).

The DTI software analyzes the brilliance, fire, scintillation, and efficiency of a diamond based on measurements of all proportions and facets and calls it the **Light Return Index™**. DTI defines their light performance components as follows:

Brilliance – The amount of "white" light returned by the diamond

Fire – The amount of spectral color or rainbow effect returned by the diamond

Scintillation – Alternating beams of light or sparkle returned by the diamond when it is illuminated at different angles.

Efficiency – the contrast between the light and dark areas on the crown of the diamond.

The DTI Light Return Index™ is indicated separately on the report from their **Cut Quality Index**, which factors in the proportions, symmetry and polish. If the clarity or transparency of a stone has a negative effect on its light performance, an appropriate deduction will be made on the GIL report in the Light Return Index™. Figure 5.4 shows a sample GIL report. For more information, go to www.gemworldlabs.com.

Tips on Evaluating Light Performance Visually

As mentioned in Chapter 1, lighting is a key factor in evaluating brightness and fire, but the best type of light varies depending on the factor being assessed. This section provides tips on judging three light performance factors—brightness, fire and pattern.

Brightness

Strongly diffused lighting (frequently some type of diffused fluorescent lighting) is best for evaluating brightness. However, the primary light source should not be above your head (although not too close to the diamond). It should be above the diamond; otherwise your head will block a major portion of the light. A daylight fluorescent desk lamp can help resolve this problem.

Gemworld International Laboratories
2640 Patriot Blvd., Suite 240
Glenview, IL 60025
847.657.0555
847.657.0550 (F)

Diamond Grading Report

Natural Diamond

Date: January 9, 2007

Report no: 01063570001

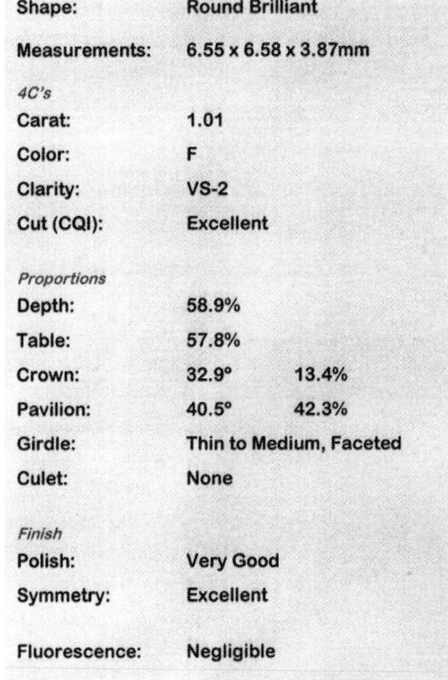

Shape:	**Round Brilliant**	
Measurements:	**6.55 x 6.58 x 3.87mm**	
4C's		
Carat:	**1.01**	
Color:	**F**	
Clarity:	**VS-2**	
Cut (CQI):	**Excellent**	
Proportions		
Depth:	**58.9%**	
Table:	**57.8%**	
Crown:	**32.9°**	**13.4%**
Pavilion:	**40.5°**	**42.3%**
Girdle:	**Thin to Medium, Faceted**	
Culet:	**None**	
Finish		
Polish:	**Very Good**	
Symmetry:	**Excellent**	
Fluorescence:	**Negligible**	

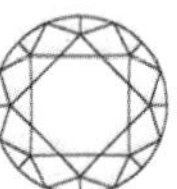

Actual Photo Facet Architecture

Poor	Fair	Good	Very Good	Excellent

Cut Quality Index (CQI)™

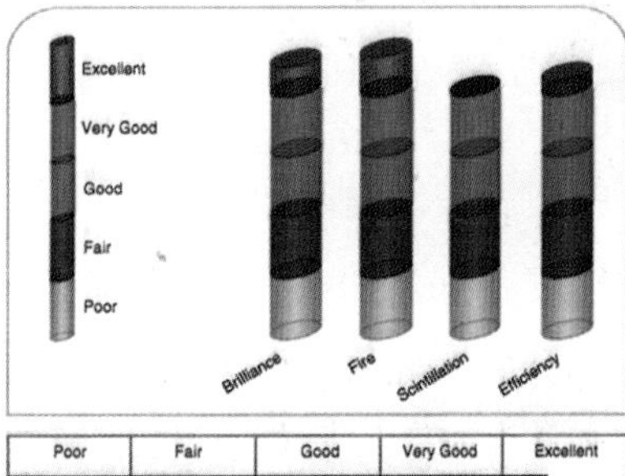

Poor	Fair	Good	Very Good	Excellent

Overall Light Return Index™

Comments: Diamond is laser inscribed with GIL report number.

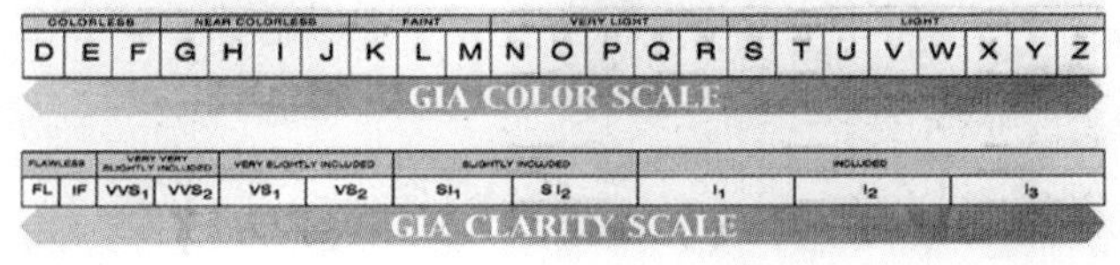

www.gemworldlabs.com

Fig. 5.4 GIL (Gemworld International Laboratories)) sample Diamond Grading Report

The environment also contributes to the quality of the light. Diamonds can reflect everything around them, including the walls, furniture and clothes you wear. It's best to wear a white shirt or blouse when grading brightness. However, it's helpful for something dark to be in the environment to provide contrast in the reflections. An all-white diamond is not as attractive and may not appear as bright as one that has a good contrast of dark and bright areas.

The GIA recommends using a gray background or tray for brightness grading. The gray background will allow you to see the background through the stone if there is light leakage, yet it won't make the stone look unnaturally dark. The GIA also recommends a viewing distance of 12 to 18 inches (30 to 45 cm) from the diamond. It can also be helpful to view the diamond closer and further from the eye. When dealers judge brightness, they sometimes place diamonds side by side in the crease between their fingers. Besides allowing them to see areas of light leakage, this indicates how the diamonds will look when worn.

When I was a diamond sorter in the 1980's, I was expected to assess the brightness of diamonds as small as .005 carat because that was a key factor in determining their price category. Lining these stones in a tray or between my fingers would have been impractical. The quickest and most accurate way of judging each diamond's brightness was to pick it up with tweezers and look at it with a loupe. The further the stone and loupe were held from the eye, the more light the stone received. It took about two to five seconds to assess the brightness, clarity, transparency and cut quality of the diamond and determine to which price pile these small diamonds belonged. The diamonds were already presorted for color and size.

The brightness of larger diamonds can also be assessed using a loupe and even a microscope, but the stones should also be judged with the unaided eye. No matter what magnification or background is used, you should look at diamonds from various angles by tilting the tray, the stone holder or your fingers. Your assessment of the diamond's brightness will be subjective.

The GIA was the first institution to publish criteria for their brightness grades. They are as follows:

- **Excellent**: very lively, even distribution of bright areas across the stone's crown with no distracting dark areas.
- **Very good**: lively, even distribution of bright areas across the stone's crown with few distracting areas.
- **Good**: has some life. Some distracting dark areas either around the culet or the upper girdle facets or both.
- **Fair**: little life. Some crown areas look bright but others might look gray. Areas of concentrated darkness may be within the table area, around the girdle or both.
- **Poor**: dull and lifeless. Few bright areas on crown. The entire table area may be very dark. The upper girdle facets might be very dark.

Fire

Diffused lighting such as fluorescent lighting suppresses fire. Sunlight, pen lights, spotlights and incandescent light bulbs increase its visibility, so these types of light sources should be used to assess fire. The GIA advises that fire grading can be done more efficiently in a dark or slightly dark room. It's difficult to visually assess differences in fire with stones weighing less than a half a carat. However, if you know their table facet percentage, you can make reasonable predictions about their potential fire. In its *Diamond Grading Lab Manual* (p. 24), the GIA states that stones with table facet percentages in the middle to upper 50-percent ranges produce more fire.

When comparing the fire of diamonds, look at them side by side under the same light source and tilt the tray so the stones can be viewed at different angles. The GIA rates fire using the following guidelines:

- **Excellent**: very fiery. Bright flashes of fire across most of the crown facets.
- **Very good**: fiery. Flashes of fire across many of the crown facets.
- **Good**: somewhat fiery. Some flashes of fire.
- **Fair**: small flashes of fire confined to small areas of the crown
- **Poor:** very few small flashes of fire

Pattern

Pattern, the size and arrangement of bright and dark areas, is evaluated with the same diffused lighting as brightness. The bright areas result from surface and internal reflections and the dark areas may be the result of light leakage or reflections of dark objects near the diamond. Something dark should be in the environment to provide a desirable contrast between the dark and bright areas (often the observer is all that is needed to create contrast against a bright environment). Tilt the tray or stone holder back and forth when making a visual assessment of the diamond's pattern. Consider the following:

- Is there a good contrast between the bright and dark areas of the pattern?
- Is the pattern well balanced and symmetrical?
- Is the diamond free of distracting dark areas?
- Do you like the pattern?

If you answer yes to all of these questions, then the diamond has a high rating for pattern.

The GIA grades and guidelines for judging pattern are:

- **Excellent**: extremely attractive with *no* distracting patterns. Very strong contrast between bright and dark areas. Area around culet is bright.
- **Very good**: very attractive. Strong contrast between bright and dark areas. *Minor* pattern problems may be present such as slight dark rings at the table edge, but the culet area is bright.

- **Good**: attractive, but has *noticeable* pattern problems such as a dark culet, moderately dark upper girdle facets, a dark ring at the table edges or radiating pavilion main facets that extend under the crown facets. Some contrast between bright and dark areas.
- **Fair:** unattractive. Little contrast between bright and dark areas. *Obvious* pattern problems such as fisheyes, dark centers, distracting dark upper girdle facets, prominent dark radiating pavilion main facets and overall grayed out appearance.
- **Poor**: extremely unattractive. Very little contrast between bright and dark areas. Overall appearance of darkness with few bright areas. *Prominent* pattern problems such as extreme fisheyes, very dark centers, and very dark pavilion main facets. Stone may appear much smaller than its actual diameter because of extremely dark upper girdle facets.

In summary, the best diamonds have even, symmetrical, bright and dark patterns across their crowns without areas of concentrated darkness under the table or around the edge of the table or girdle. Desirable patterns have high contrast and look good from all viewing angles.

6

A Closer Look at Clarity

In Chapter 2, I briefly described inclusions, blemishes, and the clarity grades established by the GIA (Gemological Institute of America.). In this chapter, I discuss the grades in more detail and show you several views of six diamonds ranging in clarity from VS_1 to I_1. As a review, the clarity chart included in Chapter 2 is repeated below.

GIA CLARITY GRADES* * For trained graders using 10-power magnification and proper lighting	
Fl	**Flawless**, no blemishes or inclusions.
IF	**Internally flawless**, no inclusions and only insignificant blemishes.
VVS_1 & VVS_2	**Very, very slightly included**, minute inclusions that are difficult to see.
VS_1 & VS_2	**Very slightly included**, minor inclusions ranging from difficult to somewhat easy to see.
SI_1 & SI_2	**Slightly included**, noticeable inclusions that are easy (SI_1) or very easy (SI_2) to see.
I_1, I_2, & I_3 In Europe: **P_1, P_2 & P_3**	**Imperfect**, obvious inclusions that usually are eye-visible face up. In I_3, distinctions are based on the combined effect on durability, transparency, and brilliance.

Clarity Grades

Flawless It's extremely rare that a diamond is flawless. Diamonds normally have at least a minor surface blemish.

According to the GIA Diamond Grading Course, a diamond can still qualify as Flawless if it has extra facets on the pavilion, naturals confined to the girdle, or internal graining that is not reflective, white or colored and that does not significantly affect transparency.

Fig. 6.0 A 13.24 emerald-cut diamond, which was originally graded by the GIA in 2000 as a Flawless, D color diamond After being worn, an updated report for a May 2007 auction stated it was a D, VVS_2 with potential, meaning it can be polished to increase the clarity grade. The ring sold for $960,000. *Ring from Joseph DuMouchelle International Auctioneers; photo by David Behl.*

Internally (IF) Diamonds with no inclusions and only insignificant blemishes, such as tiny pits and scratches, can be classified internally flawless. IF blemishes can usually be removed with minor polishing. One exception is light surface graining; it can't be polished away. If the graining is whitish, colored or reflective, the diamond is not graded any higher than VVS_1. Everyday wear can lower the grade of Flawless and IF diamonds; an example of this is shown in figure 6.0.

VVS_1 & VVS_2 These diamonds have inclusions so small that the average person would not be able to find them under 10-power magnification. Even trained diamond graders may have to view the stone from several positions to find the inclusion(s). It may only be visible through the pavilion.

Some typical VVS flaws are pinpoints, minute hairline cracks, tiny bruises, bearding, and slight graining. To grade diamonds of VVS clarities, it's best to use a microscope, rather than just a 10-power loupe. Professional diamond graders may use higher magnification than 10x on the microscope to more quickly locate VVS inclusions. Afterwards the magnification is decreased to determine if the inclusions are still visible at 10x.

VS_1 A novice would have a hard time finding the very small crystals, clouds, cracks (feathers) or pinpoints that characterize this grade. Sometimes, he or she may not be able to find them under ten-power magnification.

VS_2 Diamonds with this classification have the same types of minor inclusions as VS_1 stones but the inclusions are either more numerous, larger or easier to see.

SI_1 Even though this is the seventh clarity grade from the top, this is still an excellent grade. If you look at an SI_1 stone face-up with the unaided eye, you normally won't see any inclusions. However, they may be eye visible in large stones, especially in emerald cuts. If you look at an SI_1 diamond with 10-power magnification, you'll notice small cracks (feathers), clouds or crystals.

SI_2 Sometimes you can see the inclusions of these stones through the pavilion (bottom) of the stone with the naked eye, but normally, the inclusions are not visible through the crown. An exception to this would be with large diamonds and with emerald-cut diamonds. As the GIA points out in their diamond grading course, inclusions in such diamonds are easier to see because of their larger facets. The inclusions of the SI grades generally do not affect the durability of the stone.

SI_3 An intermediary grade between I_1 and SI_2, which was first introduced on reports by the EGL (European Gem Laboratory). It is also used by PGS (Professional Gem Sciences) and is seen on trade price lists. The GIA, IGI (International Gemological Institute) and AGS (American Gem Society) labs do not use the SI_3 grade on their reports; and to my knowledge, none of the other major laboratories listed in Chapter 14 use it either.

I_1 (P_1) The inclusions of this grade are obvious at 10-power magnification, but in small brilliant-cut diamonds, they are barely visible to the unaided eye through the crown. This can be a good clarity grade choice for people on a limited budget. Often a well-cut I_1 looks better than a poorly cut SI diamond.

I_2 (P_2) The inclusions are often easily visible to the unaided eye and may affect the beauty and durability of the diamond. Large cracks and very dense clouds are common I_2 inclusions. This grade is frequently used in discount jewelry.

I_3 (P_3) These diamonds frequently look shattered, as if they'd been hammered. Sometimes they have no cracks, but they're so filled with crystal inclusions that they have a muddy gray or whitish look. An I_3 grade would be unacceptable to someone interested in a brilliant and transparent diamond.

Clarity grading requires more than identification of diamond inclusions. An overall visual impression must be formed of the diamond with and without 10-power magnification, and the grading conditions must be considered. Keep in mind the following:

- Each grade represents a range of quality. Consequently, diamonds of the same clarity grade are not always equally desirable. That's why it is important to visually examine stones instead of just relying on grades when selecting diamonds. In some cases, a high I_1 diamond can look better than a low SI_2 stone when set.

- Prongs and settings can hide flaws. Consequently, only approximate clarity grades can be assigned to diamonds set in jewelry. If customers are interested in a stone with a high clarity, it may be best for them to buy a loose stone and have it set.
- Diamonds must be clean for accurate grading. Dirt and dust can look like inclusions. Alcohol or distilled water with a bit of dish washing liquid are helpful for cleaning diamonds.
- Big inclusions generally lower grades more than small ones. Usually one or two of the largest inclusions establish the clarity grade.
- The type of inclusion can have a dramatic effect on the grade. For example, a small feather (crack) will tend to lower a grade more than a pinpoint inclusion.
- Dark inclusions tend to lower grades more than colorless and white inclusions. Sometimes, however, white inclusions stand out more than black ones due to their position.
- Inclusions under the table (in the center) of the diamond tend to lower grades more than those near the girdle (around the edges).

Diamond Clarity Examples

A month before I started writing the first edition of this book, I photographed six diamonds, each of a different clarity ranging from VS_1 to I_1. They were selected at random and then photographed from different angles, both through the lens of a microscope and through a camera lens. No special photographic lights were used. The photos were shot with either the lighting on the microscope or with ordinary diffused incandescent desk lamps or with a combination of the two types of lighting. In some of the captions you will see the term **darkfield illumination.** This means the light is coming from the side against a black background in the microscope. It highlights the flaws and usually makes the diamond look worse than under normal lighting. The diffused overhead lighting view most closely approximates the view through a loupe with fluorescent lighting. In the overhead lighting view, the light is above the stone.

I photographed the diamonds in this manner in order to give you a fuller understanding of the clarity grades than what you would get from just seeing single face-up photos of the diamonds. Three of the diamonds happened to come with GIA grading reports and three had EGL mini certificates (shortened version of a full grading report).

With the exception of the grading and proportion information taken from the lab documents, all comments about the diamonds are based on my opinions. Other qualified trade professionals may disagree with some of my statements. I will be giving you the perspective of a gemologist with experience in the wholesale diamond trade.

Diamond 1: VS_1, H color, EGL LA, 0.995 ct

Fig. 6.1 VS_1, 7x, darkfield illumination

Fig. 6.2 VS_1, 7x, overhead lighting

Fig. 6.3 (VS_1) Clouds, which are only visible in the pavilion view and a tiny crystal. The inclusions are reflected so they appear doubled.

Fig. 6.4 (VS_1) Profile view, overhead lighting

Diamond 2: VS_2, I color, GIA, 1.00 ct; 63.3% depth; 58% table; medium to slightly thick faceted girdle; no culet, good polish, good symmetry

Fig. 6.5 VS_2, darkfield illumination

Fig. 6.6 VS_2, 7x, overhead lighting

Fig. 6.7 (VS_2) Crystal near the girdle at one o'clock position and pinpoints. Darkfield light.

Fig. 6.8 (VS_2) Profile view, overhead lighting

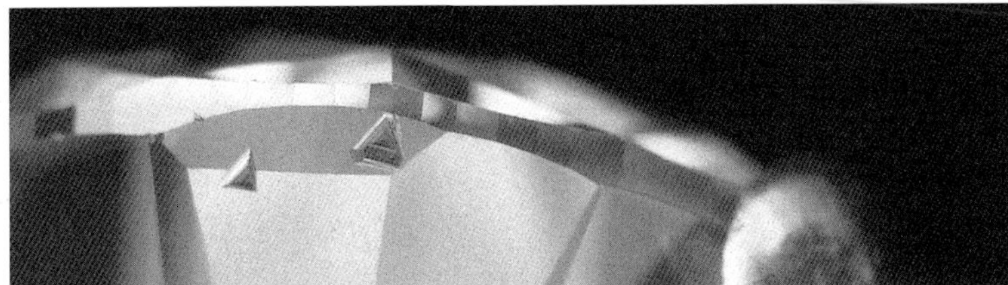

Fig. 6.9 (VS_2) Indented naturals and an extra facet that was considered a clarity feature by the lab. This is an ideal set of "birthmarks" for a diamond. They are not visible from the top view and they distinguish the stone from all other diamonds.

Diamond 3: SI_1, J color, GIA, 1.00 ct; 65.4% depth; 59% table; thin to thick faceted girdle; no culet, good polish, good symmetry

Fig. 6.10 SI_1, 8x, darkfield illumination

Fig. 6.11 SI_1, 8x, overhead lighting

Fig 6.12 (SI_1) Feather, pinpoints and tiny crystals at 9 o'clock position, small crystal and pinpoint just above the culet, darkfield lighting

Fig. 6.13 (SI_1) profile view, overhead lighting

Diamond 4: SI_2, G color, EGL LA, 0.701 ct

Fig. 6.14 SI_2, 7x, darkfield illumination

Fig. 6.15 SI_2, 7x, overhead lighting

Fig. 6.16 SI_2, 7x, darkfield & overhead light

Fig. 6.17 (SI_2), profile view

Diamond 5: SI_3, L color, EGL LA, 1.406 cts

Fig. 6.18 SI_3, 7x, darkfield illumination

Fig. 6.19 SI_3, 7x, overhead lighting

Fig. 6.20 SI_3, darkfield and overhead lighting

Fig. 6.21 (SI_3) profile view

Fig. 6.22 (SI_3) Bearded girdle and natural. Re-polishing could improve the girdle.

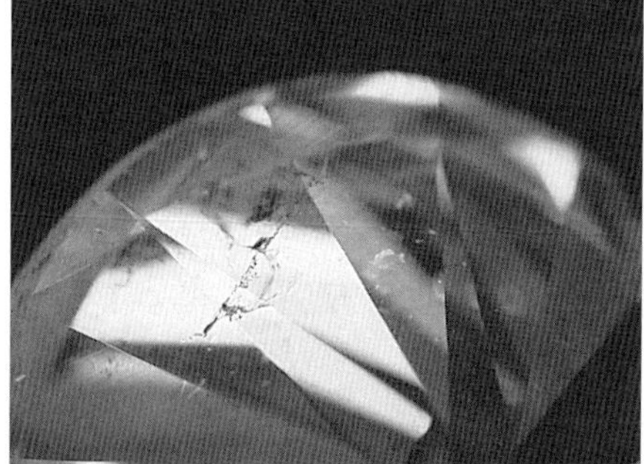

Fig. 6.23 SI_3, 17x, Inclusions that look black with overhead lighting as in figure 6.19

Diamond 6: I_1, E color, GIA, 2.20 ct; 61.1% depth; 58% table; medium to thick faceted girdle; no culet, good polish, fair symmetry

Fig. 6.24 I_1, 6x, darkfield illumination

Fig. 6.25 I_1, 6x, overhead lighting

Fig. 6.26 I_1, darkfield and overhead lighting

Fig. 6.27 (I_1) profile view

Fig. 6.28 I_1, darkfield illumination

Fig. 6.29 I_1, darkfield illumination

Fig. 6.30 Face-up views of the six diamonds. Left to right: I_1, SI_3, SI_2. SI_1, VS_2, and VS_1 (actual size). Their inclusions are not noticeable but the lower brilliance of the SI_2 diamond is apparent.

Only one of the preceding six diamonds would I advise people not to buy, and that is the 0.701 ct, SI_2, G color diamond. It has a good color grade and a respectable clarity grade, but it looks dull and dark, especially when compared to the other diamonds (fig. 6.30). This is because the crown and pavilion are n't well proportioned.

By contrast, the diamond with the lowest color grade, the 1.41 ct, SI_3, L color stone, is bright and sparkly. In my opinion, color is a matter of personal taste. For example, a blouse with a faint yellow color is not inferior to one that is white. In the diamond world, however, colorless diamonds are more rare and in higher demand than diamonds with yellowish tints. Consequently, colorless diamonds are higher-priced. If this diamond were D color, it would probably cost 75% more, all other factors being equal. When a customer has a strict budget, color can be a good factor on which to compromise.

The 2.20 carat, I_1, E color diamond would be appropriate for someone more interested in the size and color grade. A person could buy this stone for about one-third the price of an IF or VVS_1 diamond of the same color grade, all other factors being equal, or for about half the price of a VS_2 diamond. Under normal lighting this is an impressive diamond, and its inclusions are small enough that they are not visible to the naked eye.

On the subject of lighting, you should not restrict your customer's view of diamonds under magnification to darkfield illumination. Turn on the overhead microscope light so that they can see the brilliance of the diamond magnified. Darkfield lighting masks brilliance, exaggerates flaws and is seldom used by dealers in the process of buying and selling gems. They normally use loupes, and the light is above and/or to the side of the diamond over a white background. Darkfield illumination is most helpful for detecting treatments and imitation diamonds, and for grading clarities of VVS and above.

Sometimes inclusions look white under darkfield illumination, but black when viewed with a loupe or under the microscope's fluorescent lamp. Dark inclusions, especially those in the center of the table, have a greater impact on the clarity grade than those that are white. This is another reason to look at diamonds with overhead lighting.

When judging brilliance, move the stones and compare them next to other diamonds. The apparent brightness of each diamond can change depending on the distance of the diamonds from the lamp and their position in the tray. A larger view of these six diamonds is shown in the previous chapter. However, they are arranged in the order of their descending color grades instead of their ascending order of clarity.

Diamonds with clarity grades lower than I_1 are not often sent to gem labs for grading. Some examples of I_2 and I_3 grades are shown below.

Fig. 6.31 I_2

Fig. 6.32 I_2

Fig. 6.33 I_2

Fig. 6.34 I_2

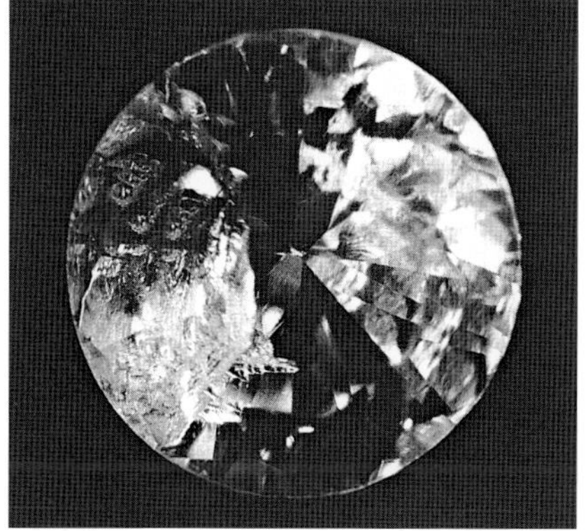

Fig.6.35 I_3,

Fig. 6.36 I_3

Fig. 7.1 Half the necklace and one earring in this composite photo are shown under normal lighting conditions (left), and the other half of the necklace and the same earring are shown as they appear under a long-wave ultraviolet lamp (right). Even though diamonds in a range of fluorescent strengths are placed next to diamonds with faint or no fluorescence (the darkest stones), the jewelry has a uniform overall appearance under normal lighting conditions. *Jewelry courtesy Harry Winston, Inc.; photos by Harold & Erica Van Pelt. Photo reprinted with permission from the Gemological Institute of America.*

7

Fluorescence

When a Burma ruby is placed under ultraviolet (UV) light, it typically will have a beautiful red or red-orange glow. This glow is called **fluorescence**, which is the emission of visible light by a material when it's stimulated by ultraviolet light, x-rays or other forms of radiation. The term "fluorescence" comes from the mineral fluorite (calcium fluoride), which is noted for displaying an array of intense fluorescent colors. Like rubies, many diamonds exhibit this characteristic.

It's helpful to understand the basic principles of light in order to understand fluorescence. The various types of light are defined in terms of wavelengths, which are measured in nanometers (one millionth of a millimeter, abbreviated nm). See graph below:

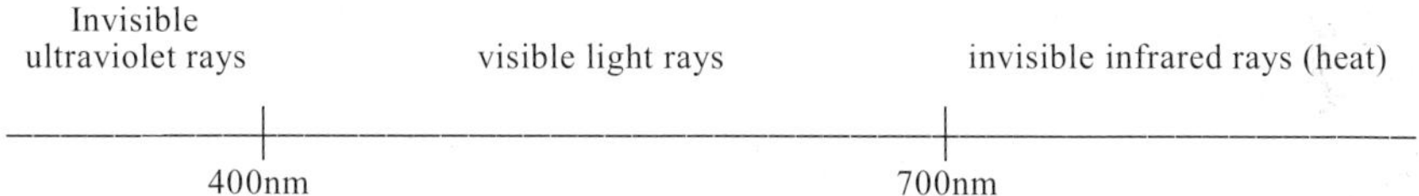

The light that the human eye can see falls approximately between 400nm and 700nm. These are the same wavelengths as the colors of the rainbow which start from violet at 400nm and extend to red at 700nm.

Light with wavelengths longer than approximately 700 nm is called **infrared light**. We can't see this light, but we can feel it as heat.

Light with wavelengths shorter than 400nm is called **ultraviolet light**. Even though we can't see or feel this light, it can still have an effect on us. For example, it can cause our skin to sunburn and tan.

Scientists divide the wavelength range of ultraviolet light into the four sections shown on the graph below.

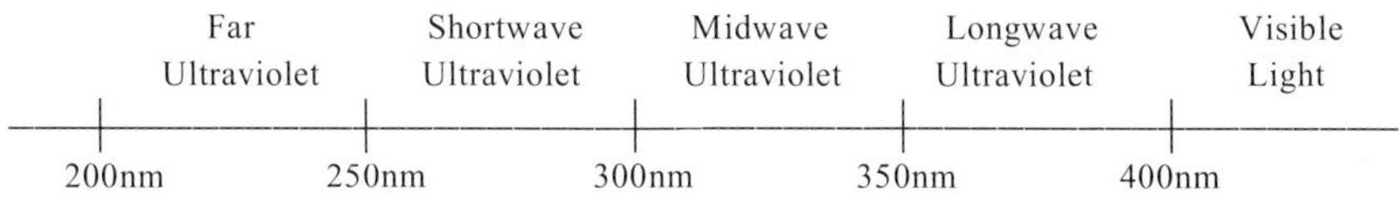

Longwave UV light is known among hobbyists as "black light." It's present in sunlight and causes some minerals to fluoresce as well as other items such as teeth, fingernails, and some paints, fabric and ink. Longwave UV light doesn't seem to have a negative effect on the skin or body.

Midwave UV light is also present in sunlight and induces fluorescence in some minerals. When its wavelengths are shorter than 310nm, it helps the body absorb vitamin D and it causes the skin to tan or burn, depending on the length of exposure.

Shortwave UV light is absorbed by the earth's atmosphere, so it is not present in sunlight. Shortwave UV lamps are especially effective in stimulating mineral fluorescence and are widely used by hobbyists as well as gemologists. When using these lamps, one must avoid overexposure because this light can also cause sunburn.

Far UV light extends from about 20 nm to 250nm. Gemologists and mineralogists are not concerned with this light because air absorbs it. Research on far UV light must be conducted in a vacuum. X-rays fall below far UV light and have wavelengths between .01 and 10–20 nanometers.

Besides being used for gem and mineral identification, UV light has a variety of practical applications, which include:

- Treatment of skin disorders and eye problems
- Detection of counterfeit bills
- Destruction of bacteria, sterilization
- Study and analysis of cell cultures and biological samples
- Water purification
- Detection of metal stress and cracks in aerospace and defense industries
- Quality control in the agricultural industries. Stored food, for example, can be examined for signs of rodent urine, which fluoresces.

(The material in the preceding section is primarily based on information from a chapter entitled "The Magic of Ultraviolet Light" by Thomas Warren in the book *Ultraviolet Light and Fluorescent Minerals.* Warren is the founder and president of Ultra-Violet Products, Inc.)

Diamond Fluorescence

When diamonds fluoresce under UV light, they usually display a blue color, but they may also look violet, green, yellow, orange, red or white; or they may show a combination of colors. The fluorescence is often patchy or in bands. Sometimes the diamonds continue to glow after the UV light is turned off. This continued emission of visible light after the light source is removed is called **phosphorescence**.

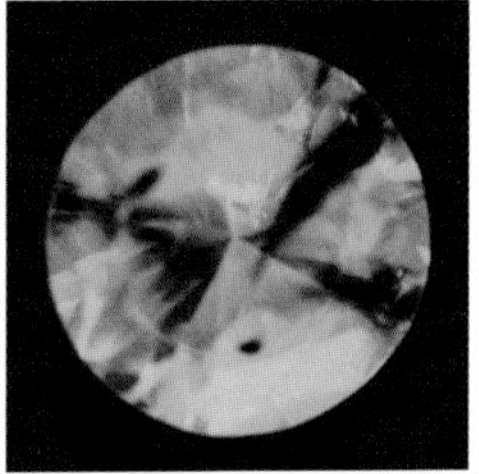

Fig. 7.2 Fluorescence in a blue synthetic diamond. *Photo: Alan Hodgkinson.*

Diamonds with blue fluorescence typically have a yellow-green phosphorescence, which is a positive test for diamond. If the diamond is then heated, it will glow blue again, and this effect is called **thermo-phosphorescence**. Under X-rays, diamond will usually have a uniform bluish white glow. Cathode radiation (electron radiation) gives the most brilliant fluorescent effects and causes some diamonds to glow different colors on different faces (from Eric Bruton's *Diamonds).*

Lab reports usually indicate the strength and color of a diamond's fluorescence to longwave UV light. The description is not a grade; it is just a further means of identifying the diamond. The GIA Gem Trade Laboratory categorizes the levels of strength as "none," "faint," "medium," "strong," or "very strong,"

Not all labs use the same categories. The AGS (American Gem Society) Laboratories has four categories: "negligible," "medium," "strong" and "very strong."

The following conditions may influence the observed fluorescence reactions:

- ♦ The distance of the UV lamp to the gemstone being examined. The closer the lamp is to a diamond, the stronger the reaction may be.
- ♦ The darkness of the room in which the stone is viewed.
- ♦ The strength of the fluorescence. For weak fluorescence reactions, it is sometimes difficult to accurately see and describe the fluorescence color. Use of a reference of known fluorescence color can help the observer in such situations.
- ♦ The type of lamp used. Both the UV lamp and the filters in the lamps can vary from one manufacturer to another. In addition, both the lamp and the filters can degrade over time, and this may influence observed fluorescence reactions.

What Causes Diamond Fluorescence?

Trace elements and irregularities in the atomic structure of a mineral can cause both gem color and fluorescence. Even though the chemical formula for diamond consists only of carbon, it can have traces of other elements such as nitrogen, aluminum and boron. When nitrogen and aluminum substitute together for carbon atoms, blue fluorescence can result. Single nitrogen atoms coupled with a carbon vacancy can cause yellow fluorescence. Two nitrogen atoms associated with crystal irregularities due to radiation damage can activate greenish-yellow fluorescence.

The information in the preceding paragraph is from pages 194 and 195 of *Ultraviolet Light and Fluorescent Minerals,* in a chapter entitled "Activators in Fluorescent Minerals." It's written by Earl R. Verbeek, a research geologist with the U.S. Geological Survey.

Is Ultraviolet Lighting the Same as Fluorescent Lighting?

No, it's not the same. Ultraviolet lamps emit mostly UV light, whereas fluorescent lamps emit mostly visible light. Even though both types of lamps are made from glass tubes with cathodes inserted at both ends, the fluorescent tube is coated with a phosphor on the inside walls that absorbs UV light and re-emits it as visible light.

A short-wave UV lamp, on the other hand, has a clear tube and a filter that blocks the passage of visible light and allows shortwave UV light to pass through. The primary emissions of shortwave UV lights are typically about 254 to 255 nanometers.

Longwave UV lamps use tubes with a longwave-emitting phosphor coating on the inside. These tubes are similar in appearance and construction to fluorescent tubes, but the phosphor coating is designed to emit longwave UV light rather than visible light. The primary emissions of longwave UV lamps are at about 365 to 366 nanometers. For more information, see pages 12–21 of *Ultraviolet Light and Fluorescent Minerals.*

Are Fluorescent Diamonds Undesirable?

It seems common sense that a diamond's beauty should be judged on its appearance in normal light, not under a longwave UV lamp. Nevertheless some Internet sites have advised consumers to reject diamonds solely on the basis of a lab report stating that the diamond fluoresces under UV light. Those who believe that fluorescent diamonds are bad claim that fluorescence makes diamonds look, oily, hazy or milky white, they don't mention the fact that a lot of highly transparent valuable diamonds are fluorescent (see figure 7.1).

As a result, more and more people have come to believe that fluorescent diamonds are undesirable. In fact, some consumers who chose a diamond for its beauty have wondered if it's defective simply because the stone's lab report states that it has medium or strong fluorescence in UV light.

According to the August 3, 2007 *Rapaport* magazine, faint blue fluorescence has no impact on price. However, in the D to H color grades, medium to very strong blue fluorescence can decrease the prices of diamonds with clarity grades of VS and above. On the other hand, in I to N color grades of all clarities, medium to strong blue fluorescence may increase the price slightly. This is because blue fluorescence can make diamonds look whiter in sunlight, particularly when the fluorescence is strong. Yellow fluorescence, however, can have a negative effect on price if it makes the diamond appear more yellowish than its color grade.

I used to work full time in the diamond industry, and I had the opportunity to visit the offices of many diamond dealers in the Los Angeles diamond district. I would observe how they examined diamonds during transactions. Never did I see a dealer place a diamond under a UV light and examine the stone's fluorescence in order to determine if he wanted to buy it. Fluorescence was not an issue. What mattered were quality and the overall life of the diamond.

When I sorted parcels of diamonds, I looked at each stone with a loupe under fluorescent and diamond grading light, but never under UV light. If a diamond was milky white, it was obvious when I looked at it, and the diamond was placed in a rejection pile. If the diamond was hazy, it was downgraded. Transparency was important, but this quality was determined by examining the stone under normal lighting, not under a UV lamp. Transparency is a separate phenomenon from fluorescence.

On the front cover of the winter 1997 issue of *Gems and Gemology* is a photograph of a well-matched, transparent diamond necklace and an earring by Harry Winston. Half the necklace and one earring are shown under normal lighting conditions; the other half and the same earring are shown under longwave ultraviolet light (fig. 7.1). Even though the diamonds have a range of fluorescent strengths, they have a uniform attractive appearance under normal lighting conditions.

The Harry Winston necklace is not an unusual example. Photographs of important diamond pieces viewed under fluorescent lighting used to be taken for identification purposes. If someone made a copy of the piece, it was easy to detect the copy by comparing it with the pattern of diamond fluorescence in the original piece.

If we wouldn't reject these diamonds, than why should we reject any other fluorescent diamond simply because rumors and some sites on the Internet suggest they are undesirable?

The power of the written word is sometimes amazing. In 1829, Sir Walter Scott published his novel *Anne of Gerstein*. In it, one of the characters wore a gorgeous opal that would change color depending on her mood. One day when a few drops of holy water were sprinkled on the opal, she fainted and died shortly thereafter. Convinced that this meant opals were unlucky, readers stopped buying the gem. Within a year of the novel's publication, the opal market had crashed and prices were down about 50 per cent. Even today, there are a few people who think opals bring bad luck even though it was considered a lucky gemstone prior to 1829.

My Advice Regarding Diamond Fluorescence

The preceding section was entitled, "Are fluorescent diamonds undesirable?" In my opinion, the answer is no. A diamond with fluorescence can be just as attractive as one with none. When we buy a diamond, we're buying a gemstone, not a lab report; we should pay more attention to how the diamond looks under normal lighting than to its UV fluorescence description on the report

Finding a diamond in a desired size, shape, color, quality and price range is a challenge. Why make the process more difficult by ruling out attractive transparent diamonds that happen to be fluorescent? If your customers find a good-quality diamond they like at the right price, they should consider buying it whether or not it's fluorescent. Here is some additional advice for diamond buyers:

- ♦ If a seller offers a discount because a diamond is fluorescent, accept the discount.
- ♦ If a seller asks for a premium because a diamond has blue fluorescence, don't pay it unless you can see that it has a positive impact on the diamond's color. There are plenty of other sellers who don't charge extra for such diamonds. If the fluorescence has an unusual color, the premium may be warranted. Collectors of fluorescent gems want them.
- ♦ View diamonds under various types of normal lighting—fluorescent lamps,

daylight, light bulbs. If you select diamonds that look good in the light sources under which they will be worn, it won't matter what their color or fluorescence strength is under UV light.

- If a colorless, near colorless or yellow diamond has medium to very strong blue fluorescence, be glad because this is a good indication that the diamond is natural and not synthetic. (See Chapter 7 on synthetic diamonds for more information.)
- Base your choice of diamond on its actual appearance, rather than on the description of its fluorescence on a lab report.

Two Good Sources of Information on on Diamond Fluorescence

- The book *Ultraviolet Light and Fluorescent Minerals* by Thomas S. Warren, Sterling Gleason, Richard C. Bostwick and Earl R. Verbeek
- The article "A Contribution to Understanding the Effect of Blue Fluorescence on the Appearance of Diamonds" by Thomas Moses, Ilene Reinitz, Mary Johnson, John King, and James Shigley in the winter 1997 issue of *Gems & Gemology*.

8

Synthetic Diamonds

Synthetic (man-made) diamonds were first produced in the early 1950's for industrial purposes. Around 2002, small quantities began to be sold commercially for use in jewelry. Colorless and colored lab-grown diamonds are now more widely available.

What are Synthetic Diamonds?

Synthetic diamonds are diamonds made in a laboratory that have essentially the same chemical composition and crystal structure as natural diamonds. Their physical and optical properties are almost the same as those of natural diamonds.

Cubic zirconia (CZ) is not synthetic diamond. It's a diamond imitation (termed simulant in the trade) because it has a different chemical composition than a diamond. Some CZ's are marketed in stores and on the Internet as synthetic diamonds, but this is considered an unethical trade practice. CZ's are not man-made diamonds; they're imitation diamonds.

Marketers of synthetic diamonds usually identify their diamonds with terms such as "lab grown," "lab-created," "created," and "man-made;" whereas gemologists and natural stone dealers usually refer to them as synthetic diamonds. A few sellers call them "cultured diamonds" and compare them to cultured pearls. This is misleading advertising. The next section will explain why.

How Does Growing Diamonds Differ from Culturing Pearls?

There are two basic types of lab-created diamonds—HPHT synthetic diamonds (those grown under high pressures and high temperatures) and CVD synthetic diamonds (those produced using chemical vapor deposition techniques).

Fig. 8.1 CVD single grown crystals. *Photo from the EGL USA Group.*

HPHT-created diamonds are grown by placing a carbon-containing solid in the center of a special pressure chamber and surrounding it with a metal flux such as iron or nickel (a flux is a solid material that dissolves other materials when melted). After applying extremely high pressure and high temperatures under controlled conditions, carbon is dissolved in the molten flux. The carbon atoms move to tiny diamond seed crystals near the chamber walls and begin to grow. Within a few days, new synthetic diamond crystals suitable for faceting are formed.

CVD synthetic diamonds are produced at low pressures by placing minute synthetic diamond seed crystals in an environment with carbon-containing gases. The gas molecules are broken apart during decomposition and carbon atoms are deposited on the "seeds," causing them to grow into lab-created diamond crystals.

Cultured pearls are not grown in laboratories. They grow in oysters or mussels after man implants a shell bead or a piece of tissue from the mollusk in them. The nacre (pearl coating) isn't created in a laboratory. It's secreted by the mollusk around the irritant. Cultured pearls take a few months to a couple of years to form, not just a few days like synthetics.

Some sellers are telling customers that man-made diamonds are grown just like cultured pearls. Besides being misleading, this is unfair to the pearl industry. A cultured pearl is a much more natural product than a lab-created diamond. Because of widespread misconception with the term "cultured," the Jeweler's Vigilance Committee (JVC) has petitioned the Federal Trade Commission to forbid sellers from applying the term "cultured" to laboratory-grown gems. Major trade organizations in the US and abroad fully support the JVC on this issue. Producers of man-made gems have been able to successfully market their products by identifying their products as lab grown or lab created. So there is no reason to use the term "cultured," other than to deceive buyers.

Detecting Synthetic Diamonds

Even though most jewelers are not currently able to distinguish synthetic diamonds from those that are natural, the major gem laboratories are able to identify all lab-grown diamonds since synthetics don't have all of the same physical and optical properties as natural stones. That is because they are not formed in exactly the same way.

Researchers and gem laboratories are sharing their findings with trade members, so more and more jewelers will be able to detect man-made diamonds. The manufacturers of lab-grown diamonds have been very cooperative and generous in providing samples of their products to gem labs for analysis.

DeBeers has already developed diamond instruments such as the DTC DiamondView™ and DiamondSure™ that can detect synthetic diamonds. They are working on developing lower priced synthetic diamond detectors. Some lab-grown diamonds can be identified without a special diamond tester. They may be detected with:

Magnification

The microscope is an important tool for identifying the origin of diamonds. Unlike synthetic diamonds, natural diamonds may have included minerals such as garnet, diopside and diamond. In HPHT lab grown diamonds, however, gray or black metallic inclusions are more typical. They result if bits of the molten metal flux used to grow the diamonds get trapped in the crystals.

Fig. 8.2 Metallic inclusions *Photo by Sharrie Woodring.*

Fig. 8.3 Close-up view of same metallic inclusions. *Photo by Sharrie Woodring*

Fig. 8.4 Metallic inclusion with a different shape. *Photo by Sharrie Woodring.*

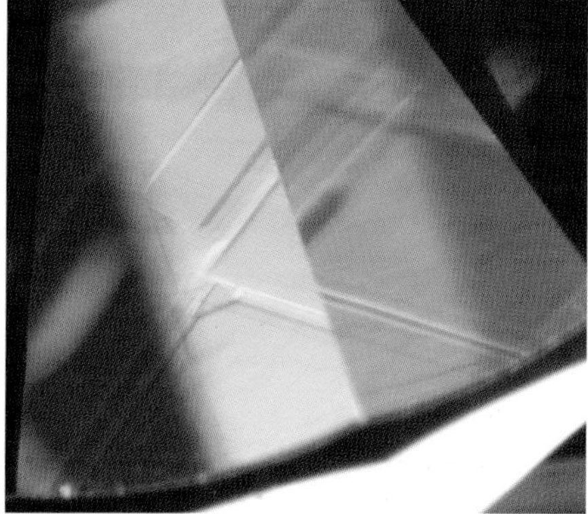

Fig. 8.5 Graining in the form of an X. *Photo by Sharrie Woodring.*

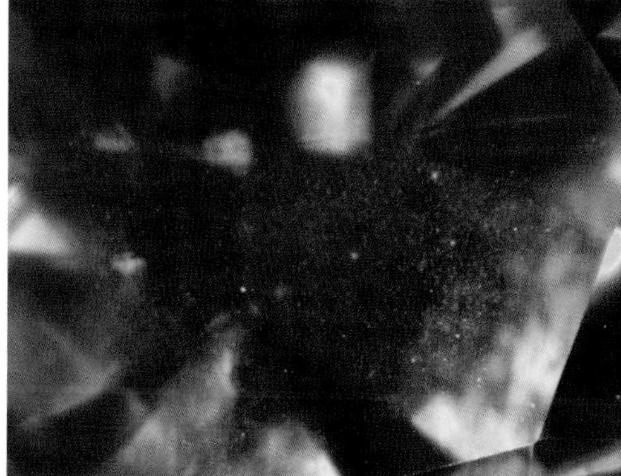

Fig. 8.6 A cloud of pinpoint inclusions. *Photo by Sharrie Woodring*

Fig. 8.7 Uneven color zoning in an HPHT synthetic diamond. *Photo from EGL USA*

These metal flux inclusions are usually rounded, elongated or irregular in shape and have a metallic luster (figs. 8.2–4).

Some lab-grown diamonds have minute cloud particles dispersed throughout the stone, which are best revealed with fiber optic illumination (fig. 8.6). They may be difficult to find with only darkfield lighting. According to Sharrie Woodring of GCAL, these clouds are most often found in orangy to yellow colors of HPHT-grown synthetic diamonds.

Since man-made diamonds grow differently than those in nature, their growth patterns are different. For example, lab grown diamonds may display distinctive graining (fig. 8.5) Color zoning may be more pronounced than in natural diamonds (fig. 8.7).

Magnetism

Because of the presence of metallic inclusions containing iron, synthetic diamonds may be attracted to or repelled by special magnets (fig. 8.8). Natural diamonds are not magnetic.

Fig. 8.8 A synthetic diamond attracted to a magnet. *Photo by Alan Hodgkinson.*

Fluorescence

A high percentage of natural and synthetic diamonds can be distinguished from each other just by observing their fluorescence under a UV lamp (figs.8.9–10). Some of the main differences are:

- **Natural diamonds usually fluoresce stronger to LW (longwave) than to SW (shortwave) light, whereas most synthetics fluoresce stronger to SW.** However, some synthetic diamonds that have undergone high temperature and high-pressure color treatment fluoresce stronger to LW than to SW.

- **Blue is the most common LW fluorescent color of colorless and yellow natural diamonds.** The fluorescent colors of HPHT synthetic yellow to colorless diamonds are normally greenish yellow to chalky yellow, although on rare occasions pale bluish white colors have been noted. CVD man-made diamonds typically have an orange to orange-yellow or yellow-green UV fluorescence.

  If you have a yellow, colorless, or near colorless diamond with medium to very strong blue UV fluorescence, it's a natural diamond.

- **The distribution of UV fluorescence in natural diamonds tends to be more even than in synthetic diamonds.** Some HPHT synthetic diamonds have characteristic cross and hour-glass fluorescence patterns, whereas CVD diamonds often display straight groove-like parallel lines under UV light that are difficult to see without magnification and strong short wave UV light such as that used in the DeBeers Diamond View™ Instrument.

Figs. 8.9 & 8.10 Left photo: pink diamonds in normal lighting—left, an irradiated natural round brilliant; center, natural color crystal from Argyle mine in Western Australia; right, an irradiated synthetic Chinese diamond. Right photo: Same pink diamonds under longwave ultraviolet light. *Photos by Alan Hodgkinson, author of the upcoming Alan Hodgkinson's Gem Testing Techniques.*

PHOSPHORESCENCE

Synthetic colorless to blue diamonds normally glow (phosphoresce) longer under SW UV than natural diamonds after the UV light is switched off. In fact, some synthetic diamonds continue to glow for several minutes to hours in the dark. Scottish gemologist Alan Hodgkinson reports observing a DeBeer's synthetic blue diamond that phosphoresces for several days, though the phosphorescence is very weak after about an hour. By contrast, the glow of natural diamonds typically lasts less than 30 seconds, although exceptions are encountered as with the famous Cullinan diamonds.

See Tables 8.1 and 8.2 for more detailed information on the fluorescence and phosphorescence of diamonds.

UV lamps are more affordable than most of the other instruments used by labs to detect synthetic diamonds. Small hand-held LW UV lamps are available for as low as US$25. You can find small SW UV lamps for as low as US$50. As the wattage or strength of the light goes up, so does the price. Appraisers can buy a decent LW/SW lamp for less than $300. Major labs pay more for stronger and higher-quality lamps.

Here are a few tips for judging the UV fluorescence of diamonds:

- View the diamond(s) against a black background.
- View the diamonds in a totally dark room.
- Allow your eyes to adjust to the darkness so very weak reactions can be observed.
- Place the UV lamp as close to the diamond(s) as possible.
- Avoid looking at the fluorescent UV light tube.
- It's good to wear protective eye wear when viewing diamonds under UV lamps, especially under shortwave UV. The longer the viewing time the better.

- For best results, it's helpful to have comparison stones when judging single stones. Fluorescence and phosphorescence tests can also be used effectively on parcels of diamonds to quickly sort out diamonds that are obviously natural or synthetic. Questionable diamonds can undergo further testing.

Table 8.1

Description of diamond	Intensity & color of fluorescence under longwave UV lamp	Intensity & color of fluorescence under shortwave UV lamp
Natural colorless to near colorless	occasionally none visible; weak to very strong blue or sometimes yellow or orange	none visible or weak to strong blue or sometimes yellow or orange
Synthetic colorless to near colorless	HPHT: none visible; CVD: usually weak yellow or orange	HPHT: weak to strong yellow, green-yellow or orange-yellow; CVD: very weak to strong orange-yellow or yellow- green
Natural yellow	sometimes none; otherwise weak to very strong blue or yellow; sometimes orange, rarely green	sometimes none; other-wise weak to strong blue or yellow; sometimes orange; occasionally green
Irradiated & HPHT-treated yellow	weak to strong yellow to green	weak to strong yellow to green
HPHT synthetic yellow	occasionally none; usually weak to strong yellow or yellow-green	usually weak to strong yellow to yellow-green,
Irradiated HPHT synthetic pink/purple	weak to strong reddish or pinkish orange	medium to very strong reddish or pinkish orange
Natural blue	usually none; rare: weak to moderate orange-red	usually none; occasionally yellowish to bluish white, rare: weak to moderate orange to orange-red
Synthetic blue	usually none visible, occasionally weak grayish blue or brownish orange	weak to moderate yellow, green-yellow, grayish blue, or brownish orange

The above table was based on information in "A Chart for the Separation of Natural and Synthetic Diamonds" by the GIA,.*The MicroWorld of Diamonds* by John Koivula, articles in *Gems & Gemology,* and personal communication with Branko Deljanin & Sharrie Woodring, EGL USA research and Alan Hodgkinson.

Table 8.2

Description of diamond	Phosphorescence	Distribution of UV fluorescence (best seen under magnification)
Natural colorless or near colorless	usually none, rarely weak yellow (LW & SW) lasting 30 seconds or less	usually even, but sometimes patchy, or uneven with concentric bands of octahedral growth
Synthetic colorless	weak to strong yellow, greenish yellow, or greenish blue (SW) lasting 60 seconds or more	HPHT synthetic: sometimes uneven distribution, often with a square or octagon plus a cross-shaped growth pattern through the crown and/ or an hourglass pattern from the side. CVD: even to barely visible growth striations (best seen under the DeBeers Diamond View instrument)
Natural yellow	occasionally weak to moderate yellow (LW & SW) usually less than 15 seconds	usually even, rarely uneven; may show blue and yellow fluorescent patches of color
Irradiated & HPHT **treated yellow**	very weak greenish yellow (SW), less than 15 seconds	
HPHT **synthetic yellow**	usually none, sometimes weak yellow or greenish yellow lasting several seconds	uneven distribution like colorless synthetic diamonds
Irradiated, HPHT **synthetic pink/purple**	usually none	usually even
Natural blue	very rarely bluish white to LW and almost always bluish white to SW; rarely weak to moderate, yellow orange to orange red lasting less than 15 seconds	usually even
Synthetic blue	moderate to strong yellow to SW lasting 30–60 seconds or as long as an hour	uneven distribution like colorless synthetic diamonds

The above table was based on information in "A Chart for the Separation of Natural and Synthetic Diamonds" by the GIA,.*The MicroWorld of Diamonds* by John Koivula, articles in *Gems & Gemology,* and personal communication with Branko Deljanin & Sharrie Woodring, EGL USA Research and Alan Hodgkinson..

When HPHT synthetic diamonds are of high clarity, it's difficult to identify them under magnification. This is when fluorescence and phosphorescence tests are especially helpful. Major gem laboratories use a combination of tests along with high-tech, expensive equipment like the DTC Diamond View™ and spectrometers which can detect impurities in the UV-Visible-Near-infrared spectra of synthetic diamonds. Major gem labs also have more experience identifying synthetic diamonds. Therefore, when purchasing or selling an expensive diamond, it's advisable to get a lab report stating that the diamond is of natural origin. For more information on gem laboratories, see the chapter on diamond grading reports and light performance..

If you'd like more technical information on identifying man-made diamonds, consult the following sources:

"A Chart for the Separation of Natural and Synthetic Diamonds" by the Gemological Institute of America. It includes 60 color photographs.

Diamonds: Treatments, Synthetics and Simulants; Integrity, Disclosure and Detection, a CD-ROM produced by the Diamond Trading Company and distributed by GEM-A of the British Gemmological Association.

Gems & Gemology in Review: Synthetic Diamonds, Dr. James Shigley, GIA

Guide to Laboratory-Created CVD & HPHT Diamonds: Methods of Growth, Techniques of Identification by Sharrie Woodring, Branko Deljanin, EGL USA Group, 2004

The MicroWorld of Diamonds by John Koivula: Gemworld Intl., Inc.

Periodicals:

Australian Gemmologist. (Gemmological Association of Australia), Brisbane

Gems and Gemology. (Gemological Institute of America), Carlsbad, CA

Journal of Gemmology. (Gemmological Association and Gem Testing Laboratory of Great Britain), London

Diamond Types

In the 1930's, scientists divided diamonds into two basic categories—Type I and Type II. Type I diamonds can be broadly defined as diamonds with nitrogen in their structure; Type II diamonds are those without significant nitrogen. This difference in structure affects the physical and optical properties of the diamonds. For example, Type II diamonds conduct heat better than Type I diamonds. They also absorb light differently and fluoresce in distinct ways.

If you decide to consult the preceding reference sources, it would be helpful for you to have a basic understanding of diamond types because researchers use these categories to classify lab-grown and HPHT-treated diamonds. If you only want to know how to evaluate natural diamonds, you can skip the rest of this section and go on to the next chapter.

In the 1950's, it was proposed that Type II stones be further divided into Type IIa and Type IIb. Type IIb diamonds phosphoresce and conduct electricity. Most natural blue diamonds are Type IIb.

Later Type I stones were divided into subtypes Ia and Ib. The nitrogen in Ib stones is distributed throughout the diamond crystal as single atoms and not concentrated in masses, while the nitrogen in Ia stones appears as pairs or clusters of atoms. Tables 8.3 and 8.4 summarize some of the characteristics of the four basic diamond types.

Most natural diamonds are Type Ia. Most HPHT synthetic diamonds are Type Ib, and most CVD diamonds are Type IIa. When diamonds fall in the same type category, it's harder to differentiate lab-created diamonds from those that are natural, and advanced spectrographic tests in gem labs are necessary.

Type Ia can be further divided into **Types IaA and IaB**. If the nitrogen atoms of Type Ia diamonds are in pairs, they are classified as Type IaA diamonds. If the nitrogen atoms are in large aggregates they are classified as Type IaB diamonds. For more information on diamond types, consult the previously mentioned references.

Table 8.3: Features of Type Ia & Type Ib natural diamonds (those with nitrogen)

	Type Ia	Type Ib
Color	colorless to yellowish, yellow, brown, olive, gray; rare: green	fancy yellow, a more saturated yellow than Type Ia and brownish yellow. All synthetic yellow diamonds with nitrogen fall in this category.
Rarity	most common natural type	rare in nature
LW UV fluorescence	none or typically weak to very strong blue	often none; sometimes weak yellow or orange
SW UV fluorescence and transparency	none or weak to strong blue fluorescence. Opaque to SW UV.	often none; sometimes weak yellow or orange fluorescence. Opaque to SW UV.
Phosphorescence	occasionally weak yellow (LW & SW) , lasting 30 seconds or less.	occasionally weak to moderate yellow (LW & SW), usually less than 15 seconds
Electrical conductivity	none	none
Heat conductivity	very good	very good
Trace elements	nitrogen present in aggregated forms	isolated nitrogen atoms, each replacing one carbon atom
Cleavage	relatively uneven	relatively uneven

Information in the above table is based on the *GIA Diamond Dictionary, Diamonds* by Eric Bruton, *Gemstone Enhancement* by Kurt Nassau, "A Chart for the Separation of Natural & Synthetic Diamonds" by GIA, *Gems & Gemology* and personal communication with Branko Deljanin., EGL USA Research.

Table 8.4: Features of Type IIa & Type IIb natural diamonds (without significant nitrogen)

	Type IIa (almost pure carbon with tiny amounts of nitrogen or boron)	**Type IIb** (boron substitutes for some carbon atoms)
Color	colorless, brown to light brown, and sometimes pink or blue-green	mostly blue, some gray
Rarity	very rare	extremely rare
LW UV fluorescence	none, weak to medium blue, sometimes orange in pink diamonds	usually none, rarely chalky blue-green, weak to moderate orange to orange-red
SW UV fluorescence and transparency	none or weak to medium blue or greenish gray, sometimes orange fluorescence in pink diamonds. Translucent to SW UV.	usually none, occasionally weak to moderate yellow to bluish white, rarely orange to orange-red fluorescence
Phosphorescence	usually none, however, Cullinan I, the largest faceted diamond in the world, phosphoreseces for several minutes	very rarely weak to moderate bluish-white to LW, almost always bluish-white to SW; rarely weak to moderate yellow, orange, or orange red to SW, less than 15 seconds.
Electrical conductivity	none	are semiconductors
Heat conductivity	3 to 5 times more heat conductive than Type I	varies from stone to stone
Trace elements	no significant nitrogen, occasionally a bit of boron	no nitrogen, a bit of boron
Cleavage	relatively perfect	relatively perfect

Information in the above table is based on the *GIA Diamond Dictionary*, *Diamonds* by Eric Bruton, *Gemstone Enhancement* by Kurt Nassau, "A Chart for the Separation of Natural & Synthetic Diamonds" by GIA, *Gems & Gemology,* and personal communication with Sharrie Woodring, Branko Deljanin, EGL USA and Alan Hodgkinson.

9

Diamond Treatments

Treatment is the standard term used in gemological literature for any process done to improve the appearance of a gemstone, except cutting and cleaning. **Enhancement** is often used as another word for treatment. However, it has a broader meaning as well. "Enhancement" also refers to the faceting and polishing of a gem. In addition, it sounds more positive, and occasionally leads buyers to believe that treated diamonds are even better than natural stones.

In Europe, some gem labs use the term "enhancement" on their colored gem reports to refer to routine treatments that are well accepted in the trade, such as heat treatment. In these reports,"treatment" is reserved for unaccepted treatments. This policy has the effect of turning treatment into a negative term, when in fact it's a neutral term by dictionary definition.

Generally speaking, diamond treatments are less accepted than colored gemstone treatments because the supply of untreated diamonds has been sufficient to meet the needs of the trade. For example, many jewelers would never consider selling irradiated diamonds. However, they will sell irradiated pink tourmaline and blue topaz. No matter how well accepted a treatment is, the trade has come to agree that all treatments should be disclosed to buyers.

Besides disclosing treatments, sellers should avoid suggesting that their treated diamonds are just as valuable as natural diamonds, because this is not true. When heat and pressure treated colorless diamonds were first introduced to the market, a few jewelers bought them at a prices below those of natural diamonds and then resold them to their retail customers at premiums of 5–10% above the price of natural diamonds of the same quality. Even though they disclosed the treatment, these jewelers misled their customers into thinking the diamond value was higher than it was. It's fine to market treated diamonds as an attractive and affordable alternative to natural ones. It's wrong, however, to suggest that treated stones have the same value and prestige as completely natural diamonds. Auction sales and secondary-market prices confirm that untreated diamonds of natural origin are the most highly valued.

Even if you only sell natural diamonds, you should have some fundamental knowledge about treatments in order to answer your customers' questions and so that you'll be less likely to unknowingly misrepresent a treated diamond as untreated. It's becoming harder and harder to consistently detect treatments. Independent lab documents are becoming more necessary, but it may not be financially worthwhile to get them for small diamonds.

Techniques that aren't treatments may also be used to make a diamond appear more valuable. Sometimes two pieces of diamond are cemented together to form a larger stone called a **doublet**. Diamond doublets are normally created to make a stone appear larger. A colored cement can also be added to change

Figs. 9.1a–c A diamond doublet shown as an assembled and unassembled stone. Because the separation plane can be easily hidden by a bezel setting, careful microscopic examination is required to rule out a doublet. Some diamond doublets use a non-diamond pavilion, but thermal conductivity testers will test positive on these stones if only the crown is tested. *Information and photos by Paul Cassarino.*

the face-up color of the composite stone. This is classified as a deceptive practice when it is not disclosed. An example of one diamond doublet is shown in figures 9.1a–c, but no further discussion is included in this chapter because the process of assembling diamonds is not considered a treatment.

Methods for Changing Color

Diamonds are treated to improve either their color or clarity. Methods for changing color include:

- foilbacking
- irradiation
- annealing
- coating, tinting, painting
- high pressure and high temperature (HPHT)
- high temperature heat treatment

FOILBACKING

For probably 4000 years, foil backings have been used to add color and brilliance to gems. As gem-cutting techniques progressed and brought out more brilliance in stones, these backings became less popular. Today foil backings are not normally used on diamonds because it's easier to tint or coat them. Foil backings are more likely to be seen on rose cuts and on glass imitations, especially in antique and estate jewelry. **Beware of closed-back settings**. Something such as foil or a coating may be concealed underneath the stones. Select jewelry pieces in which the pavilion of the diamond(s) is visible. If it isn't visible, make sure the diamond(s) comes with a respected lab report.

COATING

Coating is also an old technique, but recent advancements to the technology have caused a resurgence of coatings in the commercial market. Slightly yellowish or brownish diamonds can be transformed into more expensive-looking orange, yellow, blue, green, red, pink, or purple diamonds, or they may make a diamond appear colorless or near colorless by masking color (fig. 9.2). The coating sometimes covers the entire stone, but more often than not it's applied just to the pavilion and/or the girdle. A bit

Fig. 9.2 Left: A diamond that appears near colorless because of a temporary bluish coating, which neutralizes the yellowish diamond color. Right: Same diamond after a thorough rubbing with a diamond cloth. *Photo from EGL USA Group.*

Diamond Coating

Fig. 9.3 Coated diamonds ranging from 0.58–0.86 ct. *Photo by Sharrie Woodring.*

Fig. 9.4 Coated diamond melee ranging from 0.01–0.05 cts. *Photo by Sharrie Woodring.*

Fig. 9.5 Damaged coating. *Photo by Sharrie Woodring*

Fig. 9.6 Coating peeled off in the form of a heart. *Photo by Sharrie Woodring.*

Fig. 9.7 Coating with worn facet edges, scratches and pitting. *Photo by Sharrie Woodring.*

of color on one facet near the girdle can make it appear evenly colored when viewed face up. EGL USA has seen anywhere from a one to four color grade shift. Some coatings are relatively durable; others can be easily rubbed off.

The coating, tinting or painting agents may include ink, colored plastic, fingernail polish, paint, and chemical films such as calcium fluoride doped with gold or various metal oxides. One noteworthy case occurred in 1983 when a 9.58-carat diamond was put up for sale at a major auction in New York. It was supposed to be a fancy pink diamond valued at $500,000. Someone managed to switch it with a light yellow diamond coated with pink nail polish that was worth about one fourth of the appraised value. The deception was discovered a day before the sale.

The Spring 2007 issue of GIA's *Gems & Gemology* had a 19-page article on coated colored diamonds produced by Serenity Technologies, Inc. The thin-film coatings were applied only to the pavilions of the samples that GIA examined, but the color appears evenly distributed. GIA issues identification reports on coated diamonds, but not quality and color grading reports. These diamonds are identified as "Surface Coated" on the report and an additional comment explains that "A foreign material has been artificially applied to the surface, which precludes quality analysis." The biggest problem with coated diamonds is that the treatment is not permanent. It can wear away and be damaged by high heat, polishing compounds, chemicals, flux, rhodium plating, retipping, and setting.

Coatings can be detected by:

- **Magnification with diffused reflected light.** This is the easiest way to detect coated diamonds. Transmitted light is also helpful. Interference colors, small uncoated areas, irregularities in the coating, and damage such as abrasions and chipped coating along the facet edges can indicate coating. For best viewing, use 45X magnification or higher.
- **Immersion in methylene iodide.** Areas of concentrated color in the surface area can confirm the presence of coating.
- **Chemical analysis.** Expensive, high-tech equipment is required.

In some cases, unusual UV fluorescence or spectroscopic features may indicate coating.

IRRADIATION

Light yellow and brown diamonds are sometimes irradiated to produce green, blue, yellow, orange, black (which are actually very dark green) and occasionally pink, purple, or red diamonds. Usually the treatment is followed by heating (annealing) at about 800°–1000°C and sometimes higher to improve the irradiated colors, which are often very dark. The color of irradiated diamonds is basically stable, but some stones can change color if they come into contact with a jeweler's torch.

Diamonds are irradiated after cutting either with high-energy electrons in a linear accelerator or with neutron bombardment. Both of these processes produce a uniform face-up color because of their good penetration. Government agencies regulate the amount of radioactivity allowed in gemstones. Geiger counters can detect radioactivity.

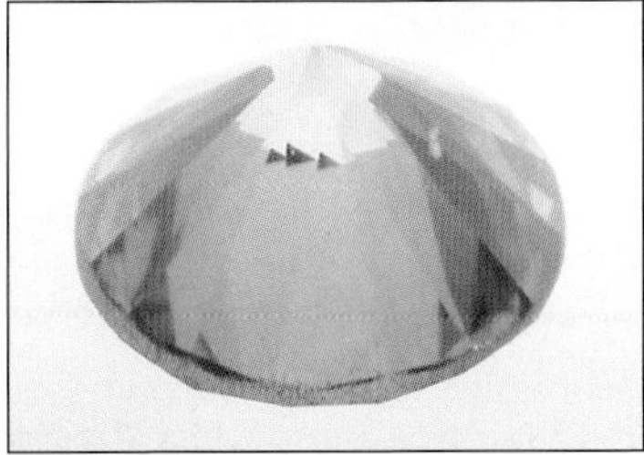
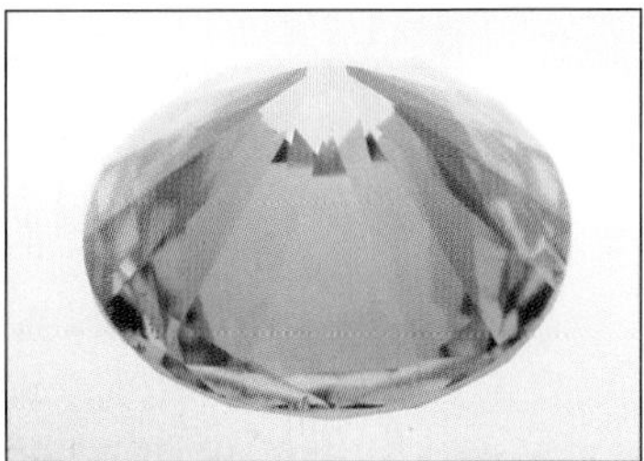

Figs. 9.8 & 9.9 Irradiated diamonds left and center with color concentrations at the culet indicating treatment. Face up they are Fancy Intense Blue and Fancy Intense Yellow. The diamond on the right is HPHT treated, but, like natural colors, it doesn't have color concentrated near the culet and/or girdle. *Photos by Sharrie Woodring.*

Irradiation is detected by:

- **Magnification**. Color concentrations in the culet area of a diamond, sometimes resembling an umbrella and color zoning following facet patterns indicate irradiation treatment. The 'umbrella' effect is best seen by looking through the table and focusing at the culet. The 'umbrella' is then visible around the culet. This often is seen in older cyclotron-treated diamonds.

  The irradiation treatments more commonly used today produce color concentrations like those in figures 9.8 and 9.9; the zoning can be seen by placing the diamond table down and viewing it with diffused transmitted light. These concentrations do not appear as an umbrella when looking through the table at the culet. If the stone was treated from the crown, a dark colored ring of color zoning may appear just inside the girdle.

  Green naturals (trigon markings) on the girdle are typical characteristics of natural-color green diamonds. A dark green color can be seen in irradiated black diamonds when viewed against a strong light. Natural-color black diamonds do not have this forest green color.

- **Spectroscopy**. This is the most important identification technique for irradiated diamonds. The spectroscope is often used with cooling, either with an aerosol refrigerant-gas, dry ice, or liquid nitrogen in order to make the absorption lines more prominent. Reflected light techniques with the spectroscope work much better than those which use transmitted light (p. 90 of *Identifying Man-Made Gems* by Michael O'Donoghue).

  Most Type Ia diamonds have a prominent absorption line at 415 nm and a weaker line at 478 and other weaker lines. Irradiated diamonds have additional absorption lines at points such as 497, 503, and 595 (*Gemstone Enhancement* by Kurt Nassau). The *Handbook of Gem Identification* (p 143 & 144) by Richard T. Liddicoat provides colored spectra examples of various treated and natural color diamonds. Spectroscopy may not differentiate natural-green diamonds from those that are irradiated because natural radiation causes the color in natural-color green diamonds. For this reason, the color origin of natural green diamonds is often classified as undetermined on lab reports. Some green diamonds, however, do receive reports from labs such as the GIA stating that their color is natural.

Laboratories use spectrophotometers for identification. Spectrophotometers can detect absorption from the UV to the infrared and are much more sensitive than handheld spectroscopes. Often, advanced instruments are needed for identification. For example the 741nm line in green and blue irradiated cannot be viewed by handheld instruments.

Fig. 9.10 Irradiated and heated diamonds allowed the designer to create an evenly colored blue surface for this sombrero Tahitian pearl ring by A & Z Pearls. *Photo by Diamond Graphics.*

- **Fluorescence.** Irradiated pink and reddish diamonds have a characteristic strong orange fluorescence, especially under long-wave UV light. Naturally pink diamonds may also have a strong orange fluorescence, but they have different spectra. A chalky fluorescence is suspicious as this occurs more often in treated diamonds.
- **Phosphorescence**. Natural color Type IIb blue diamonds usually show phosphorescence under short-wave UV radiation. Irradiated blue diamonds do not normally phosphoresce. However, synthetic blue and colorless diamonds often phosphoresce.

Annealing (Heating Combined with Another Treatment Process)

In its diamond course, the GIA defines **annealing** as a controlled heating and cooling process which is used to stabilize and change irradiated colors or alter the color of yellow to brown synthetic diamonds. Irradiated diamonds followed by annealing are normally described as simply irradiated or treated on lab reports. It doesn't matter whether a lab-grown diamond is heat treated or not because the stone is not of natural color.

High Pressure high temperature (HPHT) Treatment

HPHT treatment was first used by researchers to change the color of diamonds in the 1970's. Laboratories were able to produce yellow and green colors by heating diamonds to temperatures above 1900°C under extreme pressure. It wasn't until 1999 that the trade learned it was possible to turn inexpensive brown diamonds colorless using the same treatment process. In other words D, E and F color diamonds can be produced by HPHT treatment. Sometimes these diamonds are identified as "processed."

Colored HPHT treated diamonds were introduced to the commercial market in 2000. Yellowish-green and greenish-yellow colors are the most common but other colors such as blue, pink, red and orange are also being produced. This has become the preferred method of color-treating diamonds because the colors are

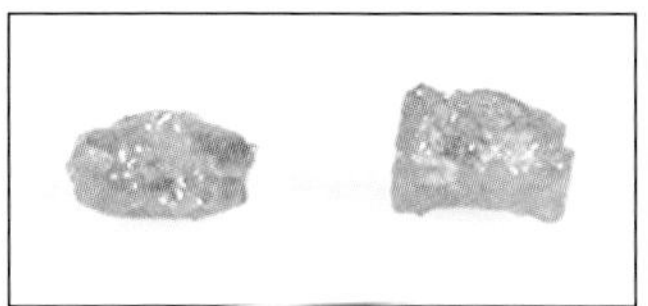

Figs. 9.11 & 9.12 Type IaB diamonds before and after HPHT treatment. *Photos from EGL USA Group.*

Fig. 9.13 Type IaAB diamonds before HPHT treatment. *Photo from EGL USA Group.*

Fig. 9.14 Type IaAB diamonds after HPHT treatment. *Photo from EGL USA Group.*

Figs. 9.15 & 9.16 Type IaAB daimonds after HPHT treatment. *Photo by EGL USA Group.*

Figs. 9.17 & 9.18 Type IIa diamond before (left) and after (right) HPHT treatment. *Photo by EGL USA group.*

stable and do not wear away, and no radioactivity is present. Not all heat treatment methods are equally accepted.

Within the colored gemstone market, low temperature heat treatment is preferred to high temperature heat treatment because high temperatures are more destructive of internal characteristics of diamonds and pose a greater risk to the durability of the gemstone. The GIA defines "low temperature" as temperatures under 1000° C (from GIA Chart of Commercially Available Gem Treatments).

HPHT treated diamonds are detected by:

- **Magnification**. Some characteristics of HPHT-treated diamonds are burned surfaces and facet edges; etched or frosted naturals; fine cracks under the table and in the girdle region; corrosion on the girdle; laser inscriptions on the girdle such as GE POL; small tension cracks around mineral and graphite inclusions; and white granular cleavage cracks with a frosted texture with graphitization.

  Yellow graining with green luminescence is somewhat common in HPHT treated yellow-color-range diamonds (figs. 9.23 & 9.24) and rare in natural colored diamonds; brown graining is more common in natural colors.

Fig. 9.19 Burn marks on the surface of the diamond. *Photo by Sharrie Woodring.*

Fig. 9.20 Circular stress crack created by expansion of the crystal during HPHT treatment. *Photo by Sharrie Woodring.*

Fig. 9.21 White granualar cleavage crack (feather) with a frosted texture. *Photo by Sharrie Woodring.*

Fig. 9.22 Close-up view of feather in figure 9.21. *Photo by Sharrie Woodring.*

Fig. 9.23 Colored planar graining showing green luminescence. Strong transmitted darkfield light was used. *Photo by Sharrie Woodring.*

Fig. 9.24 The planar graining looks yellowish when viewed with a white diffuser plate (or white paper) over the darkfield light well. *Photo by Sharrie Woodring*

Green luminescence to visible light is also rarer in natural diamonds but more common in HPHT treated (yellow color range) diamonds. See the Summer 2000 issue of *Gems & Gemology*, pages 128-137 for more information.

- **Spectroscopy**. Greenish yellow HPHT-treated diamonds have additional distinct absorption lines at 495 nm and 503 nm even at room temperature.
- **Fluorescence**. A strong chalky greenish fluorescence to long wave UV light is characteristics of some HPHT treated diamonds.
- **Photoluminescence and cathodoluminescence**. These high-tech methods are often necessary for detecting HPHT-treated colorless diamonds, especially those of very high clarity.

Irradiation + HPHT Treatment

The newest form of diamond treatment is irradiation followed by HPHT treatment. It can produce diamond colors that are not possible with irradiation and heat treatment without high pressure.

High Temperature Heat Treatment

Fig. 9.25 Heated black diamond. *Photo: EGL USA*

In 2000 and 2001, around the time that HPHT diamonds entered the market, a significant number of black diamonds began to appear in gem labs. They did not have the characteristic dark green color of irradiated black diamonds. The SSEF lab in Switzerland discovered that these stones were the result of high temperature heat treatment without pressure.

When HPHT treaters learned that diamond graphitizes at high temperatures if inadequate pressure is applied during heating, they decided to make the best of the situation. They heat treated inexpensive diamond bort with a lot of cracks to temperatures above 1900°C until diamond graphite formed and entered the cracks. This process transformed industrial bort into jewelry-quality treated black diamonds that have fooled many labs. However, now that labs have experience with these heated black diamonds, they can often detect the high temperature heat treatment simply with magnification because the inclusions of these heated diamonds are different than those of natural black diamonds. The heat treatment can be confirmed with high-tech tests such as luminescence spectroscopy at liquid nitrogen temperature.

Methods for Improving Clarity

Laser Drilling

The purpose of laser drilling is to get rid of dark inclusions. During this process, a focused laser beam is used to drill a narrow hole to a dark inclusion. If the inclusion is not vaporized by the laser itself, then it's dissolved or bleached with acid. After the treatment, the hole looks like a white dot face-up and like a thin white line from the side, and the diamond is more marketable.

Fig 9.26 Profile and pavilion view of traditional laser drill holes in a diamond. *Photo by author.*

Fig. 9.27 Diamond in figure 9.26 viewed face up. *Photo by author.*

Fig. 9.28 Curved laser drill holes. *Photo from the EGL USA Group.*

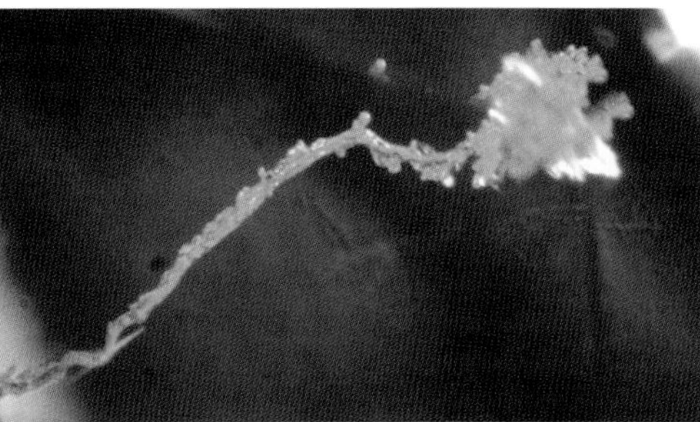

Fig. 9.29 Close-up view of curved drill hole in figure 9.28. *Photo from EGL USA Group.*

Fig. 9.30 Fracture-filled diamond with reddish flash. *Photo by Sharrie Woodring.*

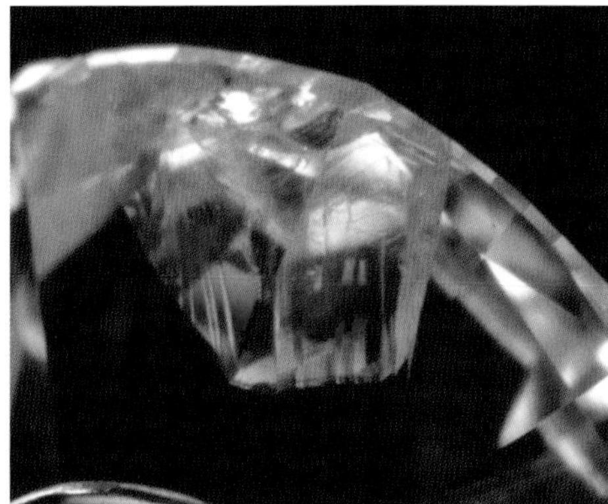

Fig. 9.31 Iridescent colors and feathery appearance of a natural (unfilled) diamond cleavage. *Photo by Sharrie Woodring.*

Internal drilling is a newer technique. The internal channel can expand the inclusion and become a surface reaching crack, which can be penetrated by bleaches. The drilled arca is harder to detect because it resembles a natural inclusion instead of being an obvious drill hole

An even newer lasering process creates a curved hole to the dark inclusion, which may be subjected to a caustic solution (fig. 9.32). At high temperature, the solution etches the inside of the hole and makes it look frosted, giving it an entirely new look. This can confuse viewers who aren't familiar with this process. (Information from Nick DelRe and Branko Deljanin, of EGL USA)

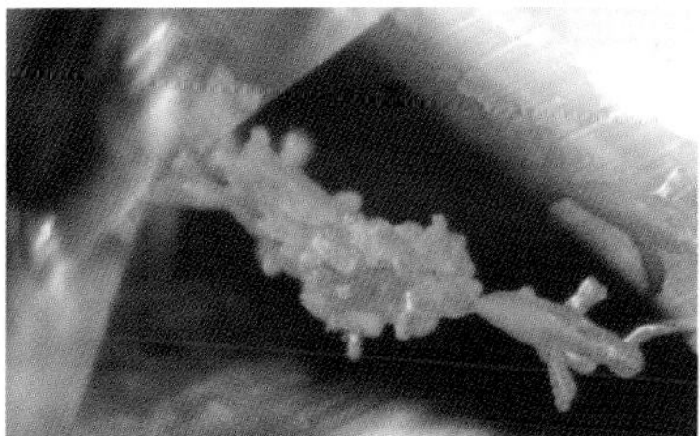

Fig. 9.32 Close-up view of a drill hole that was subjected to a caustic solution. *Photo from EGL USA Group.*

If a drilled hole or crack is treated with a special filler that makes the drilled areas less visible, detection is more difficult. Such a stone is considered to be both filled and drilled.

Lasering is an older and more accepted form of treatment than fracture filling, irradiation, and HPHT treatment. It dates back to the early 70's. Many dealers will sell lasered diamonds even though they may refuse to carry other types of treated diamonds in their inventory. It's more accepted because it's a permanent treatment; it doesn't add a foreign substance to the diamond; it doesn't decrease the durability of the diamond; and it only affects the drilled area of the diamond instead of altering the overall internal character of the diamond the way high temperature heat treatment can.

FRACTURE FILLING

Fracture filling is a method of improving clarity and transparency by filling cleavages or breaks with a substance that makes them almost invisible. These cracks aren't large gaps; they're extremely narrow. The filler used is a glass-like thin film, so the filling process does not add measurable weight to the stone. Even though you may not see them, the filled cracks are still present in the diamond. Three other names for the diamond filling process are **glass infilling**, **clarity enhancement** and **clarity treatment.** Laser drilling, mentioned above, is also a clarity enhancement and treatment.

The main advantage of fracture-filled diamonds is cost. A stone that looks like it's worth $2000, may sell for only $1500. That's because the purchase price of the diamond before treatment was based on its unfilled appearance. In addition, the companies that process the stones have encouraged jewelers to pass on the savings to consumers. A major disadvantage of this treatment is that it's not always permanent.

Normally the goal of fracture filling substances is to improve clarity by making fractures optically invisible, but it can also be used to improve or change color. For example, emeralds can look greener with green fillers. Nick DelRe and Branko Deljanin of EGL USA examined a diamond with an unusual infilled material (fig. 9.33). The material was not opaque to x-rays and the x-ray fluorescence detector did not indicate any element akin to those found in typical fracture-filled diamonds. They speculate that the diamond was filled with a bluish filler to improve the color grade in an attempt to partially cancel out its yellowish body color.

Fig. 9.33 Unusual infilled material in a diamond. *Photo from EGL USA Group.*

The GIA Gem Trade laboratory did an extensive study of filled diamonds from three of the chief commercial sources—Yehuda/Diascience, Koss & Shechter/Genesis II and Goldman Oved/Clarity Enhanced Diamond House. The results were published in the Fall 1994 issue of *Gems & Gemology*. Regarding the durability of diamond fillings, the GIA scientists concluded that "prolonged exposure—or numerous short exposures—to commonly employed cleaning methods may sometimes damage filling substances." They also found that "repolishing or jewelry repair procedures involving direct exposure to heat (as in retipping prongs) will damage and partially remove the filler from such treated diamonds." However, "jewelry repair procedures involving indirect heating (as in sizing a ring) might not damage the fillings." In addition, extended exposure to the ultraviolet radiation of sunlight might cause fillings containing bromine to cloud and discolor. The Yehuda-treated diamonds tested by the GIA did not show any changes when exposed to ultraviolet radiation. Diamond fillers have improved over the years, but they can still be negatively affected by heat and chemicals.

Many of the jewelers who sell fracture-filled stones as an affordable alternative to untreated diamonds inform their customers about the treatment and its durability problems. Unfortunately, not everyone does. The three treatment firms mentioned above have publicly urged sellers to disclose fracture-filled diamonds.

Treatments should be identified when possible so buyers can be advised if special care is needed. Table 9.1 discusses stability and care requirements of the various types of treated diamonds.

Fracture-filled diamonds can be detected by using a binocular microscope along with a variety of illumination techniques. Three of the most common features seen in these diamonds are:

- **Color flashes**. Fracture-filled diamonds display flashes of color in their filled areas as the stones are rotated or rocked. Yehuda-treated diamonds of the 80's showed an orangy flash that changed to blue when the background of the break became bright. The fillings in the more recent Yehuda stones flash violet to purple to pink against a black background and green to yellow against white. Similar colors were seen in the Koss- and Goldman Oved-treated stones but the colors tended to be either less saturated or more subtle.

Table 9.1 Treated diamonds: care, durability & stability issues

Types of treated diamonds	Stability and durability issues and care tips
Coated, foil-backed	May scratch, turn cloudy, fade, show wear and be damaged by setting or repeated ultrasonic cleaning. Avoid retipping, chemicals and high heat. Do not use coated diamonds in rings for everyday wear.
Irradiated	May change color if heated. Avoid high heat and sudden temperature changes.
Irradiated+ annealed	May change color if heated
HPHT	The color is stable.
Laser Drilled	Stable unless drilled areas are infilled
Fracture filled, Filled drilled area	Diamond fillers have improved over the years, but the GIA still recommends removal of any filled diamond from its setting before doing repair work. Fillers can be damaged by chemicals and high heat such as a jeweler's torch. Repeated ultrasonic cleaning may damage the filler over time.

Data based on various articles in *Gems & Gemology*

Don't confuse the flash effects of filled diamonds with the flashes of blue and orange seen off the facets of untreated diamonds. These normal color flashes appear as patches of color rather than as the outline of a fracture or drill-hole. The flash effect results because the fillers don't exactly match the diamond's RI for all wavelengths of light.

♦ **Trapped bubbles in the filling**. Most filled stones show some bubbles. Sometimes they look like tiny pinpoints and in other cases they may be fairly large.

♦ **Cloudy filled areas**. Glass-infilled stones may show "white clouds" in part of the filling. Some of these clouds may be groups of minute bubbles.

Filled stones can often be detected with just a 10-power loupe. Normally, stones must be rotated, rocked and viewed from several angles. It's especially important to view the pavilion of the stone from the bottom and the sides. Loupes with built-in lights (darkfield loupes) can be helpful.

Unfortunately, not all filled diamonds are easy to detect with a loupe. The flash effects of stones with small cracks, thick fillings or subtle flashes may be hard to see with a loupe and may require microscopic examination along with special lighting techniques such as fiber-optic illumination. Mounted stones, in particular, can pose problems because the viewing angles and visibility are restricted.

Another complication is the fact that fractures in untreated diamonds can also display colors. These normally consist of a sequence of rainbow-like colors (fig. 9.31), but sometimes only one or two colors can be seen. Typically, unfilled cracks have a feathery appearance unlike filled cracks, but this is easiest to see with the high-power magnification of a microscope. The viewing angle is important when determining if a crack is filled or not. As the GIA points out, "Iridescent colors in unfilled breaks are usually best seen at a viewing angle roughly perpendicular to the break, whereas flash effects in filled breaks are usually detected when looking almost parallel (edge-on) to the break."

A loupe can be very helpful in spotting many fillings, but as GIA researchers have stated, *a 10x loupe cannot be relied on to detect characteristic features in all filled diamonds. Instead a binocular microscope with a range of lighting options should be used.* More detailed information on filling detection is provided in the fall 1994 and summer 1995 editions of *Gems & Gemology*. They can be ordered by calling the GIA at (800) 421-7250, extension 7142.

In October 2009, the GIA's New York lab reported a new treatment process, probably involving HPHT annealing and subsequent irradiation and annealing at relatively low temperatures. It was used to induce the color of a large (8.44 ct) Fancy Vivid orangy pink pear shape. This diamond had an even color distribution and was internally clean. Spectroscopic analysis revealed a very low concentration of aggregated B-form nitrogen and trace amounts of isolated nitrogen. Strong absorptions from NV centers at 575.0 and 637.0 nm were the main cause of the treated-pink color.

10

Judging Fancy Colored Diamonds

Consumers are becoming increasingly eager to add diamonds of various colors to their jewelry collection. Some of the key factors for the recent popularity of colored diamonds are:

- **The developments of new cuts which maximize color**. Yellowish diamonds were always available during the 1900's, but it wasn't until the late 1970's that diamond cutters discovered that the face-up color of light yellow and other yellow diamonds could be strengthened by changing the shape, proportions and faceting of a diamond.

- **Increased availability of colored diamonds**. The discovery of the Argyle mine in Western Australia during the late 1970's was a major turning point because of its supply of brown and pink diamonds. Since then, new deposits have been found. (See Table 1 for sources of colored diamonds).

- **Auction sales**. The 1987 Christie's New York sale of a 0.95-carat purplish red diamond (the Hancock Red) for more than $926,000 per carat was another major event in popularizing colored diamonds. Since then auction sales of many other notable colored diamonds have attracted significant media attention.

- **Establishment of the Natural Colored Diamond Association (NCDIA)** in 2003. The NCDIA sponsors fashion shows and media events and has launched a website www.ncdia.com to provide consumers and trade members with information about colored diamonds.

- **Increased availability of treated colored diamonds**. High pressure high temperature (HPHT) technology and other treatment processes have produced colors of diamonds that were previously unavailable, especially in commercial quantities. The publicity generated by producers of these treated colored diamonds has also increased public awareness of natural-color diamonds.

In the jewelry trade the term **fancy** means "different than the norm." Therefore, a **fancy cut** refers to any cutting style other than a round brilliant or single cut. The GIA Diamond Dictionary defines a fancy color diamond as any *naturally* colored diamond with a noticeable depth of body color. From a technical standpoint, the GIA definition of a fancy colored diamond is more complex. Page 196 of *Gems & Gemology in Review: Colored Diamonds* states,

Fig. 10.1 A 2.70 ct Fancy blue-gray round brilliant in a platinum diamond ring by Landau Ideal™ Diamonds. *Photo by Leonard Derse.*

Fig. 10.2 A 6.02 ct Fancy Intense yellow cushion flanked by two D VS_1 half-moon diamonds. *Ring and photo from Abe Mor Diamond Cutters.*

"Unlike other colored diamonds (except brown), yellow diamonds with grades of Faint, Very Light, and Light are not considered to be fancy colored diamonds, but are part of GIA's D-to-Z color grading scale." In other words, fancy colored yellow and brown diamonds must have a greater depth of color than other colored diamonds in order to be classified as **fancies** or **fancy diamonds**, two other terms for fancy colored diamonds. For example, a K (faint yellow) diamond is not considered to be a fancy colored diamond, but a Faint pink diamond with the same lightness of color as a K-color diamond is a fancy colored pink diamond. However, a Faint pink diamond is noticeably lighter than a Fancy pink diamond. In this latter context, the term "fancy" is being used as a color grade, not as a general category of diamonds.

As more and more treated colored diamonds have entered the market, sellers have applied the term "fancy" to these diamonds as well. This trend has encouraged some natural-color diamond dealers to advertise their diamonds as natural color diamonds instead of fancy color diamonds.

The color of fancies results from a variety of factors. Some of the most common causes are missing carbon atoms, or impurities such as nitrogen, hydrogen, and boron. Natural radiation can produce green or greenish colored diamonds, and fluorescence can contribute to diamond color. Inclusions can make diamonds look black or white. Table 10.1 briefly identifies the causes of color in various colored diamonds. Keep in mind that the process of creating color in diamonds is a lot more complex than the table makes it appear.

Evaluating Fancy Color Diamonds

The rarer the color, the greater the role of color in determining a diamond's value. For example, the Hancock 0.95 carat purplish red diamond has eye-visible inclusions such as a deep cavity in the table (top center facet). Despite its low clarity grade and relatively small size, it still holds the record price per carat for any gem ever sold at auction.

Table 10.1: Natural Fancy Colored Diamonds: Sources and Causes of Color

Basic color	Sources	Causes of color
Red	Australia, Brazil, South Africa	Irregularities in the crystal's atomic structure as a result of deformation
Violet	South Africa, Australia	Hydrogen impurities
Purple	Russia (main source), South Africa, Democratic Rep. of Congo	Irregularities in the crystal's atomic structure as a result of deformation
Green	Borneo, Brazil, Central African Republic, South Africa	Natural radiation; hydrogen, green fluorescence may occasionally make a diamond appear greenish
Blue	South Africa (main source), Borneo, Brazil, Central African Republic, India (historic)	Boron impurities, sometimes radiation
Orange	Democratic Republic of Congo, Botswana, South Africa	Probably chemical impurities and structural distortion
Pink	Australia (main source), Angola, Borneo, China, South Africa, Tanzania, India (historic)	Structural defects combined with various impurities of nitrogen or hydrogen
Yellow	Angola, Borneo, Brazil, Central African Republic, Guinea, Ivory Coast, Russia, Sierra Leone, South Africa, Venezuela	Isolated nitrogen atoms that randomly take the place of individual carbon atoms or aggregates (clusters) of 3 nitrogen atoms
Green-Yellow	Brazil, Ivory Coast, Venezuela	Natural radiation, hydrogen, nitrogen
Olive*	Central African Republic, Sierra Leone, Borneo, Russia	Natural radiation, hydrogen, nitrogen
Black	Central African Republic, South Africa	Black inclusions
Brown	Australia, Angola, Borneo, Brazil, Democratic Republic of Congo, Ivory Coast, Russia, Venezuela, South Africa	A defect in the atomic structure of the crystal probably caused by tremendous pressure and evidenced by colored graining
Gray	Central Africa, Congo	Hydrogen impurities
Chameleon**	Central Africa	Natural radiation, hydrogen and nickel impurities. Cause of color change not certain. Nitrogen, nickel and/or hydrogen may be involved.

Sources: Gems & Gemology *in Review: Colored Diamonds*, edited by John M. King, "Nature of Color in Diamonds" by Emmanuel Fritsch in *Nature of Diamonds* edited by George Harlow, *Collecting and Classifying Coloured Diamonds* by Stephen C. Hofer, and ncdia.com.

* Olive: a common color term for grayish yellowish green or grayish greenish yellow used by some dealers but not the GIA

** Chameleon diamonds show a color change typically from olive green to brownish yellow when heated to 150° C or when stored in darkness for a few days, but the reverse change is possible.

Likewise for blue, green and orange diamonds, color is by far the most important value factor, so they are cut to maximize their color. On the other hand, size, clarity and cut quality are more important for yellow and brown diamonds because there is a much greater supply of them.

Shape can greatly increase the price of round fancy colored diamonds for two reasons—normally more weight is lost from the rough for rounds than for fancy shapes. In addition, if rough is cut into a round diamond, it may get a lower color grade than if it's cut as, say a radiant or princess cut. For example, a Fancy yellow round diamond may be graded as a Fancy Intense yellow diamond if it were cut as a radiant. To offset the lower color grade and loss of weight, a high premium must usually be paid for round fancy colored diamonds.

Overall, the relative importance of color for fancy diamonds does appear to be changing for some fancy colors like yellow. In *Gems & Gemology In Review: Colored Diamonds* (p xx), John M. King points out that requests for color-only GIA reports for fancies have decreased in proportion to those for comprehensive reports. By 2003, 75% of the GIA fancy color diamond reports were comprehensive reports. This suggests that factors other than color are becoming more important in the sale of many fancies.

The percentage of fancy color diamonds receiving lab reports has also greatly increased. A prime reason for this is more awareness of sophisticated treatments and synthetic diamonds that require special lab equipment and skills to detect. Chapters 8 and 9 dealt with treated and synthetic diamonds. The rest of this section provides basic information about the evaluation of color in fancies. Cut and clarity grading information is given in Chapters 2–6.

Before discussing color evaluation, three fundamental color terms should be defined and explained. GIA color terminology and examples are presented because their diamond color terminology and grades are the ones most widely used throughout the world:

Hue: Basic spectral colors such as yellow, green and orange as well as transition spectral colors such as greenish yellow and orangy yellow. White, gray and black aren't hues because they're not part of the color spectrum; however. GIA uses 27 hues to describe their diamond color grades seven of which are basic one-word colors—red, orange, yellow, green, blue, violet and purple. Even though black, brown, gray and white are not listed in the GIA color chart wheel, their grading system sometimes treats them as hues. For example, a GIA grading report may identify a diamond as a Fancy brown or Fancy black diamond.

Primary hues tend to be rarer and more highly valued than transitional hues with secondary colors. But there are many exceptions. As mentioned earlier, the diamond color that has fetched the highest per-carat price was purplish-red.

Tone: The amount or lightness of color. (In some color systems, this is called "lightness," "value" or "saturation"). For example, the GIA color grades of D to Z indicates the tone of the diamond and the amount of yellow, brown or gray present.

Fig. 10.3 Fancy color diamond bracelet courtesy Jennifer Phelps-Montgomery for Michael Werdiger Inc.

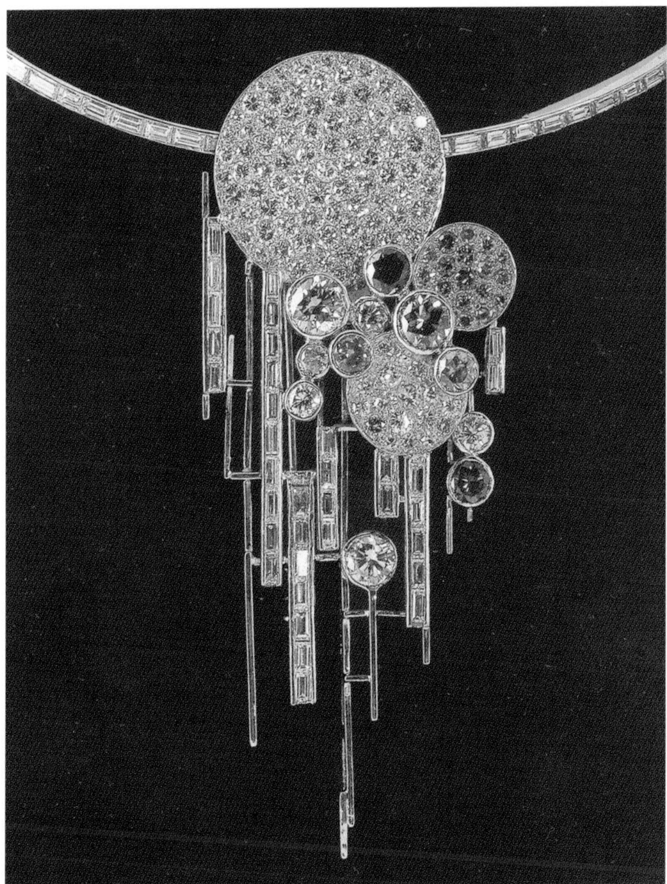

Fig. 10.4 Brooch-pendant set with various shades of yellow, brown and olive green diamonds created by Jean Vendome. *Photo from Jean Vendome/Paris.*

Fig. 10.5 Ring set with olive green diamonds. *Ring and photo from Michael Werdiger Inc.*

Fig. 10.6 Fancy Light pink heart shape diamond flanked by two Fancy Light blue tapered baguettes. *Ring from Overland Gems, photo by Pete Flusser.*

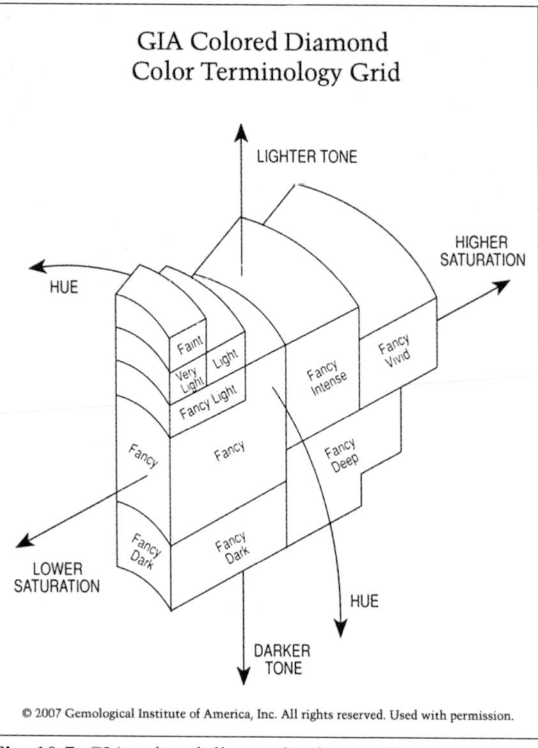

Fig. 10.7 GIA colored diamond color terminology grid

Diamond tone is described with terms such as colorless, near colorless, faint, very light, light, fancy light and fancy. This is different than the GIA tone terminology for other transparent colored gemstones, which have seven GIA tone levels ranging from very light to medium to very dark. Faint to medium tones of red are described by the GIA with terms such as "Faint pink" and "Fancy pink."

In general, the lighter the tone, the lower the value, with the exception of dark and very dark tones, which often are less valuable because their color is not as intense and rich as hues with medium tones. Blue diamonds can have darker hues than other colors and still maintain their desirability.

Saturation: **The strength, purity, or intensity of the hue** (also called chroma in color science). When the saturation decreases, cool hues like green, blue and violet become grayish, and warm hues like red, orange and yellow become brownish. Colors with medium tones can have higher saturation levels than those with light and dark tones. In other words, colors with medium tones and no brown or gray modifying the color have the highest saturation level which is described by the GIA as "vivid." The next highest saturation level is "intense." Diamonds graded as "dark" have a lower saturation because a lot of gray or brown masks their color, which lowers their value. (See figure 10.7 above.)

Fig. 10.8 Fancy Light grayish brown cushion-shape diamond (1.25 ct)

Fig. 10.9 Fancy Vivid purple pink round brilliant diamond (1.10 ct)

Fancy Intense yellowish green

Fancy Vivid yellowish orange

Fancy Intense bluish green

Fancy grayish yellowish green (chameleon)

Fig. 10.14 Fancy Deep blue oval diamond (1.10 ct)

Fig. 10.15 Fancy Deep orange round brilliant (1.52 ct)

The diamonds and photos on this page are from **Arthur and Natacha Langerman, Antwerp.** All of the diamonds are of natural color and origin.

Fig. 10.16 Moussaieff Red (5.11cts) the world's largest Fancy red diamond. It was cut from a 13.90 ct crystal found by a Brazilian farmer in an alluvial deposit. All red diamonds are very rare and highly valued, but what's even more unique about this stone is that the GIA graded its hue as an unmodified red, instead of as a purplish red or brownish red. *Photo and diamond from Moussaieff Jewellers.*

Fig. 10.17 The **Black Korloff** Diamond (88 cts). It belonged to the Korloff Sapojnikoff family of Russian nobility until it was sold in 1920. *Diamond and photo from Korloff Paris.*

Fig. 10.18 A Fancy gray diamond (1.42 ct). In the GIA fancy-color-diamond nomenclature, gray and brown can be hues or saturation adjectives modifying another hue. *Diamond and photo from Arthur and Natacha Langerman.*

When evaluating colored diamonds, keep in mind the following:

- Unlike traditional diamonds, **fancy colored diamonds are graded in the face-up position**, instead of primarily face-down. Face-up does not mean exactly straight up in one position. GIA graders rock the diamond slightly in the tray in search of the best angle to see the stone's characteristic color—the overall color seen in the stone face-up. This is not easy to determine because faceted gems tend to present a mosaic of colors. A diamond's shape, faceting style and cut quality can influence its apparent face-up color. The trade and labs have agreed that the face-up color seen when fancies are worn is more important than the impression of their overall color when viewed face-down.

- **The highest value for fancies is based on the presence of color**, whereas the highest value for diamonds on the D–Z scale are is based on the absence of color.

- **A consistent environment is very important for comparing color**. See Chapter 1 for tips on lighting and viewing diamonds. The GIA Gem Trade

Laboratory grades colored diamonds in a white illumination box with 6500° Kelvin fluorescent lighting.

- **The GIA saturation terms of "fancy," "intense" and "vivid" have different meanings depending on the color.** For example a GIA Fancy yellow diamond has a higher saturation than a Fancy blue diamond or pink diamond. A Fancy red diamond has a higher saturation than a Fancy purple diamond.
- **The range of saturations possible varies depending on the hue.** For example, yellow diamonds occur in a much wider range of saturations than blue diamonds, so the GIA boundaries for fancy grades in the yellow hue range allow for greater depths of color than in the blue hue range (Lesson 13, p 25 of GIA's *Diamonds and Diamond Grading).*
- **There are noticeable differences of color within each GIA colored diamond grade.** For example, one Fancy pink diamond can look distinctly lighter than another one also graded as Fancy pink. Therefore it's especially important that you visually examine colored diamonds before buying them.
- **Diamonds with an even distribution of color are more highly valued** than those with an uneven color distribution. Examine the stone from the side and face down to determine if the color is layered or concentrated in one area. A small area of color at the culet, can make the entire diamond appear colored when viewed face up.
- **Gem laboratories can vary in the way they grade and define color**. Even though some non-GIA labs use the GIA fancy color grading system, some don't. Some of these labs, however, may give a GIA "equivalent" grade. This is another reason why it's difficult to visualize the appearance of a fancy colored diamond, just by reading a lab report for it.
- **The mounting can have a noticeable impact on the apparent color of a diamond.** For example, rose gold may emphasize the color of a pink diamond. On the other hand, the contrast of a Fancy yellow diamond set against platinum or palladium may make the yellow appear stronger.

Fancy Colored Diamond Rarity

According to the GIA *Diamonds & Diamond Grading Course* (#12, p 18), "pure orange—with no hint of brown—is probably diamond's rarest color."

If you ask five colored-diamond specialists to list colored diamonds in the order of their rarity, you'll most likely get five different answers for a variety of reasons.

- They might each define and categorize basic diamond colors differently. Even gem labs may vary in the way they categorize diamond color.
- "Rarity" can refer to either natural or commercial rarity. In other words, specific diamonds colors may be unavailable because they're not frequently found in nature and/or because the demand is a lot higher than the supply.

Fig. 10.19 A Fancy pink diamond that looks like a Fancy *Intense* pink diamond when mounted because it's set in pink gold.

Fig. 10.20 The pink diamonds that surround this Fancy Intense pink diamond make it appear larger by complimenting its color.

Mounting Tips from AMGAD

The appearance of colored diamonds can be enhanced by mounting them properly. Each diamond is different and requires personal consideration when being set. Here are a few tips from the specialists at Amgad Natural Color Diamonds.

- Rose gold prongs or bezels can strengthen the natural color of pink diamonds. Platinum and white gold are also recommended for pink diamonds as they do not detract from the diamond's pink color the way yellow gold does.
- Higher karat gold prongs or bezels (18K or 22K) can visually enhance the color of lighter yellow diamonds.
- Bezel settings can make a colored diamond appear darker than if it were prong set.
- Enclosed basket settings can increase the apparent color saturation of a fancy diamond by reducing the amount of light leaving the diamond.
- The color of a fancy diamond can be enhanced by surrounding it with other colored diamonds or by offsetting it with white diamonds.
- The apparent size of a diamond can be increased by setting it with smaller side stones, by surrounding it with pavé or bead-set diamonds, or by using a bezel setting instead of a prong setting.

The way a diamond appears loose is not always the way it will appear when mounted. Show your customers why they should deal with an expert jeweler by giving them practical advice on how to enhance the colored diamond(s) they select. The mounting makes a world of difference.

All rings and photos on this page are from **Amgad Natural Color Diamonds.**

Fig. 10.21 A Fancy brownish-pink diamond. The pink gold setting brings out the pink, and the brownish color modifier deepens the tone.

Fig. 10.22 The 18K yellow gold bezel makes the diamond appear larger and deeper yellow. The colorless diamonds provide contrast.

Demand and desirability play a large role in the price of a colored diamond. If you ask dealers what's the rarest color, their answers will probably be influenced by the difficulty of finding specific colors for purchase.

- Primary diamond colors are usually modified by secondary colors. For example diamonds are seldom pure red; their red is often modified by purple..
- The saturation levels of diamond colors can vary. A highly saturated vivid pink diamond is more rare than a light blue diamond and vice versa.
- There is no record of all the fancy colored diamonds in existence, so it's impossible to objectively classify and count them.

Stephen Hofer, a gemologist and diamond cutter discusses the problems of assessing colored diamond rarity in his classic book *Collecting and Classifying Coloured Diamonds.* He analyzed the rarity of diamonds with pure and composite colors in terms of five categories of natural and commercial rarity. The four category names and rarity ratings in the following chart are based on pages 109-113 of Hofer's book.

Natural rarity	Basic fancy colors	Comments
Exceptional	red, orange, green, blue, purple	The perceived value of purple is less than the that of the other colors
Notable	pink	A 10.04 ct Fancy Vivid pink diamond ring sold for 6.2 million in 2006 (Sotheby's)
Reasonable	olive, orange-yellow, purplish pink	A 4.77 ct Fancy Intense orange-yellow diamond was sold in 1990 for $821,803 per carat; A 7.37 ct Fancy Intense purplish pink diamond was sold in 1995 for $819,201 per carat
Nominal	brown (the most common color), black, gray, yellow	A 13.83 ct Fancy Vivid yellow diamond sold for $238,792 in 1997

As you can see from the table, the stones that fetch the highest prices do not necessarily have the rarest colors. The quality of the color and the stone, as well as its size and desirability also have a major impact on the value of a diamond. A diamond can be beautiful without having a rare and pure color.

Don't rely too heavily on color grading terminology. Use it as a basis for narrowing down your selection and determining a fair price, but select the diamond(s) that you find most visually pleasing. Keep an open mind regarding diamond color, and consider all factors when comparing colored diamond prices and beauty.

Fig. 10.23 Jewelry by LJ West Diamonds; photo courtesy of Natural Color Diamond Association.

Fig. 10.24 Record-shattering Fancy Vivid pink diamond. Mounted in a platinum ring by Graff, this 5-carat VS_1 cushion-cut beauty achieved the highest per-carat price ever paid for a diamond—about US$2.1 million. The ring fetched a total of $10.8 million on December 1, 2009 at the Christie's Hong Kong fall auction. "The Vivid Pink" was the most expensive jewel sold at auction in 2009. *Photo copyright Christie's Hong Kong.*

11

Antique Cuts & Jewelry

The History of Diamond Cuts

It wasn't until the mid-1300's that European and Indian gem cutters began to cut and shape rough diamond. Compared to modern cuts, old cuts were very plain. The first was probably the **point cut**, which preserved the diamond crystal's octahedral shape and resembles two pyramids base to base. The sides were polished against a stationary polishing surface coated with diamond grit and olive oil.

The next to appear was the **table cut**, an octahedral shape with its top point cut away, creating a square-shaped, flat-top table facet. Frequently, cutters also removed the lower point of the stone to form a smaller square facet called a tabular. This gave the stone a total of ten facets—five on the crown (top) and five on the pavilion (bottom).

When such stone is viewed from above, the table cut looks like a square within a square. The table cut greatly improved the amount of light returned to the viewer, giving diamonds more brilliance and fire than point-cut gems. As a result, point-cut diamonds were gradually reshaped into table cuts. These dominated diamond jewelry through the 1500's.

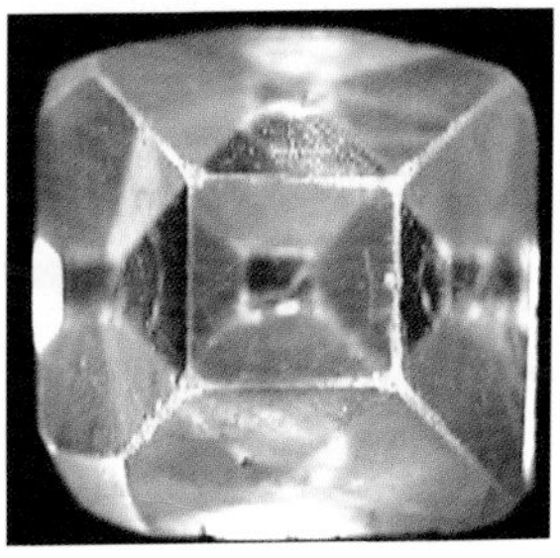

Fig. 11.1 Sawn octahedron (2.58 ct) set in a hand forged and fabricated ring by Todd Reed. *Photo by azadphoto.com.*

Fig. 11.2 (Upper right) Octahedron diamond crystal.

Fig. 11.3 (Lower right) Table cut. *Both photos by Paul Cassarino of the Gem Lab.*

Fig. 11.4 Briolette. *Pendant & photo from Harry Winston, Inc.*

Fig. 11.5 & 11.6 Left: Center-diamond rose cuts set in an early 19th century cuff link. Right: Rose cuts in a late 18th century cufflink. Cufflinks and photo from Bertrand Pizzan, who has one of the world's most important collection of cuff links.

The rose cut was probably developed in India in the early 1500's. **Rose-cut** diamonds are dome-shaped with flat bottoms and they have rose-petal-like triangular facets that radiate out from the center in multiples of six. From above, the rose cut may be round, oval or pear shape. Rose-cut diamonds can display considerable brilliance, but they don't have as much fire as a full-cut brilliant cut. The famous Orlov diamond is a form of rose cut.

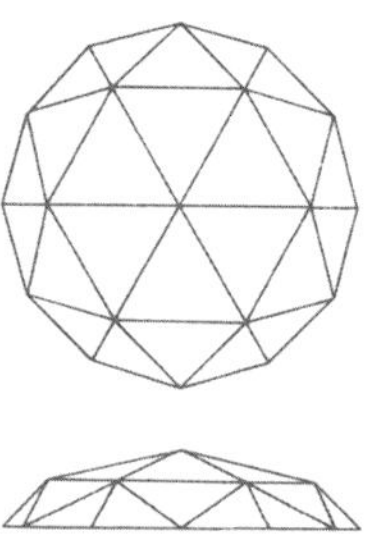

Rose Cut

During the 18th and 19th centuries, both Amsterdam and Antwerp spec-ialized in rose cuts. The Dutch rose cut was more pointed than most others, while the Antwerp style was not as high or as steeply inclined. Most rose cuts were round. Oval and pear shapes were far more rare.

Variations of this cut are the **double rose** and the **briolette,** an elongated double rose that has a tear-drop shape. In recent years, rose cuts and briolettes have become very popular. In fact most rose cuts on the market are new, typically cut in India or Turkey. The demand for rose cuts started with designers, who use it for reproductions. The newer rose cuts tend to be more symmetrical while the shape and facets of most old rose-cut diamonds are normally irregular.

In the mid-1600's, the **single cut** was introduced. It had more potential for brilliance than the table cut because there were more facets: a table, eight crown facets, eight pavilion facets and sometimes a culet (the small facet on the pointed bottom of the pavilion). This cut served as the basis for the modern brilliant cut, and it is still used for small diamonds weighing less than one-tenth of a carat.

Fig. 11.8 Single cut. *Photo by Paul Cassarino.*

The **Mazarin cut** or **double cut** was also introduced in the 1600's. It consists of a cushion shape cut with seventeen facets above the girdle and seventeen below, including the culet. (A **cushion shape** has a rectangular or squarish outline with curved sides and rounded corners. It's an intermediary shape between a round and a square or an oval and a rectangle) The modern version of the double cut is the **Swiss cut**, a round 34-facet brilliant cut which is sometimes used for small stones.

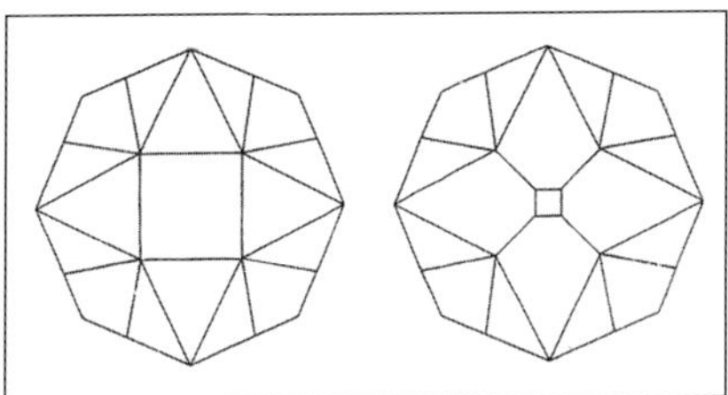

Fig. 11.9 Double cut (Mazarin cut)

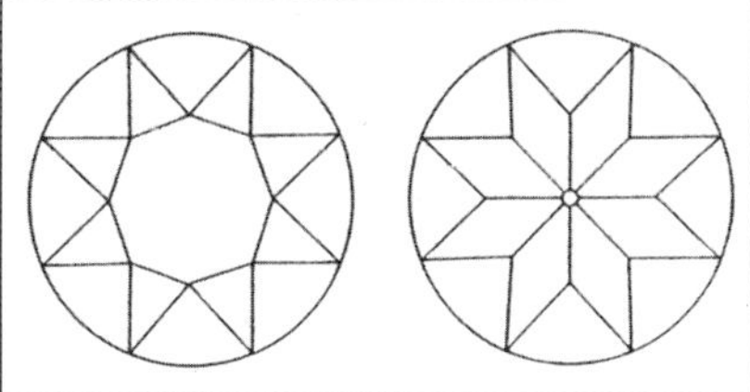

Fig. 11.10 Swiss cut

New developments in diamond cutting were aided by the industrial revolution and the discovery of diamonds in Brazil in the 1700's. Improved gas lighting, an increasing interest in optical science and a greater availability of diamonds encouraged diamond cutters to experiment with new faceting styles such as the **old-mine cut**—a cushion shape with a high crown, deep pavilion, large culet and 58 facets similar to the modern brilliant. "Old-miners" became the most popular cut diamonds of the eighteenth century.

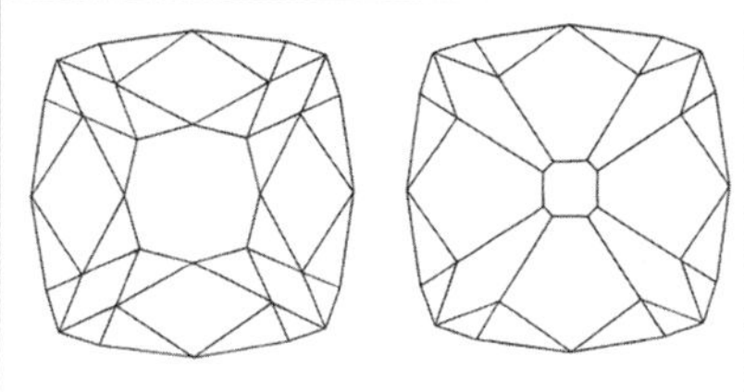

Fig. 11.11 Old mine cut

Fig. 11.12 Old mine cut, face-up view

Fig. 11.13 Side view of stone in figure 11.12

Variations of the old-mine cut were the Brazilian and Lisbon cuts, which were fashioned from Brazilian diamonds. The generic name for these cuts is brilliant-cut cushion or simply **cushion**. This shape gradually went out of style for diamonds after the 1920's, but is becoming increasingly popular again.

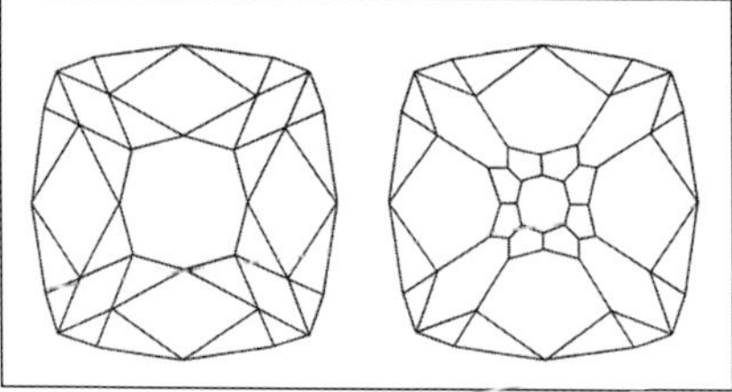

Fig. 11.14 Brazilian cut

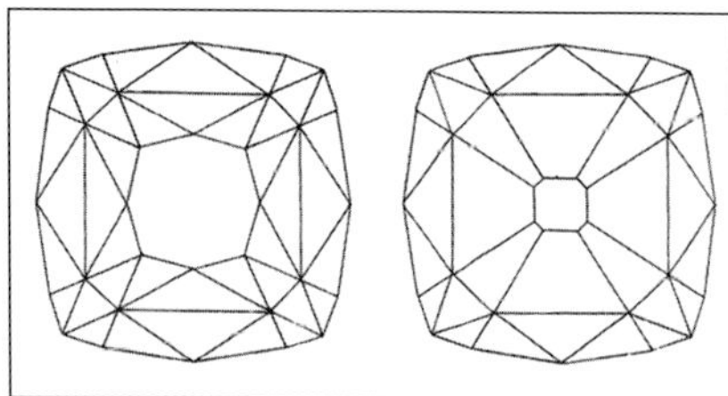

Fig. 11.15 Lisbon cut

Michael Goldstein, a specialist in old-cut diamonds, prefers the well-made cushions from around 1910 to many of those cut today. He says that a lot of people cutting cushions haven't looked at older ones. Consequently they're unable to cut cushions that look like antique diamonds.

Fig. 11.16 Modern cushion-cut diamond, flanked by two pear shapes (tw ≈20 cts). *Ring and photo from Harry Winston, Inc.*

The next cut to appear was the **old European cut**, which was similar to the old mine cut except it was round and sometimes less bulky. This new round cut is the direct ancestor of the modern brilliant cut. The old European cut is the most common diamond cut seen in antique jewelry. Don't expect to find true old-European cuts with high color grades. Their color grades tend to be lower than G color because the mines from which many of them originated, such as the Premier Mine in South Africa, did not produce much colorless rough.

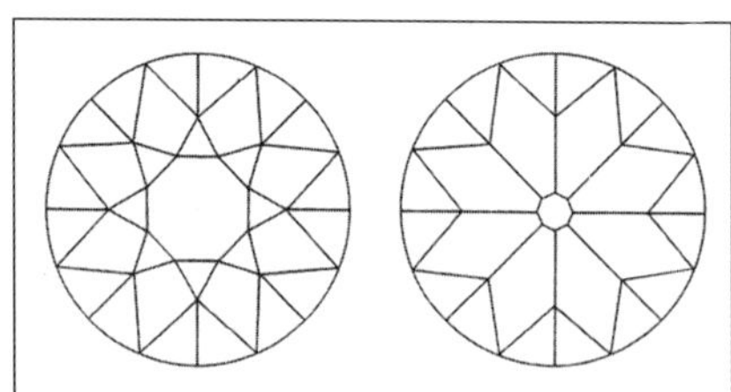

Fig. 11.17 Old European cut

Old mine and old European cuts are sometimes recut as modern cuts in order to make them brighter and more symmetrical (figs 11.18–11.25). They may also just be repolished. However, occasionally modern cuts are recut as old European cuts.

Fig. 11.18 Old mine cut, 1.13 ct

Fig. 11.19 Recut to 0.78-ct radiant cut

Fig. 11.20 Old mine cut, 0.64-ct

Fig. 11.21 Recut to 0.41-ct radiant cut

Fig. 11.22 Old mine cut, 1.71 ct

Fig. 11.23 Recut to 1.39 round brilliant cut

Figs. 11.18–11.23 Compare the diamonds above. As diamond cutting has progressed, the culets have become smaller and the shapes more symmetrical. The diamonds in these photos were recut for customers of Joe & Paul Cassarino at the Gem Lab in Rochester, New York. *All photos by Paul R. Cassarino.*

Fig. 11.24 Old European cut, 1.24 ct with a diameter of 6.72 mm before being recut. *Photo by Paul R. Cassarino.*

Fig. 11.25 Same diamond recut to 1.03 ct, 6.50 mm, round brilliant ideal cut. *Photo by Paul R. Cassarino.*

According to Debra Sawatzky, an antique jewelry specialist, there's been an unusually high demand lately for Old European cuts. It's sometimes easiest to meet this demand by recutting round brilliants. So don't assume that rings mounted with old European cuts are antiques. Even if the diamonds are truly old, this doesn't mean the ring is old. It's not uncommon to remount old stones in new jewelry.

A Boston diamond cutter, Henry Morse, is credited with proposing the proportions and angles for the modern round brilliant cut in the late 1800's, but the old-European and old-mine cuts remained popular into the 20th century. The **modern round brilliant cut** has a lower crown, a smaller culet and more brilliance than its predecessors, but it has the same number of facets—33 on the crown and 25 on the pavilion, including the culet. Since about 1920, it's been the best-selling diamond cut. The diamond cutter, Marcel Tolkowksy, helped popularize the modern round brilliant by publishing his recommendations for its best proportions in 1919 in a treatise called *Diamond Design*.

The girdles of high-quality diamonds are usually faceted to help reflect light internally and to give the diamond a more finished look. This means that most round brilliants have more than 58 facets. The brilliant cut is also applied to shapes other than round such as the marquise, pear, oval and heart shapes.

Another cut that appeared in the late 1800's was the square or rectangular **emerald cut**, which had step-like, four-sided facets that are parallel to the girdle, unlike the brilliant cut which has triangular facets and kite-shaped facets. In addition, the corners of the stone were cut off creating eight sides and a more rounded look. Joseph Asscher is credited with developing this style. Consequently old square or rectangular emerald cuts are often called **Asscher cuts** or simply Asschers.

Fig. 11.26 Old Asscher cut. *Photo by Gail Levine from the Auction Market Resource.*

Fig. 11.27 Royal Asscher® Cut. *Photo from the Royal Asscher Diamond Co.*

Unlike modern emerald cuts, old Asschers had smaller tables, higher crowns and deeper pavilions. Despite their greater depth, they are noted for their high brilliance and dispersion. Nevertheless, many were recut into flatter emerald or radiant cuts to create a more contemporary look. Today old Asscher cuts are in high demand and are selling at a premium, so it would be pointless to recut them.

In 2001, the Royal Asscher Diamond Company introduced a new patented square emerald cut to the market called the Royal Asscher® Cut. It's an offspring of the original Asscher diamonds, but it has 16 additional facets giving it a total of 74 facets.

The Royal Asscher Company did two years of research and computer simulations to determine which combinations of angles and proportions would maximize the brilliance of a square emerald cut. Besides optimizing the life of the stone, the new Royal Asscher utilizes the rough more efficiently. As a result, it looks larger for its weight face up because the total depth is less. Royal Asscher diamonds are cut and polished exclusively in Amsterdam, Holland and are inscribed with the Royal Asscher Cut logo and an identification number held by the company.

Unlike the Royal Asscher, the old Asschers are not perfect squares. Some look more rectangular than square. In addition, old Asschers had smaller tables, higher crowns and no girdle inscriptions. So it's not hard to distinguish between the two Asschers. No matter which Asscher you might own, they are both beautiful diamond cuts.

Some diamonds that were cut in the 1930's and 1940's are called **transitional cuts**. Dealer Michael Goldstein says these stones usually have the overall faceting of modern brilliants but still may have a slightly open culet and a bit of the faceting of an old European cut. According to Goldstein, the term "transitional cut" can also refer to a stone that is a cross between a cushion cut and an old European cut or it may mean a stone that is out of round with

Fig. 11.28 Original Radiant Cut. *Diamond & photo from RCDC Corp.*

Fig. 11.29 Diamond macles in a ring by Todd Reed. *Photo by azadphoto.com.*

attributes of the cushion cut. A transition is the process of changing from one state (cutting style) to another, hence the term "transitional.

In 1977, Henry Grossbard of New York patented a rectangular brilliant- and step-cut diamond with slanted corners. He called it the **radiant** cut, (fig 11.28). It was the first rectangular cut to have brilliant-cut facets on both the crown and the pavilion. When the patent expired, the diamond became a well-accepted cutting style used by many manufacturers. In 2002, Grossbard's company relaunched their diamond as the Original Radiant Cut Diamond brand.

The **princess cut** appeared around 1980. It was a square brilliant cut that retained its 90-degree-angle corners. In other words, it had a true square shape. The Quadrillion® is a precision-cut square brilliant that was patented in 1981. It has 49 facets and a star-shaped pattern on the pavilion.

Some diamond crystals are flattened and triangular in shape with two individuals sharing a common face. These twinned crystals are called **macles** and are typically fashioned into heart, pear and triangle shapes to make efficient use of the rough. Originally the triangles were given a tabular or step cut, but in the 1950's, cutters began to experiment with new faceting patterns to increase their brilliance.

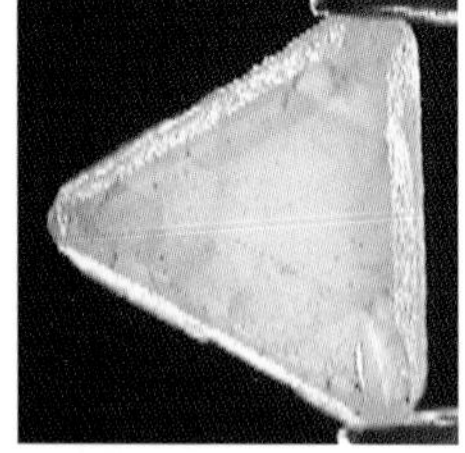

Fig. 11.30 Macle. *Photo: Paul Cassarino.*

The Royal Asscher Diamond Company produced a brilliant-cut triangle with arching sides in 1960 and named it the **trilliant**. In 1962, Irving and Milton Meyer created an American version with straight sides called the American trilliant. Then in 1978 Leon and Marvin Finker trademarked their version of a triangular brilliant-cut the **trillion**.

It had equilateral sides and straight edges. They re-registered their cut as the **Trielle®** because "trillion" had passed into common use as a name for any triangular brilliant cut.

Knowing when the various diamond cuts first entered the market can help you determine the age of a jewelry piece. For example, if someone shows you an antique-style ring with a princess-cut diamond, it's probably safe to bet that it wasn't made before 1980.

Pricing Antique Diamonds

The main types of antique diamonds found on the market today are old European cuts , old mine cuts, briolettes and rose cuts. Old Asscher cuts are hard to find and most come with old mountings, which helps differentiate them from the modern Asscher-cut diamonds. Because of their rarity, old Asscher cuts normally cost more than modern emerald cuts.

Antique diamonds are priced using the same color, clarity and weight criteria as modern cuts. However, there are some fundamental differences:

- Old cuts are worth more mounted in their original mounting than when they are loose. With antique jewelry, the sum of the whole is worth more than the sum of the parts.
- Old cuts are subject to wider variations in pricing than modern cuts. This is partly because there's a more limited supply of antique diamonds and partly because they have enormous differences in symmetry since they were not cut with modern machinery.
- The proportions of antique diamonds are not as important as they are for new diamonds. Usually the older the diamonds, the poorer the cut by today's standards because weight retention of the rough was once more important than brilliance. Nevertheless cut does matter. Large, poorly cut diamonds may be worth as much as 50% less than well-proportioned stones of similar color and clarity.

  The way a stone is cut can indicate whether it is an antique diamond or a newly cut antique-style diamond. Newly cut diamonds often have thicker girdles, lower crowns and different faceting patterns than their earlier counterparts; thus reflecting the light differently. Conversely, knife-edge girdles are common on old cushion cuts.

Appraisers determine the value of antique diamonds by a variety of methods. Sometimes they base the value on the hammer prices of similar diamonds at auctions. The best and most convenient source of diamond prices at auctions is the *Auction Market Resource* by Gail Levine. Sales of selected pieces from all the major auction houses are listed together with detailed descriptions and sales prices. For more information consult www.auctionmarketresource.com.

Appraisers often consult the prices listed on antique diamond websites such as www.antiquediamond.com or they may call antique dealers or jewelers for price information. Price lists of new diamonds are also used as a reference tool. No matter which method is used, the value will vary depending on the purpose of the appraisal—estate, insurance replacement, orderly liquidation (through auctions) or quick liquidation.

The quick liquidation value is the immediate cash amount that you can get for a diamond or jewelry piece if you try to sell it. The least expensive way to determine this value is to show the piece to some antique dealers or jewelers that sell estate jewelry and ask them how much they'd pay for it. If you're looking for the highest possible price, don't take the jewelry to a general pawn shop. Most likely the pawn shop will only give you a low scrap price; they're not normally trained to know the antique value of jewelry unless they happen to sell a lot of estate jewelry.

No matter what type of appraisal you get, expect differences of opinion among appraisers and sellers. There is no one true value for an antique diamond or any other diamond, for that matter. For information on selecting an appraiser, consult the appraisal chapter in this book.

Period Jewelry (European & American)

Antique dealers often describe their styles of jewelry with a period name based on the rule of monarchs or art movements. Many of the periods overlap, and the beginning and starting dates vary depending on the historical source. The dates and information in this section are based largely on Christie Romero's *Warman's Jewelry*, Gail Levine's *Auction Market Resource*, and Anna Miller's *Buyer's Guide to Affordable Antique Jewelry* .

Before listing the various jewelry periods, let's define some related terminology:

Antique jewelry: Any jewelry one-hundred or more years old, as defined by the United States Customs Bureau. Webster's dictionary defines the term "antique" more loosely—any work of art or the like from an early period.

Heirloom, estate, or vintage jewelry: Jewelry that has been previously owned by someone and that is typically passed on from one generation to another. It can range from a few decades to 100 or more years in age.

Collectibles: Items gathered from a specific designer, manufacturer, or any period or periods in time. The items are collected according to the buyer's interests, and normally they are no longer in production, but they don't have to be as old as antiques. For example, retro jewelry pieces are considered collectibles, but they are not true antiques. Hence the phrase, "antiques and collectibles."

Circa dating: Establishing an approximate date of origin for a jewelry piece. It covers a ten-year window on either side of the date. A circa date of 1900 means the piece was probably made some time between 1890 and 1910.

Jewelry Periods

Here's an outline of jewelry eras starting from the 18th Century followed by brief descriptions of each period.

Georgian	1714–1837 (reigns of King George I – King George IV)
Early Victorian	1837–1860 (Queen Victoria 1837–1901)
Mid-Victorian:	1860–1885
Late Victorian:	1885–1901
Arts & Crafts:	1890–1914
Art Nouveau:	1890–1910
Edwardian:	1890–1915 (King Edward VII, 1901–1910) (Belle Epoque)
Art Deco:	1915–1935
Retro:	1935–1955

GEORGIAN (1714–1837)

Most of the diamond jewelry during the Georgian period was hand-fabricated with 18K or 22K gold. In the early 1800's in England, gold filigree was popular. Diamonds were commonly set in silver over gold to bring out their whiteness. Diamond brilliance was intensified by foil backing the stones in closed-back mountings. The backs began to open up in the late Georgian period after 1780.

The discovery of diamonds in Brazil during this period along with the advancement of cutting techniques led to variations of the 58-facet, cushion-shaped old mine brilliant cut. Two variations were the Brazilian cut and the Lisbon cut.

In 1750, an English jeweler named David Jeffries wrote that the brilliant cut was a whim of fashion and that the rose cut would outlive it. He was wrong. Over the next two centuries many of the old roses were recut to brilliant form with a major loss of weight. Nevertheless, rose-cut diamonds can also be found in jewelry of this period.

Fig. 11.31 Georgian brooch with rose-cut diamonds. *Photo by Gail Levine.*

Fig. 11.32 Georgian brooch with rose-cut diamonds. *Photo by Gail Levine.*

Fig. 11.33 Georgian brooch with rose-cut diamonds. *Photo by Gail Levine.*

Fig. 11.34 Georgian ring. *Photo by Gail Levine.*

The themes of the jewelry designs were often from nature—flowers, leaves, acorns, birds and feathers. The designs began to combine colored gemstones such as aquamarine, garnets and pink topaz with the Brazilian diamonds.

Both women and men wore a lot of jewelry during the Georgian era. Men even wore jeweled buttons on their coats and jeweled buckles on their shoes. Women had full or partial ensembles of jewelry with matching necklaces, earrings, brooches, rings and bracelets. The full ensembles were called **parures** and the partial ensembles, **demiparures**. One unusual type of jewelry piece was the aigrette, a hair or hat brooch ornament. Some aigrettes trembled when the wearer moved.

VICTORIAN (1837–1901)

Queen Victoria was a diamond lover, and she was the trend-setter for the wealthy people of Britain's new industrial society. In the early Victorian period, most diamonds were rose cuts or old mine cuts, but by the end of the 19th century, they were outnumbered by the old European cut, which some people called the Victorian cut.

Fig. 11.35 Portrait brooch accented by diamonds and pearls. *Brooch from D & E Singer; photo by Robert Weldon.*

In the mid and late Victorian periods, diamonds were plentiful, especially after the discovery of diamonds in South Africa in 1867 and the introduction of electric lighting in the 1880's, which helped diamonds sparkle indoors and at night. Closed and foiled settings were gradually replaced with open-back mountings, and there was a greater variety of setting styles—bezel, prong, gypsy and wirework settings. In 1886, Tiffany & Co. introduced a high-prong setting for diamond solitaires that became the standard for engagement rings; it was appropriately called the "Tiffany setting."

Fig. 11.36 Victorian brooch, rose-cuts

Fig. 11.37 Victorian bracelet, old European cut

Fig. 11.38 Victorian brooch

Fig. 11.39 Victorian ring

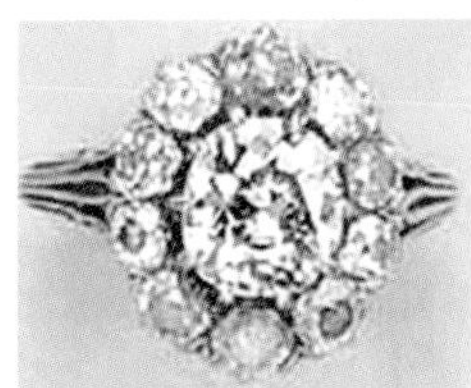
Fig. 11.40 Victorian ring

Fig. 11.41 Victorian brooch set with old European cut diamonds

Fig. 11.42 Victorian brooch

Figs. 11.36–11.42 Photos of Victorian jewelry from Gail Levine. These pictures can be viewed in color on www.auctionmarketresource.com along with over 12,000 other photographs of antique jewelry and collectibles.

Gold was also readily available during the Victorian period, thanks to discoveries in California (1848), Australia (1851) Black Hills, South Dakota (1874), South Africa (1886), Yukon, Canada (1895), and Alaska (1898). Most of the early Victorian diamond jewelry was hand-crafted using 18K to 22K gold, some of it tricolor. But in 1854, the British government made 9K, 12K, and 15K gold legal in order to meet foreign competition. Jewelers in Britain were not required to mark their jewelry during most of the nineteenth century, so it's not uncommon for jewelry during this period to be unmarked.

By the end of the Victorian era, a high percentage of the gold jewelry was machine-made and mass produced. Platinum jewelry had also been introduced to the market, but it was generally made by hand.

Victorian jewelry displayed a wide variety of motifs—branches, shells, knots, buckles, plants, flowers, vines, insects, clasped hands and women with flowing hair. After the death of Queen Victoria's husband Prince Albert (1861), mourning jewelry with black onyx or jet became popular.

Many of the World's most famous jewelry firms were founded during the Victorian period; for example, Tiffany's in 1837, Cartier in 1847, and Boucher on in 1858.

ARTS & CRAFTS MOVEMENT (1890–1910)

The Arts & Crafts movement coincided with three other schools of design—traditional Edwardian, Art Nouveau (New Art) and Late Victorian. It was a reaction to the mass-produced jewelry of the industrial revolution and the lavish ornamentation of the Victorian era.

Arts & Crafts jewelry was entirely hand-made and the materials were inexpensive. Instead of gold and platinum, silver, brass and copper were the preferred metals. Cabochon turquoise, agate, amber, moonstones and opals replaced diamonds, rubies and emeralds and were usually bezel set. The designs were either abstract or featured themes of nature such as flowers, leaves and birds.

ART NOUVEAU (1890–1910)

The "New Art" period is known for its flowing curved lines, botanical motifs and bright colors. It was the beginning of modern jewelry design. Many French jewelers adopted this style, but the one best known for his designs and artistry was Ren Lilac. He combined expensive gems with inexpensive materials like ivory and horn and set them in 18K gold. One of the techniques Lilac is noted for and that became associated with Art Nouveau is *pique à jour* enameling—translucent enamel with no metal backing, which resembles a stained glass window.

In contrast to earlier periods, diamonds, rubies, emeralds and sapphires were used mainly as accents for larger cabochon-cut semi-precious stones such as lapis lazuli, moonstone, malachite, carnelian, marcasite and conch pearls. Synthetic rubies and emerald triplets (two pieces of colorless beryl joined with a layer of green cement) made their appearance in Art Nouveau jewelry. The motifs most frequently seen are women with flowing hair, human forms with insect wings, butterflies, peacocks, bees, swans, snakes and flowers. Silver, gold, copper and plated metals were all used in this jewelry.

Fig. 11.43 Art nouveau brooch with old European cut diamond. *Photo by Gail Levine.*

Fig. 11.44 Art nouveau brooch. *Photo by Gail Levine.*

EDWARDIAN (also known as BELLE EPOQUE) (1890–1915)

The heavy use of diamonds, platinum and pearls in delicate, lacelike mountings are chief characteristics of this jewelry. Even though the reign of Edward VII was only from 1901–1910, the lavish court style of the era influenced fashion in the decades before and after his rise to power.

Edwardian jewelry was also inspired by the French courts of Louis XV and Louis XVI. In fact, it was the French jeweler Louis Cartier (1875– 1942) who was in the forefront of developing this style and who was an official jeweler for the English court. As a result, it is also identified as *belle epoque*, the French term for "beautiful era." Another expression that is sometimes used is the "garland style" (*style garlande* in French) because garlands (wreaths) of flowers and leaves were typical motifs for this jewelry. Other motifs included horseshoes, doves, fish, ducks, hearts, sun, stars, moon and bows and arrows.

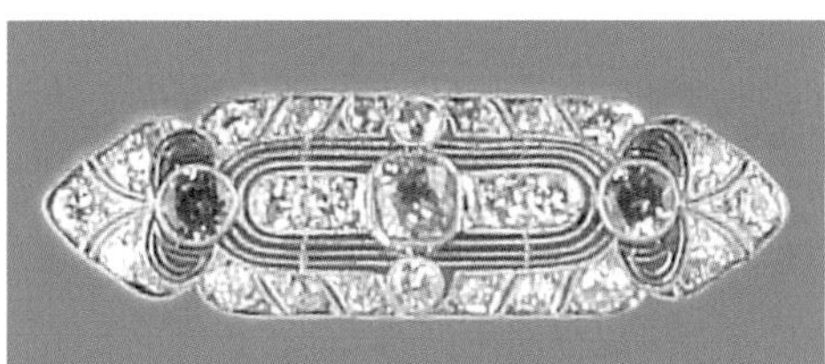

Fig. 11.45 Edwardian platinum, diamond bar pin *Brooch and photo from Joseph DuMouchelle Intl. Auctioneers; David Frechette Photography.*

New cuts such as the marquise, the emerald cut and the baguette emerged during this period, thanks to improvements in diamond-cutting technology. Calibrated stones of standardized sizes and shapes became available for use in mass produced jewelry. Cushion cuts, old European cuts and rose cuts remained popular; and briolette diamonds were often suspended in earrings.

Fig. 11.46 Edwardian lavalier

Fig. 11.47 Edwardian diamond brooch

Fig. 11.48 Edwardian rose-cut barrette

Fig. 11.49 Edwardian pendant

Fig. 11.50 Pin-pendant

Fig. 11.51 Old European cut diamond ring

Fig. 11.52 Edwardian pendant

Figs. 11.46–11.52 Photos of Edwardian diamond jewelry from Gail Levine. These pictures can be viewed in color on www.auctionmarketresource.com along with over 12,000 other photographs of antique jewelry and collectibles.

After the development of a torch hot enough to work platinum (about 1890), platinum became the most common metal for fine pieces. For awhile, platinum was laminated to gold much like silver had been. But gradually it became evident that platinum was strong enough to be used by itself for intricate mountings and secure diamond settings. Millegrained (raised beaded edges) platinum settings were used to make diamonds look larger and knife-edge settings were created to make the mounting appear invisible. Much of the metalwork was open, allowing fabric to show through. During World War I, white gold came into common use because platinum was temporarily banned for use in jewelry

Even though Edwardian jewelry was mostly white, pastel colors were also in fashion and later it was set with darker colored gemstones such as amethyst, alexandrite, amethyst, chrysoprase and demantoid garnets.

Some of the noted French houses who created Edwardian jewelry were Boucher on, Cartier, Chaumet, Georges Fouquet and LaCloche Frères. In the United States, it was made by Tiffany & Co., Black Starr & Frost, Marcus & Company, etc. Most of the pieces of the Russian Imperial court jeweler Peter Carl Fabergé (1846–1920) can be classified as Edwardian, but others have Art Nouveau lines and motifs.

Some of the noted French houses who created Edwardian jewelry were Boucher on, Cartier, Chaumet, Georges Fouquet and LaCloche Frères. In the United States, it was made by Tiffany & Co., Black Starr & Frost, Marcus & Company, etc. Most of the pieces of the Russian Imperial court jeweler Peter Carl Fabergé (1846–1920) can be classified as Edwardian, but others have Art Nouveau lines and motifs.

Art Deco (1915–1935)

Geometric patterns, straight lines and bold color contrasts characterize Art Deco designs. Platinum, diamonds and white gold continued to be used extensively, but there was a greater use of colored gemstones, some of which were synthetic. Lapis, jade, coral and black onyx were especially popular.

Even though old European, single and rose cuts were still present, the modern brilliant cut in round and fancy shapes was more commonplace. New shapes for side stones emerged in the form of bullets, half moons and shields.

One of the most popular articles of jewelry was the diamond straightline bracelet, which in the 1980's was revived and called the tennis bracelet. The cocktail wristwatch, pendant watch and dress clip were other innovations of the Art Deco period.

Fig. 11.53 Art Deco diamond and emerald brooch from Gemstone Designs. *Photo by Ron Litolff.*

The motifs most often found were geometric, abstract, floral, Oriental and Egyptian.

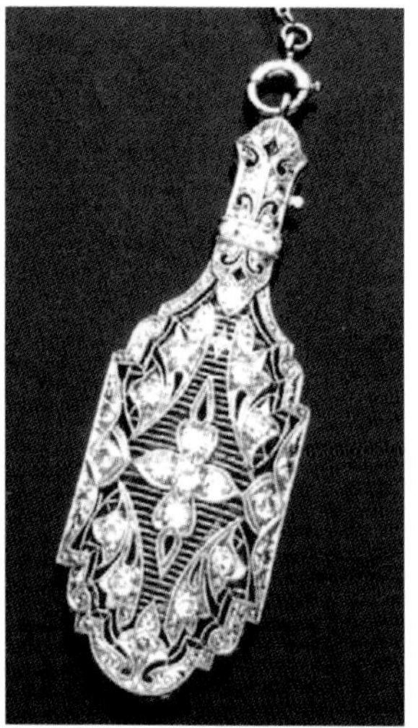

Fig. 11.54 Art Deco lorgnette

Fig. 11.55 Watch

Fig. 11.56 Art Deco brooch

Fig. 11.57 Art Deco brooch

Fig. 11.58 Ring

Fig.11.59 Lapel watch

Fig. 11.60 Art Deco watch

Fig. 11.61 Art Deco clips

Fig. 11.62 Art Deco brooch

Figs. 11.54–11.62 Photos of Art Deco diamond jewelry from Gail Levine. These pictures can be viewed in color on www.auctionmarketresource.com along with over 12,000 other photographs of antique jewelry and collectibles.

Fig. 11.63 Retro brooch

Fig. 11.64 Watch

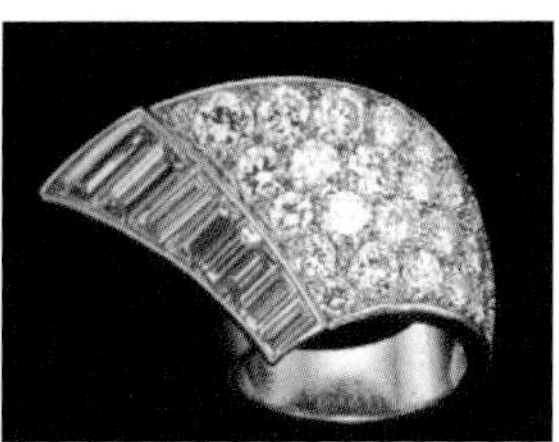
Fig. 11.65 Retro ring

Fig. 11.66 Retro watch ring

Fig. 11.67 Watch $ clip

Fig. 11.68 Retro ring

Fig. 11.69 Watch

Fig. 11.70 Retro ring

Figs. 11.63–11.70 Photos of Retro Period diamond jewelry from Gail Levine. These pictures can be viewed in color on www.auctionmarketresource.com along with over 12,000 other photographs of antique jewelry and collectibles.

Fig. 11.71 Art Deco platinum and diamond bracelet from Joseph DuMouchelle Intl. Auctioneers.

Art Deco Oriental and Egyptian motifs followed the discovery of King Tutankhamun's tomb in 1923 and new trade agreements between Japan and the US.

Louis Cartier is the most famous Art Deco designer. The works of Van Cleef and Arpels also had a strong influence on the period. Other leading designers and houses were Mauboussin, Jean Fouquet, Boucher on, Chaumet, LaLoche and the American firms of Tiffany & Co, Black, Starr & Frost, J.E. Caldwell & Co., C.D. Peacock, Harry Winston, and Shreve, Crump & Low.

Retro (1935–1955)

The all-white look of diamonds and platinum began to fade during the Great Depression of the early 1930's. Then when platinum was declared a strategic metal by the US government during World War II, it was no longer used as a jewelry metal in America. It was replaced in fine jewelry by yellow gold and rose gold, and later by white gold.

Fig. 11.72 Retro platinum, diamond and ruby, rose- and yellow-gold brooch from Joseph DuMouchelle International Auctioneers.

Colored gems such as citrine, aquamarine and tourmaline were typically used instead of diamonds, although diamond pavé did continue to enhance designs. Masses of baguettes were used in channel-set jewelry. Hollywood stars influenced fashion more than royalty, and France was no longer the jewelry design center of the world. The designs were bold, bracelets had heavy links, pendants were large and were made so they could convert to brooches.

In 1948, DeBeer's launched their famous slogan "a diamond is forever." Platinum returned after the war and was used to create lighter weight jewelry and wire settings that held clusters of diamonds, many of which had pear, oval and marquise shapes. By the end of the Retro period, diamonds were once again a girl's best friend.

12

Recutting Diamonds

Even though diamonds are the hardest substance on earth, they can break and chip. Fortunately, though, if they are damaged, recutting can usually make them look like new. Other reasons why diamonds are recut:

- To make them look more modern
- To make thcm look antique
- To improve their brilliance
- To improve their cut grade
- To improve their color grade
- To intensify the color of fancy color diamonds
- To improve their clarity

Perhaps you're wondering why diamonds aren't always initially cut to maximize their brilliance and produce the best possible color and clarity. Usually it's because the cutter wanted to retain as much weight as possible from the original diamond crystal in order to maximize its value. As the weight of a diamond goes down, its value can decrease in two ways:

a. **Its per-carat price can go down.** When a diamond moves down from one weight category to another, its price per carat may go down. There's an especially large decrease in price when a diamond falls below a true half carat or full carat. That's because one-carat diamonds are in high demand and they are more rare. Diamonds with the highest color and clarity grades have the highest price differentials as they move up or down from one weight category to another.

b. **Its total price will go down.** For example, a 0.95-carat diamond that sells for $7000 per carat would cost $6650 (0.95 x $7000), which is $350 less than a one carater of the same per-carat price.

When diamonds are cut with excellent proportions, they usually weigh less than if they were poorly cut. In order to make up the difference in price, sellers have to charge more for well-cut diamonds than for those that are cut mainly for weight retention.

Diamond cutting is an art and skill that involves making a compromise between two factors—maximum beauty and maximum value. However in most instances, the potential value and salability of the finished diamond is what determines how a diamond is initially cut and whether a diamond is worth recutting.

Fig. 12.1 A rough culet in a VS_1 diamond

The diamond in figure 12.1 is an example of how cutters maximize value. This VS_1 diamond has a rough culet and weighs 0.995 carats (1.00 carat when rounded to two decimal points). Polishing away the roughness might have brought the weight down to 0.99 carats, but it would not have increased the clarity grade. Consequently, the culet was left unpolished. The rough culet is not visible to the naked eye, nor does it decrease the brilliance of the diamond. Buyers who depend only on grades and who don't examine diamonds under magnification would never notice it. If the roughness prevented a sale, the stone could be easily repolished, but with a possible loss of weight.

Because of technological advances, the concept of diamond beauty has evolved over the years. Five hundred years ago, it wasn't possible to cut a round brilliant diamond. At that time, viewing poorly polished, unsymmetrical rose-cut diamonds was probably a breathtaking experience because they were so unusual and they sparkled more than existing table cuts. Times have changed.

The previous chapter showed examples of two old mine cuts that were recut as radiants and one that was recut as a round. When the diamonds were first fashioned, they may have been considered exquisite, but after the new owners compared their brilliance to contemporary cuts, they decided recutting was worthwhile, even though their stones would become smaller.

There are times, however, when people choose to retain the old cutting style because it can enhance the value of antique jewelry. Sometimes estate dealers send old European and old mine cut stones to cutters just for a spruce-up job. The abrasions and bruises may just be polished away and the size of the culet may be reduced.

As I mentioned in the previous chapter, many diamonds are being fashioned with antique-style cuts. Nevertheless they are being cut with better symmetry and a higher polish than was possible two hundred years ago, which is one way of distinguishing newly cut diamonds from authentic old ones.

Figures 12.2a–12.4b show how both the brilliance and value of diamonds can increase with recutting. These stones were recut for clients of Joe and Paul Cassarino, jeweler-gemologists at The Gem Lab in Rochester, New York. Not only was there a major improvement in the cut grade of the first diamond in figure 12.2a, but its clarity went up five grades from an SI_2 to a VVS_2, and its color went up one grade from an M to an L.

Fig. 12.2a Old mine cut, 2.40 ct, M/SI$_2$, before it was recut as a round brilliant

Fig. 12.2b Recut to 1.80-carat, L/VVS$_2$, ideal cut

Fig. 12.3a Old European cut, 1.24 carats

Fig. 12.3b Recut to 1.03-carat ideal cut

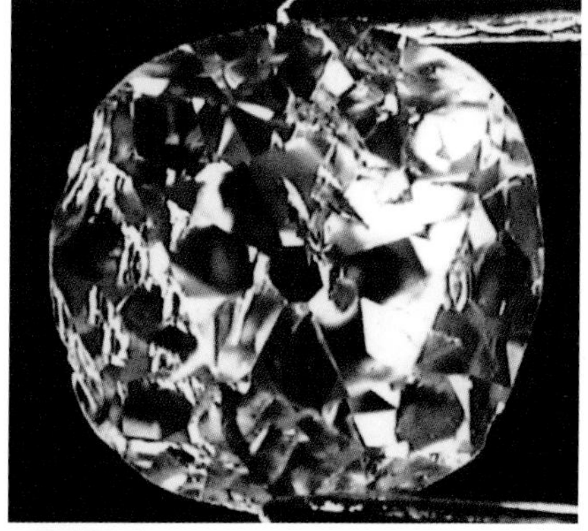

Fig. 12.4a Old mine cut, 0.77 carats, JI$_1$, AGS cut 10

Fig. 12.4b Recut to 0.57 carat, I/I$_1$, ideal AGS cut 0

All photos on this page were taken by Paul R. Cassarino of The Gem Lab.

A chip was removed from the old European cut in fig. 12.3a, and it was also recut to American ideal proportions, while remaining above one carat in weight.

The color also went up one grade for the diamond in figure 12.4a, and it can now be sold at a premium because it has an AGS ideal cut grade of 0. This stone, by the way, is an example of how a diamond with an imperfect clarity grade can still be very desirable.

How do Cutters Modify Diamond Color?

Yellowish tints of color can be removed from diamonds by subjecting them to high-temperatures and high pressure. That is considered an unnatural color change. The color grade can also be improved without subjecting the diamond to any unnatural processes. A cutter can sometimes raise the color grade of a diamond by:

a. **The removal of excess weight**. The heavy pavilions of old mine cuts often intensify the color. That is why the color grade of diamonds 12.2a and 12.4a went up when their pavilions were cut to modern standards.

   In the case of fancy color diamonds, cutters want to intensify the color. That's why it's not uncommon for fancy color diamonds to have excess weight. Maximum color is more important than maximum brilliance.

b. **The choice of shape and faceting style**. For example, a fancy light yellow round brilliant can sometimes be recut into a fancy intense yellow radiant. However there may be a weight loss of 20–25%. Because of this, yellow rough is more often than not cut as radiants or princess cuts. The color is intensified and more weight is retained. Rounds typically undergo a greater weight loss and can look lighter. Consequently fancy intense yellow round brilliants typically sell at premiums of 15–100% over radiants of the same size, color and clarity grade.

   You may wonder how cut can change the color of a diamond. It doesn't actually change it; it just makes the color appear different face up. The round and radiant in the above example had the same color when viewed from the side. Unlike colorless diamonds, fancy color diamonds are graded face-up instead of from the side. The way the facets are designed to reflect light back to the eye can change the apparent color of a diamond, giving the diamond a different color grade.

c.. **The way the girdle is cut**. If the bruted (unpolished) girdle of diamonds with G–D color grades are faceted, their color can improve by one grade. Curiously, the opposite effect can occur with stones below H color. For example, if you facet the girdle of a low J-color diamond, it can become a K color. (Source: Barry Rogoff, a diamond cutter in Los Angeles).

d. **The position of color zoning within the stone**. Sometimes diamonds have bands or sections of color called **zoning**. If a cutter orients the stone so the color falls in an area such as the culet, the color may reflect throughout the stone.

Fig. 12.5a Damaged 0.86-ct round brilliant

Fig. 12.5b Same diamond recut to 0.70 ct

Fig. 12.6a Chipped 1.01-ct old European cut

Fig. 12.6b Recut to 0.78 round brilliant

Fig. 12.7a Damaged 1.15 ct round brilliant

Fig. 12.7b Same diamond recut to 0.86 ct

All photos on this page were taken by Paul R. Cassarino of The Gem Lab

One unusual example, according to Rogoff, involves a 22-carat octahedral rough diamond that was vivid pink. The owner wanted to make a matching pair of rounds. When the cutter sawed the crystal in half, one part remained pink and the other was D color. The color zoning of the rough had not been visible prior to cutting. Unfortunately, there was a major reduction in value because vivid pink diamonds are extremely rare and sell for a lot more than D color diamonds.

Getting Diamond(s) Recut

You may have diamonds that you think are beyond repair. It is amazing how a badly damaged stone can be transformed into a beautiful one (See examples 12.5a–12.7b). Or you may have dull-looking diamonds that you wish had more life. If so, consider having them recut.

There is always a risk of breakage when recutting diamonds. In addition, it takes a lot of skill to bring out their maximum beauty. Consequently, it's to your advantage to have your diamonds assessed by an experienced professional.

After you find one who offers recutting services, ask to see an example of what the diamond will look like when recut. Then place the stone next to your diamond. If you see a dramatic difference in appearance, recutting could be worthwhile. Find out how much weight could be lost and ask about the risk of breakage.

Good cutters will look for inclusions in the diamond that might threaten its durability, and they will probably check it with a viewing instrument called a polariscope to determine if there is stress. If the stone displays vibrant colors between the crossed polarized lenses of the polariscope, this indicates strain in the diamond. If a diamond is not a good candidate for recutting, the cutter will probably advise against it, but this is rarely necessary. Most diamonds can be safely recut. The cutter will also estimate the weight loss.

The cost of cutting varies depending on the weight of the diamond and the amount of work required. Simple polishing and minor repairs will cost less. If the diamond breaks, it's considered an "act of God" and no liability is assumed. When dealing with skilled cutters, breakage is typically not a problem.

The cutter may propose different options. For example, if you had a chipped 3.06-carat stone, he might propose keeping the stone at 3 carats by smoothing away the chip and leaving the stone out of round. The cutter may also propose recutting the entire stone to excellent proportions despite the fact that the stone may end up weighing just 2.25 carats. There are often a variety of options—simple repolishing, minor repairs, no action, or complete recutting. In the end, your goals and your wallet will determine the best course of action.

13

Branded Diamonds

Finding a well-cut round brilliant is much easier than it used to be. There are many dealers now that promote them. Jewelers don't have to order a specific brand in order to get round brilliants of high quality; they only need to deal with suppliers who specialize in well-cut diamonds.

Finding a well-made fancy cut is more difficult. Some jewelers have discovered that they can often save money by buying brand-name fancy-shape diamonds because they don't have to waste money returning poorly made stones, nor do they have to lose time sorting through parcels to find fancy shapes that are well-cut. As a result these jewelers are opting to feature brand-name fancies in their stores. In sum, they like the consistent quality of cut many branded diamonds offer.

Another advantage of some of these branded cuts is that they have distinctive shapes or faceting patterns that attract customers who are looking for something different than the traditional round brilliant.

Brand names are also used to market lab-grown diamonds and treated diamonds in addition to natural diamonds with various color and clarity grades. So whether you buy a branded or a generic diamond, you should verify its quality and ask if it is natural. In other words, judge branded diamonds just as you would any other diamond.

The July/August 2007 *Gem Market News* states that most branded diamonds cost anywhere from zero premium to a 10% premium. Some are branded names without extra faceting or ideal proportions. Others with premium cuts or more facets may cost 3–5% more to produce with an end result of 5–10% premium.

Listed below are some brands that are not sold exclusively in one retail store or one chain of stores and that are different than that of the standard brilliant cut.

Ashoka®

Ashoka®

Patented by William Goldberg Corp in 2002

A modified antique cushion cut with a rectangular girdle outline and rounded corners. It has 62 facets and ranges from D to K color and IF to SI_2. Based on the famous diamond of the same name, the Ashoka® is named after the Buddhist warrior-emperor Ashoka Maurya. The English translation of *Ashoka* is "the power to remove sorrow."

Barocut™

Barocut™
Patented by Baroka Creations in 2003

A rectangular mixed cut referred to as "The Two Heart Diamond" because two hearts are visible meeting point to point at the culet. It has 81 facets and is available in sizes from 20 points and up.

Context Cut®

Context Cut® From Wild & Petsch patented by Dr. Ulrich Freiesleben in 1995

A square octahedral shaped diamond. When viewed from the top, it exhibits a four-pointed, star-shaped diagonal cross. Context cuts® are expensive to make and are used mostly by high-end designers.

Corona™

Corona™
registered by Yuval Harary Diamonds in 2001

A square cut with high brilliance. The Corona has a total of 65 facets, 40 on the pavilion and 25 on the crown. It's available between 0.05 and 2 carats in clarities IF through I_1.

Crisscut®

Crisscut® Patented by Christopher Designs and Lili Diamonds in 1998
A step cut with 77 crisscrossed facets and a rectangular or an octagonal shape. Rectangular Crisscuts come in calibrated sizes ranging from 0.05 to 20 carats and are used mainly for jewelry, whereas octagonal Crisscuts ranging in size from 0.15 carats and up are usually sold as solitaires.

Cushette®

Cushette® Cut
Patented by Diamco in 2003

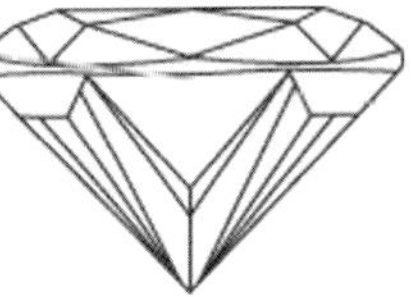

A cushion shape with the brilliance of a round diamond. It's hand cut with 33 facets on the crown and 44 on the pavilion. Cushettes range in size from 0.25 to 10 carats and are certified by GCAL.

Eighty Eight®

The Eighty-Eight®
Patented by Steven Gad of Finesse Diamonds in 2003

An eight-sided roundish diamond with 88 facets. It plays on the Asian belief that 8 is a lucky number, which brings prosperity. Eighty-Eight® diamonds are available mounted or loose in sizes from 0.05 to 5 carats, in colors ranging from D to J and in clarity from SI3 and up.

Flanders Ideal Square Cut®

Flanders Ideal Square Cut®
Square brilliant-cut diamond with cut corners and 62 facets, including the culet. Developed in the late 1980's, the Flanders Cut is available in sizes from 0.05 to 5 carats and in clarities of I_1 to IF. It bears the name of the region where it was first polished, the northern Federal Region of Belgium—Flanders.

Gabrielle® cushion cut

Gabrielle® Patented by Gabriel Tolkowsky/ Suberi Bros in 2002

A "triple brilliant" cut named after its creator, Gabi Tolkowsky. It comes in nine shapes— round, pear, oval, marquise, heart, cushion, shield, octagonal square and octagonal rectangle. Most of the shapes have 105 facets. Gabrielle® diamonds are available in clarities from IF down to I_1 and in sizes 0.10 cts and up.

Jubilant Crown®

Jubilant Crown®
Patented by Edwin Bruce Cutshall in 2001

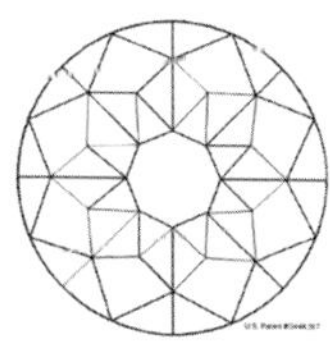

A modified round brilliant with a smaller table and 16 more crown facets than a traditional round brilliant. Table sizes range from 40 to 45%, and carat weights start at 0.19 carats. The Jubilant Crown® is available in clarities from I_1 and up in D to K colors.

Korloff Cut

Korloff Cut
Patented by Korloff in 2002

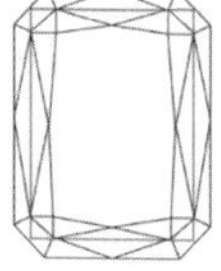

An emerald-cut shape with 65 brilliant-style facets—41 facets on the crown and 24 on the pavilion. The Korloff Cut is available mounted or loose in sizes ranging from 0.05 ct and up.

Lily Cut®

Lily Cut®

Patented by Lili Diamonds in 1997

A flower shaped diamond with a square table. It has 65 facets and comes in D through M/N colors and in calibrated sizes from 0.20 carats and up. The Lily Cut® is often used in women's rings and earrings in addition to line bracelets.

Quadrillon®

Quadrillion®
Patented by Ambar Diamonds in 1981

A square diamond with 49 brilliant style facets: 21 crown, 24 pavilion, and 4 girdle facets. When the quadrillion was developed in the early 1980's, it was the first brilliant-style square cut (the original princess cut). Before then, square diamonds were step cut. Bez Ambar has made improvements to the cut and now calls it Quad 2000.

Lucére® Diamond

Lucére® Diamond
from Cut by Gauge Diamonds

A mixed-cut, square diamond with cut corners that has a three-tiered, step-cut crown with 25 facets and a modified, brilliant-cut pavilion with 40 facets. Carat weights start at 0.25 carats and table sizes range from 54 to 63%. The Lucére diamond is available with GIA, AGS, or PGS lab reports in clarities of IF to I_1 and in colors D through M.

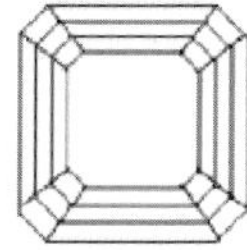
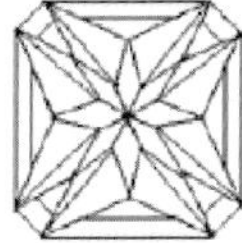

Original Radiant Cut®

Original Radiant Cut®
developed and patented by Hentry Grossbard in 1977

When the patent expired, the diamond became a well-accepted cutting style used by many manufacturers. In 2002, Grossbard's company relaunched their diamond as the Original Radiant Cut Diamond brand, the only radiant to meet the standards established by its inventor.

PrinceCut®

PrinceCut®,
patented by Avi Paz Group in 2000

An emerald-cut shape with 111 brilliant-style facets designed to give it greater brilliance and sparkle than a traditional emerald cut. The PrinceCut® ranges in sizes from 0.10 carats to +10 carats and in colors from D to I.

Princette®

Princette Cut®

Trademarked by Mark Silverstein Diamond Import Company

48-facet "princess cut" baguettes. Used mainly as a bridal stone, the Princette® is sold mounted in designer jewelry. It is available in G to D colors and SI_1 to IF clarities. The most popular sizes are 0.10 to 0.20 carats.

Royal Asscher®

Royal Asscher®

Patented by Royal Asscher Diamond Co. 2002

A 74-facet modern Asscher (step-cut square). See Chapter 11 for more details.

Royal Brilliant®

Royal Brilliant®

Patented by Exroyal Co. in 1986

An 82-facet round brilliant with 10 double bezel facets and 10 pavilion mains, which creates patterns of ten hearts and ten arrows instead of the usual eight.

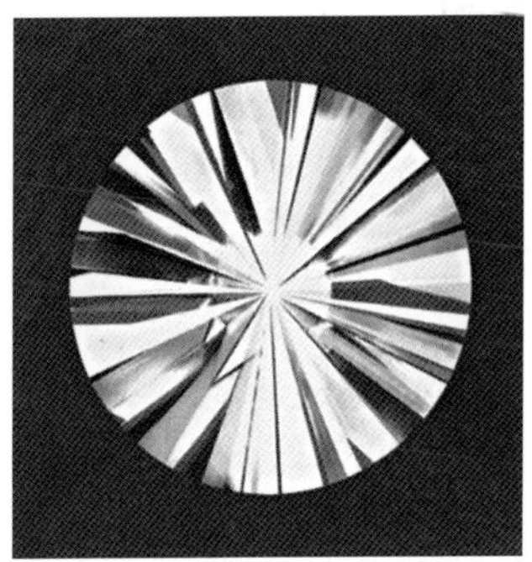
Spirit Diamond®

Spirit Diamond® or **Spirit Sun®**
From Wild & Petsch
patented by Dr. Ulrich Freiesleben in 1997

A modern round diamond, which has 16 equal crown facets and 16 equal pavilion facets radiating outwards. The Spirit Diamond® is most often used in high-end designer jewelry.

Tiana®

Tiana®
Registered by Britestar Diamond Co. Ltd

A modified cushion cut, which is square or rectangular and has 73 facets. Sizes range from 0.50 to 2.5 carats. The Tiana® comes in D to K colors and IF to I_1 clarities. Each diamond is lab graded by either IGI or AAG.

Tycoon Cut®

Tycoon Cut®
Patented by Tycoon Jewelry in 2002

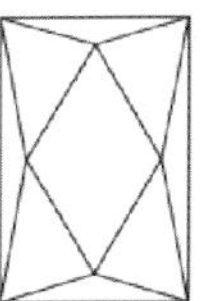
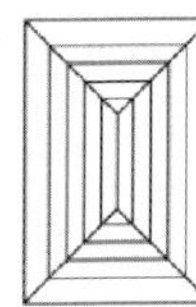

A rectangular diamond with 24 facets on the pavilion and nine on the crown. The top center facet is in the shape of a diamond, making it the "only diamond with a diamond on the top." Sizes start at 0.05 carats. Every Tycoon cut above 0.50 carat is accompanied by a GIA diamond grading report.

Trielle®

Trielle®

Registered by the Trillion Diamond Company

An equilateral triangle, brilliant-cut with 50 facets. In 1978 it was patented as the Trillion, but the name was changed to Trielle in1991 becausc the term "trillion" was being used to refer to any brilliant-cut triangle. Every Trielle diamond from 0.20 on up is cut with identical proportions, so they are fairly easy to match.

Virtue Cut®

Virtue Cut®

A step-cut diamond shape with 21 facets. Carat weights are 0.20 to 3 carats and clarities are VS and up. Color grades range from D to G and fancy yellow to vivid yellow. Virtue Cuts are featured in designer jewelry, which is sold at very high-end independent retailers.

WebCut®

WebCut®

Patented by the Dali Diamond Co. in 2003

Designed like a spider's web, the WebCut® has 24 facets on the pavilion and 24 on the crown plus the table. It's available in 0.20 to 3 carats in D to I colors from IF to SI_1. An HRD certificate is included with each WebCut® diamond.

14

Diamond Grading Reports

The first diamond grading reports were issued by the GIA (Gemological Institute of America) Gem Trade Laboratory in 1955. The GIA intentionally chose not to call them "certificates" because doing so would appear to validate the diamond itself, rather than objectively reporting information about the stone. Some other labs use the term "certificate," and trade members often refer to grading reports as "certs."

The color and clarity grades of the GIA grading report are based on a system developed by the GIA in 1952. Prior to that time, diamond color was described inconsistently in the trade with terms such as "River" and "Top Wesselton" or with multiple grades such as "A," "AA," and "AAA."

Since the GIA was the first to develop a diamond grading system and report, their diamond reports are the best known in the industry and enjoy a world-wide reputation (fig. 14.1). Another internationally respected diamond grading report is the one issued in Antwerp Belgium by the HRD (abbreviation of the Flemish name Hoge Raad voor Diamant). First introduced in 1976, the HRD Diamond Certificate is better known in Europe, Africa and Asia than in North America (fig. 14.2). The volume of diamonds graded at the HRD and GIA is so high that it can sometimes take weeks to receive a grading report. This is one reason why other labs have emerged.

Two other laboratories that issue a high volume of diamond grading reports are IGI (International Gemological Institute) and the EGL USA Group, and there are also several more. Some labs are known for being more strict than others in their grading. Since reputations can vary from one lab and location to another, it's best to do some research on the labs in your area. Ask a few trade professionals and maybe a couple of auction houses what type of lab report they would want on a diamond if you were to sell it to them. When sellers buy gemstones, they tend to want a report from a lab known for strict grading. When they sell, they sometimes want their stones graded by a lab known for lenient grading and/or minimal information, if their customers don't specify what type of report they want.

A true diamond grading report is not an appraisal and does not have a value or price indicated on the report. It's simply an independent report that identifies and describes an unmounted diamond. The moment a report has a price included, it becomes an appraisal.

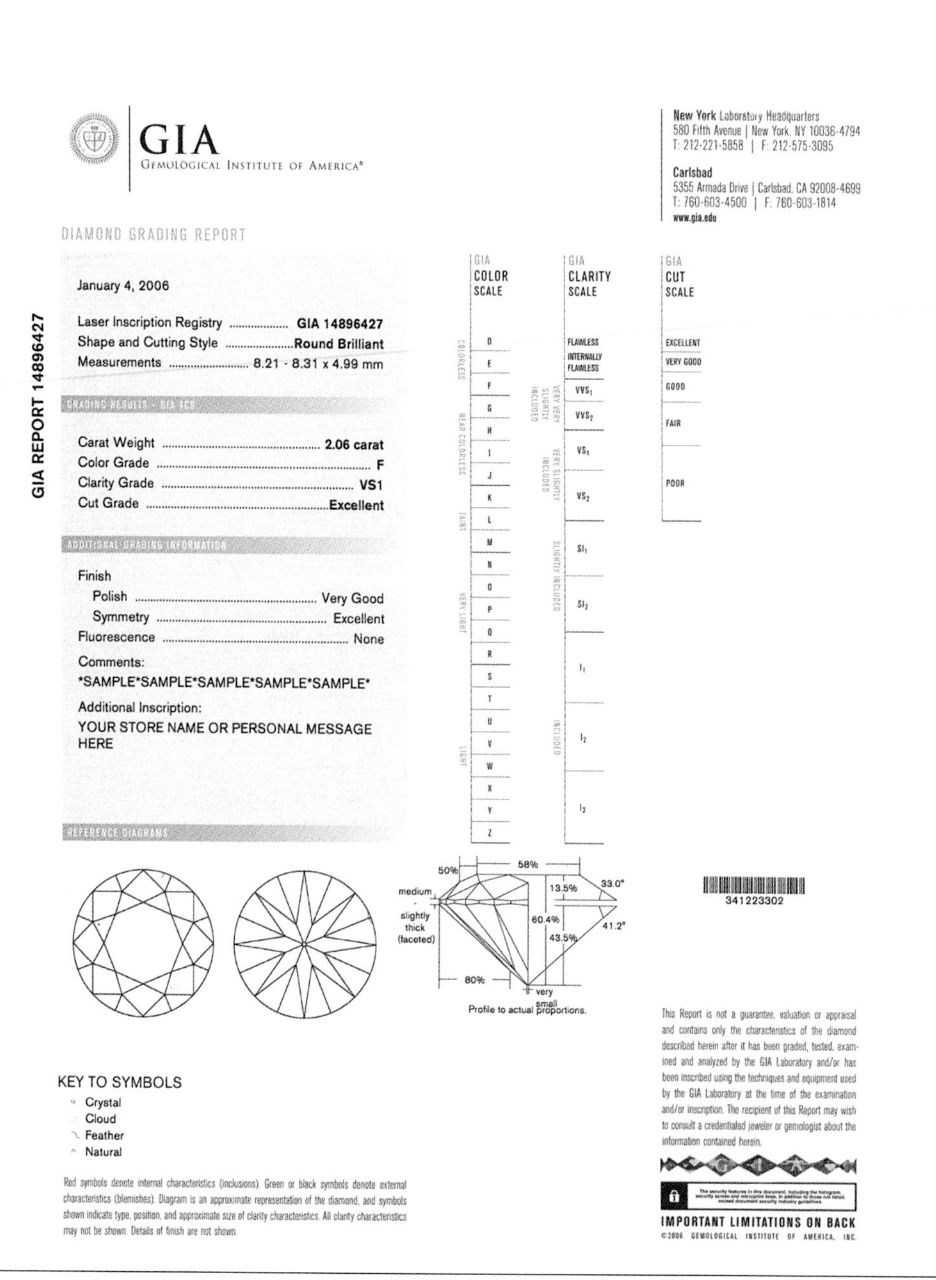

GIA
GEMOLOGICAL INSTITUTE OF AMERICA®

New York Laboratory Headquarters
580 Fifth Avenue | New York, NY 10036-4794
T: 212-221-5858 | F: 212-575-3095

Carlsbad
5355 Armada Drive | Carlsbad, CA 92008-4699
T: 760-603-4500 | F: 760-603-1814
www.gia.edu

DIAMOND GRADING REPORT

GIA REPORT 14896427

January 4, 2006

Laser Inscription Registry .... GIA 14896427
Shape and Cutting Style .... Round Brilliant
Measurements .... 8.21 - 8.31 x 4.99 mm

GRADING RESULTS - GIA 4CS

Carat Weight .... 2.06 carat
Color Grade .... F
Clarity Grade VS1
Cut Grade .... Excellent

ADDITIONAL GRADING INFORMATION

Finish
Polish .... Very Good
Symmetry .... Excellent
Fluorescence .... None

Comments:
*SAMPLE*SAMPLE*SAMPLE*SAMPLE*SAMPLE*

Additional Inscription:
YOUR STORE NAME OR PERSONAL MESSAGE HERE

REFERENCE DIAGRAMS

GIA COLOR SCALE
COLORLESS: D, E, F
NEAR COLORLESS: G, H, I, J
FAINT: K, L, M
VERY LIGHT: N, O, P, Q, R
LIGHT: S, T, U, V, W, X, Y, Z

GIA CLARITY SCALE
FLAWLESS
INTERNALLY FLAWLESS
VERY VERY SLIGHTLY INCLUDED: VVS_1, VVS_2
VERY SLIGHTLY INCLUDED: VS_1, VS_2
SLIGHTLY INCLUDED: SI_1, SI_2
INCLUDED: I_1, I_2, I_3

GIA CUT SCALE
EXCELLENT
VERY GOOD
GOOD
FAIR
POOR

341223302

KEY TO SYMBOLS
Crystal
Cloud
Feather
Natural

Red symbols denote internal characteristics (inclusions). Green or black symbols denote external characteristics (blemishes). Diagram is an approximate representation of the diamond, and symbols shown indicate type, position, and approximate size of clarity characteristics. All clarity characteristics may not be shown. Details of finish are not shown.

This Report is not a guarantee, valuation or appraisal and contains only the characteristics of the diamond described herein after it has been graded, tested, examined and analyzed by the GIA Laboratory and/or has been inscribed using the techniques and equipment used by the GIA Laboratory at the time of the examination and/or inscription. The recipient of this Report may wish to consult a credentialed jeweler or gemologist about the information contained herein.

IMPORTANT LIMITATIONS ON BACK

Fig. 14.1 Sample GIA Diamond Grading Report. *Reprinted with permission from the Gemological Institute of America.*

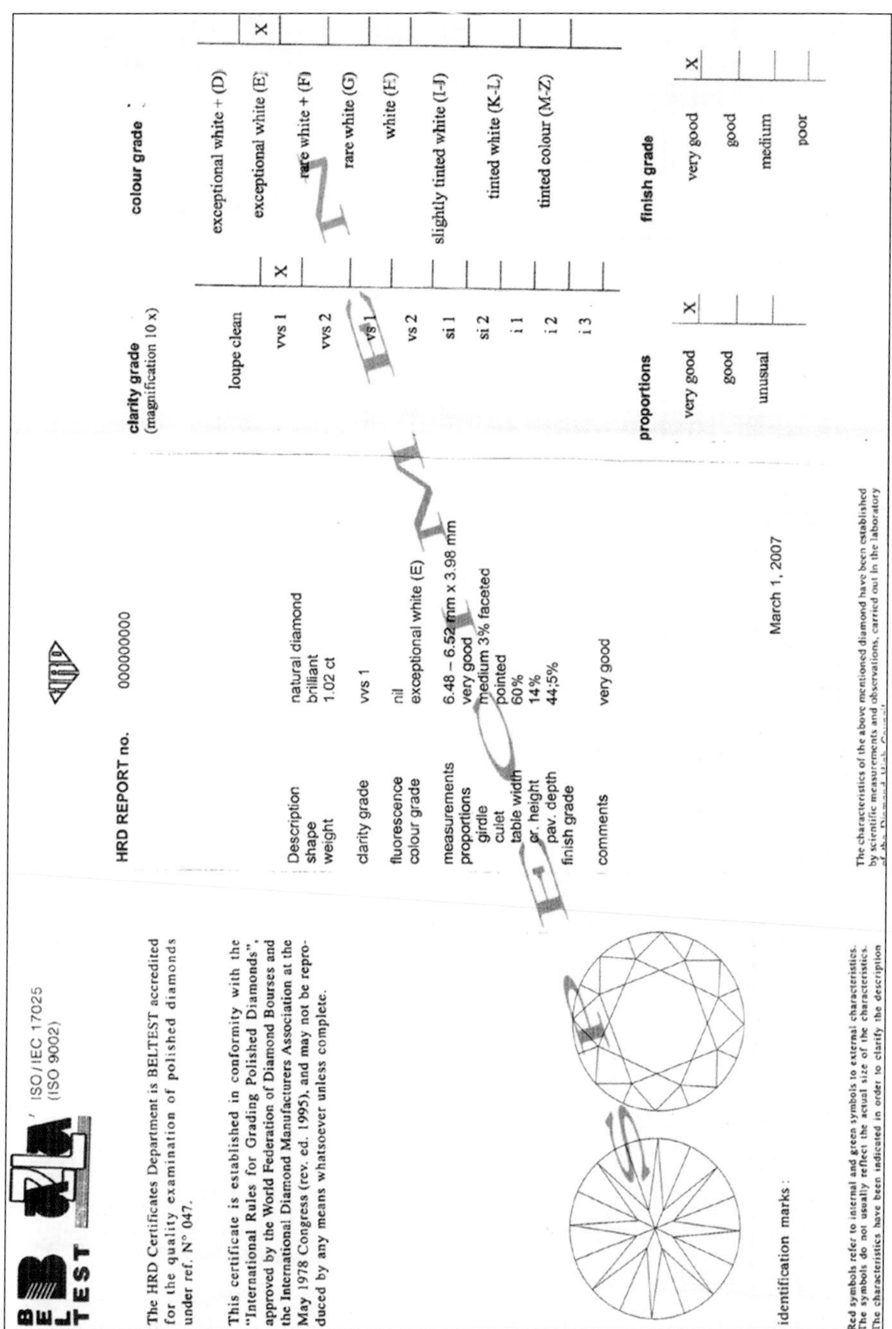

BELTEST

ISO/IEC 17025
(ISO 9002)

The HRD Certificates Department is BELTEST accredited for the quality examination of polished diamonds under ref. N° 047.

This certificate is established in conformity with the "International Rules for Grading Polished Diamonds", approved by the World Federation of Diamond Bourses and the International Diamond Manufacturers Association at the May 1978 Congress (rev. ed. 1995), and may not be reproduced by any means whatsoever unless complete.

identification marks :

Red symbols refer to internal and green symbols to external characteristics. The symbols do not usually reflect the actual size of the characteristics. The characteristics have been indicated in order to clarify the description

HRD REPORT no. 000000000

Description	natural diamond
shape	brilliant
weight	1.02 ct
clarity grade	vvs 1
fluorescence	nil
colour grade	exceptional white (E)
measurements	6.48 – 6.52 mm x 3.98 mm
proportions	very good
girdle	medium 3% faceted
culet	pointed
table width	60%
cr. height	14%
pav. depth	44,5%
finish grade	very good
comments	very good

March 1, 2007

The characteristics of the above mentioned diamond have been established by scientific measurements and observations, carried out in the laboratory

clarity grade
(magnification 10 x)

loupe clean	
vvs 1	X
vvs 2	
vs 1	
vs 2	
si 1	
si 2	
i 1	
i 2	
i 3	

colour grade

exceptional white + (D)	
exceptional white (E)	X
rare white + (F)	
rare white (G)	
white (H)	
slightly tinted white (I-J)	
tinted white (K-L)	
tinted colour (M-Z)	

proportions

very good	X
good	
unusual	

finish grade

very good	X
good	
medium	
poor	

Fig. 14.2 HRD Specimen Diamond Certificate. *Reprinted with permission from HRD (Hoge Raad vorr Diamant.)*

Some sellers wonder why customers should have a lab report when appraisals also provide identification, treatment and quality information. Major laboratories have greater expertise, more sophisticated equipment and more opportunities to examine important gems than the average jeweler, dealer or appraiser. As a result, they're better equipped to detect enhancements and synthetic gems. Now that more and more treated and synthetic diamonds are entering the market, it's increasingly important to get diamond reports from independent labs that conduct research. If you are asking a high, natural-color price for a colored diamond, it's essential that you get a lab report stating the color is of natural origin. This can offer you protection from unknowingly selling a treated diamond as a natural color-diamond. If it turns out that the lab was mistaken, it will be easier to defend yourself from being accused of fraud.

Another advantage of having a grading document from a major lab is that their documents usually carry more weight than appraisals when gems are bought and sold. If you plan to sell an expensive gem on the international market or through an auction house such as Christie's or Sotheby's, it should be accompanied by a recent report from an internationally recognized lab.

In addition to the grading certificate, it's advisable for buyers to get a separate appraisal report for expensive diamonds after they're mounted in jewelry. Besides being useful for insurance purposes, an appraisal can help verify that the diamond matches the one described in the diamond report. Appraisers offer appraisals on both mounted and unmounted diamonds. However, the GIA, HRD and some other labs will only grade unmounted diamonds. Prongs can hide inclusions, and the apparent diamond color can be influenced by the metal surrounding the stone. In addition, accurate color grading requires comparing the diamond side by side with other unmounted diamonds.

If you'd like more information on appraisals and appraisers, see Chapter 14 in the *Gem & Jewelry Pocket Guide* by Renée Newman. A list of independent appraisers who are gemologists and who have completed formal education on appraisal procedures, ethics and law can be found at www.reneenewman.com. Click on "appraisers."

Mini-certs

Several labs offer shortened versions of their full grading reports. Diagrams of clarity features are not normally included in these less detailed reports, which are sometimes referred to as mini-certs. The GIA calls their brief report the GIA Diamond Dossier. The HRD calls it the HRD Diamond Identification Report.

Some mini-certs indicate the shape, weight, color and clarity of a diamond without giving any details about its proportions, polish or symmetry. To a consumer, it might appear that the 4 C's of cut, carat weight, color and clarity are all included. However, shape is a separate price factor from cut quality, which includes the proportioning and finish qualities of the diamond. If a diamond is poorly proportioned, it's not good quality, even if its color and clarity grades are high. Don't be misled into thinking that the cut of a diamond is just its shape.

Mini-certs have the advantage of costing less than full reports, and they can normally be processed quicker. More often than not, they are issued for diamonds weighing less than one carat. For fine quality diamonds of a carat or more, it's advisable to have a full report because it offers you more protection and information.

How Reproducible are Lab Grades?

Some consumers assume that the grades on lab reports are absolute and exact when in fact color and clarity grades are highly subjective. This is one reason major labs often have at least three graders examine each diamond, and they don't guarantee that their grades are one hundred percent accurate.

Most of the time, gemologists agree on the grades. However it's not un-common for color or clarity to fall on a transition point between two grade ranges. In these cases, the majority of the labs assign only one grade per category, and invariably they give the stone the higher grade. A few labs give split grades or place an asterisk next to the grade indicating that it is borderline.

This means that grades are not always reproducible. If you were to resubmit certain diamonds to the same lab for a grade and they were unable to look it up in their data base under the number inscribed on the girdle, the stone could re-ceive a different grade the second time. Because of this, the gem trade accepts a tolerance of plus or minus one grade.

If you were to resubmit the same diamond to different labs, there's an even greater chance that there could be a difference in grades. A difference of two grades or more would indicate that there's a problem with one of the labs. The lab with the higher grades might be catering to retailers or manufacturers who send them a lot of stones for grading. Lab documents are used to sell stones; and the higher the grade, the more the seller can ask for the stone or the better deal the customers think they are getting.

This underscores one of the main themes of this book: you should base your choice of diamond on its appearance, not just on its grading report. If you don't visually examine diamonds before you buy them and compare them side by side with other diamonds, you could make a poor choice. When you get a grading report from a gem laboratory, keep in mind that the document is not necessarily the last word. It is at best an independent expert opinion.

Addresses of Some Diamond Grading Labs

Listed below are some of the better known diamond grading laboratories:

AGL (American Gemological Laboratories, Inc.) (founded 1977)
580 Fifth Ave. Suite 706, New York, NY 10036
Phone (212) 704-0727, Fax (212) 764-7614, www.aglgemlab.com
Specializes in colored diamond and colored gem reports and diamond verification

AGSL (American Gem Society Laboratories) (only for the trade)
8917 W. Sahara Ave., Las Vegas, NV 89117
Phone (702) 255-6500, Fax (702) 255-7420, www.agslab.com
AGSL is especially noted for its "ideal-cut" diamond reports.

AIGS (Asian Institute of Gemological Sciences) (founded 1978)
Jewelry Trade Center, 6th floor,
919 Silom Road, Bangkok 10500, Thailand
Phone (662) 267-4325/7, Fax (662) 267-4327, www.aigsthailand.com

CCIP Gemological Laboratory (Chambre de Commerce et d'Industrie de Paris Laboratory, also called the French Gemological Laboratory)
2 Place de la Bourse, 75002 Paris, France
Phone (33) 1 40 26 25 45, Fax (33) 1 40 26 06 75, www.diamants.ccip.fr

CGL (Central Gem Laboratory) (founded 1970)
Miyagi Building, 5-15-14 Ueno,
Taito-ku, Tokyo 110-0005, Japan
Phone (81) 3 3836-1627, Fax (81) 3 3832-6861, www.cgl.co.jp

CISGEM (Centro Informazione e Servizi Gemmologici)
Via delle Orsole 4, 1-20123, Milano, Italy
Phone (39) 02 85155250, www.cisgem.it

DEL (Deutsch Diamant und Edelsteinlaboratorien Idar-Oberstein)
(German Diamond and Gemstone Laboratories Idar-Oberstein)
Mainzer Str. 34, D-55743 Idar-Oberstein, Germany
Phone (49) 6781-981355, Fax (49) 6781-981357, www.gemcertificate.com

EGL (European Gemological Laboratory
www.egl.co.za
branches in Antwerp, Johannesburg, Istanbul, London, Tel Aviv and Seoul

EGL USA Group (founded 1986)
6 West 48th Street, New York, NY 10036
Phone (212)-730-7380, Fax (212)-730-7453, www.eglusa.com
branches in Los Angeles, Vancouver & Toronto.
The EGL USA Group is independent of EGL labs outside of North America

GAAJ (Gemmological Association of All Japan) (founded 1981)
8F Daiwa-Ueno Bldg, 5-25-11 Ueno
Taito-ku, Tokyo, 110-0005, Japan
Phone (81) 3-3835-2466, Fax (81) 3-3839-0798, www.gaaj-zenhokyo.co.jp
Specializes in colored diamond and colored gem reports

GCAL (Gem Certification and Appraisal Lab)
580 Fifth Avenue, Lower Lobby, New York, NY 10036
Phone (212) 869-8985, Fax (212) 869-2315, www.gemfacts.com

Gem A (Gemmological Association and Gem Testing Laboratory of Great Britain) (only for the trade) (founded 1925)
27 Greville Street, London EC1N 8TN, UK
Phone 44 (207) 404-3334, Fax 44 (207) 404-8843, www.gem-a.info

GIL (Gemworld International Laboratories)
2640 Patriot Blvd., Suite 240, Glenview, IL 60026
Phone (847) 657-0555, Fax (847) 657.0550, www.gemworldlabs.com

GIA Gem Trade Laboratory Inc. (only for the trade) (founded 1949)
5355 Armada Drive, Carlsbad, CA 92008
Phone (800) 421-7250 & (760) 603-4500, www.gia.org
580 Fifth Ave., New York, NY 10036, Phone (212) 221-5858

GGL (Gübelin Gem Lab Ltd)
Maihofstrasse 102, CH-6000 Lucerne 9 / Switzerland
Phone (41) 41 429 1717, Fax (41) 41 429 1734, www.gubelinlab.com

GIT (Gem & Jewelry Institute of Thailand)
Chulalongkorn University, Phayathai University
Phayathai Road, Patumwan
Bangkok 10330 Thailand
Phone (662) 218-5470-4, Fax (662) 218-5474, www.git.or.th

HKGL (Hong Kong Gems Laboratory) (founded 1987)
4/F Tung Hip Commercial Building
248, Des Voeux Road, Central Hong Kong
Phone (852) 281 51880, Fax (852) 285 43970, www.hkgems.com.hk

HRD (Hoge Raad vorr Diamant) (founded 1976)
Hoveniersstraat, 22, B-2018 Antwerp, Belgium
Phone (32) 3 222 06 31, Fax (32) 3 222 06 05, www.hrd.be
A branch will open in New York in 2005

IGI (International Gemological Institute) (founded in Antwerp in 1975)
589 Fifth Avenue, New York, NY 10017
Phone (212) 753-7100, Fax (212) 753-7759, www.igiworldwide.com
branches in Antwerp, Bangkok, Cavalese, Dubai, Los Angeles, Mumbai, Seoul, Tel Aviv, Tokyo, and Toronto

PGS (Professional Gem Sciences) (founded 1980)
5 South Wabash, Suite 1905, Chicago IL 60603
Phone (312) 920-1541, (888) 292-1888, Fax (312) 920-1547, www.progem.com

SSEF (Swiss Foundation for the Research of Gemstones) (founded 1974)
Falknerstrasse 9, CH-4001, Basel, Switzerland
Phone (41) 61 262-0640, Fax (41) 61 262-0641, www.ssef.ch

Glossary

Absorption spectrum: The dark lines or gaps produced in a continuous spectrum by absorption of certain wavelengths by specified materials.

AGS: American Gem Society.

Angle of incidence: The angle at which light strikes a surface.

Angle of reflection: The angle at which light bounces off of a surface.

Angle of refraction: The angle between a refracted ray and a line perpendicular to the surface between the gemstone and air at the point of refraction.

Antique jewelry: Any jewelry one-hundred or more years old.

Asscher cut: An emerald-cut stone with a smaller table, higher crown and deeper pavilion than a modern emerald cut. (See Chapter 11 for more information.)

Bearding: Hairline cleavages along the girdle (outer edge) of diamonds that look like whiskers and hairs extending into the diamond.

Bezel facets: Any of the four-sided, kite-shaped facets on the crown of a round brilliant-cut diamond.

Blemish: A flaw on the surface of a gemstone such as a scratch, pit, or abrasion.

Brightness: The actual and/or perceived amount of light return. In the case of a diamond, it is the combined effect of its surface and internal white light reflections.

Brilliance: Brightness with an attractive distribution of dark and bright areas that display good contrast. (This is based on the AGS brilliance definition of "brightness + positive contrast.")

Brilliant cut: The most common style of diamond cutting. The standard brilliant cut consists of 32 facets plus a table above the girdle and 24 facets plus a culet below the girdle. Other shapes besides round can be faceted as brilliant cuts.

Briolette: A gemstone with a tear-drop shape, a circular cross-section and brilliant-style facets or occasionally rectangular, step-cut style facets.

Canary colored: Yellow.

Carat: A unit of weight equaling 1/5 of a gram.

Champagne colored: Light brown.

Clarity: The degree to which a stone is free from external characteristics called **blemishes** and internal features called **inclusions**.

Cleavage: The tendency for a mineral to split along specific crystal planes; a break that follows the grain of the diamond.

Cloud: A cluster of small pinpoint inclusions.

Cognac colored: Brown.

Collectibles: Items gathered from a specific designer, manufacturer, or any period or periods in time.

Contrast: The degree of difference between light and dark tones. AGS defines contrast as the light and dark patterns seen when observing a faceted diamond.

Critical angle: The largest angle from the normal at which light rays can escape from the interior of a gemstone. If light strikes an inner surface at an angle greater than the critical angle it will not exit the gem. It will be internally reflected.

Crown: The upper part of a faceted gemstone above the girdle.

Crown angle: The angle between the girdle plane and the bezel facets. (any of the four-sided, kite-shaped facets on the crown of a round brilliant-cut diamond.

Crown height percentage: The distance between the girdle and table planes expressed as a percentage of the average girdle diameter.

Culet: The tiny facet on the pointed bottom of the pavilion, parallel to the table.

Cushion shape: A rectangular or squarish shape with curved sides and rounded corners.

Density: The degree of compactness of a substance; mass per unit volume.

Dispersion: The separation of white light into spectral colors. "Dispersion" also refers to the numerical difference in the refractive indices of a red ray and violet ray passing through a gem material. The dispersion value of diamond is always 0.044. However, the amount of dispersion (fire) that a diamond displays varies depending on how it is cut and the lighting under which it is viewed.

Doublet: An imitation gem composed of two pieces of gem material or glass and cemented or fused together.

Durability: Resistance to scratching, abrading, chipping and breaking.

Estate jewelry: Jewelry that has been previously owned by someone and that is typically passed on from one generation to another. It can range from a few decades to 100 or more years in age.

Eye-clean: Having no eye-visible inclusions or blemishes.

Facets: The flat, polished surfaces or planes on a gem.

Fancy colored diamond: Any naturally colored diamond with a noticeable depth of body color. Fancy colored diamonds are also called **fancies**. See Chapter 10 for a more complete description.

Fancy shape: Any shape except round. A pear shape is an example of a fancy shape. Sometimes fancy shapes are simply called **fancies**.

Feather: A general term for any break or crack in a diamond.

Fire: The display of spectral colors resulting from the interaction of white light with a faceted gemstone.

Fisheye: A reflection of the girdle, which looks like a white donut-shaped circle.

Fluorescence: The emission of visible light (a glowing effect) by a material when it's stimulated by ultraviolet light, x-rays or other forms of radiation. See Chapter 7 for more information.

Fracture filling: A method of improving clarity and transparency by filling cracks with a substance that makes them almost invisible.

GIA: Gemological Institute of America.

Girdle: The narrow rim around a faceted gemstone. The girdle plane is parallel to the table and is the largest diameter of any part of the stone.

Grainer: A word used to describe the weights of diamond in multiples of 0.25 carat (one grain). A four grainer is a one-carat diamond.

Habit: The crystal form in which a mineral most often occurs.

Hardness: The resistance of a gem to scratching and abrasion.

HPHT Treatment: High pressure and high temperature treatment.

Hue: Basic spectral color such as yellow, green and orange as well as transition spectral colors such as greenish yellow and orangy yellow.

Ideal Cut: A marketing term that has been used for excellent quality diamonds with proportions similar to those proposed by Marcel Tolkowsky.

Inclusions: Flaws inside a gemstone such as crystals, clouds and graining.

Kelvin: A unit to measure light temperature.

Knots: Included diamond crystals left exposed on the surface by polishing.

Laser drill holes: Tiny holes drilled into the diamond with a laser beam, allowing black spots to be dissolved or bleached out with chemicals.

Leakage: Light that escapes out of the interior of a gemstone; areas that do not return light. Light that escapes through the pavilion is **unplanned light leakage**. Light that is internally reflected back out the crown is **planned light leakage**.

Light Performance: The degree of brightness, fire, scintillation and contrast of a gemstone and the pattern formed by its bright and dark areas. AGS defines it as an analysis of brightness, fire, leakage and contrast.

Loupe; A small magnifying glass used to view gemstones.

Macles: Diamond crystals that are flattened and triangular in shape with two crystals sharing a common face.

Make: The proportions and finish of a stone.

Master stone: A diamond of a known color grade used to grade other diamonds.

Melee: Small diamonds usually less than about one-fourth carat in size.

Mohs scale: A relative scale of gem hardness from 1 to 10, the hardest value.

Nailhead: A diamond with a dark central area.

Naturals: Part of the original surface of a diamond crystal that is left unpolished. Sometimes naturals have step-like ridges or triangular forms (called **trigons**).

Normal: An imaginary line at a 90-degree angle to a surface at which light strikes.

Old European cut: An old-style round cut with 58 facets, a high crown, a small table and a large culet. (See Chapter 11.)

Old-mine cut: An old-style cushion-shape cut with a high crown, deep pavilion, large culet and 58 facets similar to the modern brilliant. (See Chapter 11.)

Opaque: Not penetrated by light; the opposite of transparent.

Optical symmetry: The alignment of facets and consistency of angles, a direct assessment of the precision of the cut and craftsmanship.

Pattern: "The relative size, arrangement, and contrast of bright and dark areas that result form a diamond's internal and external reflections." (Page 9 of the *GIA Diamond Grading Lab Manual*.)

Pavilion: The lower part of a faceted gemstone below the girdle. It is cone-shaped on a round diamond.

Pavilion angle: The angle between the girdle plane and the pavilion main facets.

Pavilion main facets: The large pavilion facets extending from the girdle to the culet on a brilliant-cut.

Pavilion depth percentage: The distance from the girdle plane to the culet, expressed as a percentage of the average girdle diameter.

Plot: The mapping of inclusions and blemishes on a diagram for identification.

Phosphorescence: The continued emission of visible light (glowing effect) from a gemstone after the light source is removed.

Point: One-hundredth of a carat. A five-point diamond weighs 0.05 carats.

Point cut: An antique cut which preserved the diamond crystal's octahedral shape and resembles two pyramids base to base. (See Chapter 11.)

Polish: The overall condition of the facet surfaces of a polished diamond. It's a sub- category of finish. When labs evaluate polish, they examine the diamond under 10X magnification and look for surface blemishes that do not affect the clarity grade.

Princess cut: A square brilliant cut with 90-degree-angle corners.

Rose-cuts: Diamonds that are dome-shaped with flat bottoms and that have rose-petal-like triangular facets that radiate out from the center in multiples of six. From above, the rose cut may be round, oval or pear shape. (See Chapter 11.)

Refraction: The bending of light that results from the change in its speed as it passes from one material to another.

Refractive Index (RI): The ratio of the speed of light in air to its speed in a gemstone; the degree to which light is bent when it passes through a gem. The RI of diamond is 2.417.

Saturation: The strength, purity, or intensity of a hue (also called chroma).

Scintillation: Tiny flashes of light from a gemstone seen when the stone, light source or observer moves. According to the GIA, scintillation is a combination of sparkle and pattern.

Single cut: A cutting style with a table, eight crown facets, eight pavilion facets and sometimes a culet. This cut served as the basis for the modern brilliant cut, and it is still used for small diamonds weighing less than one-tenth of a carat.

Specific gravity (SG): The ratio of a gem's weight to the weight of an equal volume of water at 4°C. The higher the specific gravity, the greater the density is. The specific gravity of diamond is 3.52 (± .01).

Spectra: Images formed when a beam of light is dispersed and brought into focus.

Spectroscope: An optical instrument used for forming spectra.

Spread: Cut shallow to make a diamond appear larger face-up than its weight.

Symmetry: A grading term for the exactness of shape and placement of facets. It is one of two subcategories of **finish**.

Synthetic diamonds: Diamonds made in a laboratory that have essentially the same chemical composition and crystal structure as natural diamonds. Their physical and optical properties are almost the same as those of natural diamonds. See Chapter 8 for more information.

Table: The large, flat, top facet. It has an octagonal shape on a round brilliant.

Table cut: An octahedral shape with its top point cut away, creating a square-shaped, flat-top table facet. (See Chapter 11.)

Table percentage: A percentage of the average girdle diameter. For round brilliant cuts it is determined by dividing the largest table diameter by the average girdle diameter.

Tilt: The point at which the girdle of the diamond reflects under the table. A well-made round brilliant can have a greater amount of tilt before the girdle appears in the table of the stone than one which is not as well proportioned.

Tone: The amount or lightness of color. (In some color systems, this is called "lightness," "value" or "saturation.")

Total depth percentage: The depth from the table to the culet, expressed as a percentage of the average girdle diameter in a round brilliant.

Total internal reflection: The reflection of light out the crown of a gemstone without loss of any of the light that entered the stone.

Toughness: The resistance of a gem to breaking, chipping or cracking.

Transitional cuts: Diamonds that were cut in the 1930's and 1940's and that have the overall faceting of modern brilliants but with a slightly open culet and a bit of the faceting of an old European cut.

Translucent: Allowing light to pass through partially like frosted glass.

Transparency: The degree to which a gemstone transmits light. In other words, it's the degree to which the stone is clear, cloudy or nearly opaque.

Treatment: The standard term used in gemological literature for any process done to improve the appearance of a gemstone, except cutting and cleaning. See Chapter 9 for more information on diamond treatments.

Type I diamonds: Diamonds with nitrogen in their chemical structure. This affects the physical and optical properties of the diamonds.

Type II diamonds: Diamonds without significant nitrogen in their structure.

Ultraviolet light: Light with wavelengths shorter than 400nm. It's used to help identify gemstones.

Zoning: Alternating sections of color in a gemstone.

Chemical, Physical, & Optical Characteristics of Diamonds

The information below is based mostly on the following sources:
Gems by Robert Webster
GIA Gem Reference Guide
Handbook of Gem Identification by Richard Liddicoat

Chemical composition: C, Crystallized carbon

Mohs hardness: 10

Specific gravity: 3.52 (±.01)

Toughness: Good in cleavage directions, exceptional in other directions

Cleavage: Perfect in four directions

Fracture: Step-like

Streak: White

Crystal system: Cubic

Crystal descriptions: Mainly octahedrons, also cubes, rhombic dodecahedrons, twins and plates

Optic Character: Singly refractive

Refractive Index: 2.417

Birefringence: None

Dispersion: .044

Luster: Adamantine

Pleochroism: None

UV fluorescence: Inert to strong, usually blue (LW), weaker (SW)
See Chapter 8 for more details

Reaction to chemicals: None

Stability to light: Stable

Reaction to heat:
Begins to vaporize in an oxygen-rich atmosphere at 690°C to 875°C

Absorption spectra:

Cape series: 415.5 nm: is the strongest absorption line. Others are visible at 453 with a weak line 466 and a stronger one at 478.

Natural-color brown stones with green fluorescence: A weak line at 498, a slightly stronger one at 504 and a thin faint line at 533nm.

Natural-color brown Type II diamonds show no lines.

Diamonds colored by natural or artificial radiation have absorption lines at 498 and 504 nm and in Type Ia diamonds at 595.

Irradiated pink and red diamonds have absorption lines at 595 and 647nm.

Bibliography

Diamonds

Balfour, Ian. *Famous Diamonds*. London: William Collins Sons & Co Ltd., 1987.

Blakey, George G. *The Diamond*. London: Paddington Press Ltd., 1977.

Bruton, Eric. *Diamonds*. Radnor, PA: Chilton, 1978.

Cuellar, Fred. *How to Buy a Diamond*. Naperville, IL: Casablanca Press, 2000.

Dickinson, Joan Younger. *The Book of Diamonds*. New York: Crown Publishers, 1965.

Gemological Institute of America. *Diamond Grading Lab Manual*, 2006.

Gemological Institute of America. *Diamonds & Diamond Grading* Course, 2002.

Gemological Institute of America. *Diamonds & Diamond Grading* Course 1986.

Gemological Institute of America. *Diamonds* Course 1979.

Gemological Institute of America. *The GIA Diamond Dictionary*. Santa Monica, CA: GIA, 1993.

Harlow, George E. *The Nature of Diamonds*. Cambridge University Press, 1998.

Hofer, Stephen C. *Collecting & Classifying Coloured Diamonds*. New York: Ashland Press, 1998.

King, John M. *Gems & Gemology in Review: Colored Diamonds*. GIA. 2006.

Koivula, John. *The Microworld of Diamonds*. Northbrook, IL: Gemworld International Inc., 2000.

Kassoy Inc. *Everything You Always Wanted to Know about Diamonds*. New York: Kassoy Inc., 1977.

Ludel, Leonard. *Recutting & Repairing Diamonds*.1996.

Nassau, Kurt. *Gemstone Enhancement*. Oxford: Butterworth-Heinemann, 1994.

Newman, Renée, *Diamond Ring Buying Guide: How to evaluate, identify, select & care for diamonds & diamond jewelry*. Los Angeles: International Jewelry Publications, 2002.

Newman, Renée, *Diamond Ring Buying Guide: How to Spot Value & Avoid Ripoffs*. Los Angeles: International Jewelry Publications, 1989.

Newman, Renée, *Gem & Jewelry Pocket Guide*. Los Angeles, International Jewelry Publications, 2003.

Pagel-Theisen, Verena. *Diamond Grading ABC*. Antwerp: Rubin & Son, 2001.

Pagel-Theisen, Verena. *Diamond Grading ABC*. New York: Rubin & Son, 1986.

Roskin, Gary. *Photo Masters For Diamond Grading.* Northbrook, IL: Gemworld International, 1994.

Shuster, William George. *Legacy of Leadership: a History of the Gemological Institute of America.* Carlsbad, CA: Gemological Institute of America. 2003.

Spero, Saul A. *Diamonds, Love, & Compatibility.* Hicksville, NY: Exposition Press, 1977.

Vleeschdrager, Eddy. *Dureté 10: Le diamant, 3 édition, histoire-taille-commerce.* Deurne (Anvers): 1996.

Jewelry and Gems

AGTA, *1997-98 Source Directory* & Gemstone Enhancement Information Chart.

Carmona, Charles. *The Complete Handbook for Gemstone Weight Estimation.* Los Angeles: Gemania Publishing, 1998.

Cologni, Franco & Nussbaum, Eric. *Platinum by Cartier.* Harry N. Abrams. 1996.

Gemological Institute of America. Appraisal Seminar handbook.
Gemological Institute of America. Gem Identification Course.
Gemological Institute of America. Jewelry Repair Workbook.
Gemological Institute of America. Jewelry Sales Course.
Gemological Institute of America. *Gem Reference Guide.* Santa Monica, CA: GIA, 1988.

Geolat, Patti, Van Northrup, C., Federman, David. *The Professional's Guide to Jewelry Insurance Appraising.* Shawnee Mission, KS: Modern Jeweler, 1994.

Gubelin, Eduard & Franz-Xavier, Erni. *Gemstones: Symbols of Beauty and Power.* Lucerne: EMB Service for Publishers, 2000.

Hanneman, Wm. *Guide to Affordable Gemology.* Poulsbo, WA: Hanneman Gemological Instruments, 1998.

Hodgkinson, Alan. *Visual Optics: The Hodgkinson Method.* Gemworld Intl. Inc., Northbrook, IL, 1995.

Hughes, Richard W. *Ruby & Sapphire.* Boulder, CO: RWH Publishing, 1997.

Joseph, Ralph. *Jeweler's Guide to Effective Jewelry Appraising.* Northbrook, IL: Gemworld International, Inc, 1996.

LeFèvre, Sophie. *Jean Vendome.* Paris: Somogy éditions d"art. 1999.

Liddicoat, Richard T. *Handbook of Gem Identification.* Santa Monica, CA: GIA, 1993.

Matlins, Antoinette L. & Bonanno, A. C. *Engagement & Wedding Rings.* South Woodstock, VT: Gemstone Press, 1999.

Miller, Anna M. *Gems and Jewelry Appraising.* New York: Van Nostrand Reinhold Company, 1988.

Miller, Anna. *Buyer's Guide to Affordable Antique Jewelry.* New York: Carol Publishing Group, 1993.

Morton, Philip. *Contemporary Jewelry*. New York: Holt, Rinehart, and Winston, 1976.

Nassau, Kurt. *Gems Made by Man*. Santa Monica, CA. Gemological Institute of America, 1980.

Nassau, Kurt. *Gemstone Enhancement*, Second Edition. London: Butterworths, 1994.

O'Donoghue & Joyner Louise. *Identification of Gemstones*. London, Butterworth Heinemann, 2003.

O'Donoghue, Michael. *Identifying Man-Made Gems*. London, NAG Press, 1983.

O'Donoghue, Michael. *Synthetic, Imitation & Treated Gemstones*. Oxford: Butterworth-Heinemann, 1997.

Pinton, Diego. *Jewellery Technology*. Milan: Edizioni Gold Sri, 1999.

Preston, William S. *Guides for the Jewelry Industry*. New York: Jewelers Vigilance Committee, Inc., 1986.

Romero, Christie. *Warman's Jewelry: 3rd Edition*. Iola, WI: Krause Publications, 2002.

Schumann, Walter. *Gemstones of the World:* Revised & Expanded Edition. New York: Sterling 1997.

Sprintzen, Alice. *Jewelry: Basic Techniques and Design*. Radnor, PA: Chilton, 1980

SSEF Swiss Gemmological Institute. *Standards & Applications for Diamond Report,, Gemstone Report, Test Report.*.Basel: SSEF Swiss Gemmological Institute, 1998.

Suwa, Yasukazu. *Gemstones: Quality and Value* (English Edition). Santa Monica, CA: Gemological Institute of America & Suwa & Son, 1994.

Suwa, Yasukazu. *Gemstones: Quality and Value Volume 2*. Tokyo: Sekai Bunka-sha, 1998.

Wise, Richard. *Secrets of the Gem Trade*. Lenox: Brunswick House Press. 2003.

Wykoff, Gerald L. *Beyond the Glitter*. Washington DC: Adamas, 1982.

Periodicals & Miscellaneous

Auction Market Resource for Gems & Jewelry. P. O. Box 7683, Rego Park, NY 11374.

Australian Gemmologist. Brisbane: Gemmological Association of Australia.

Canadian Gemmologist. North York, Ontario: Canadian Gemmological Assn.

Canadian Jeweller. Toroto: Canadian Jeweller.

Changing the Color of Diamonds: The High Pressure High Temperature Process Explained by Branko Deljanin & Gregory Sherman. New York: EGL USA, 2000.

Gems and Gemology. Carlsbad, CA: Gemological Institute of America.

Gems & Jewellry. London. Gemmological Association of Great Britain.

The Guide. Northbrook, IL: Gemworld International Inc. 1999 & 2000.

IDEX. Ramat Gan, Israel: Idex Online. S.A.

Instore Magazine. New York: Instore Magazin.

Jewelers Circular Keystone. New York: Reed Business Information.

Jewelry News Asia. Hong Kong, CMP Asia Ltd.

JQ Magazine. San Francisco, CA. JQ Publishing.

Journal of Gemmology, London: Gemological Association and Gem Testing Laboratory of Great Britain.

Lapidary Journal Jewelry Artist. Loveland, CO: Interweave Press.

Modern Jeweler. Melville, NY:Cygnus Publishing Inc.

National Jeweler. New York: Nielsen Business Media.

New York Diamonds. New York: International Diamond Publications, Ltd.

Palmieri's Market Monitor. New York: Gem Certification & Assurance Lab, Inc.

Professional Jeweler. Philadelphia: Bond Communications.

Rapaport Diamond Report. Las Vegas: Rapaport USA Inc.

Southern Jewelry News. Greensboro, N.C: Southern Jewelry News.

Techniques of Identification by Sharrie Woodring and Branko Deljanin, Egl USA 2004Group

Index

Other Books by RENÉE NEWMAN

Graduate Gemologist (GIA)

Ruby, Sapphire & Emerald Buying Guide

How to Identify, Evaluate & Select these Gems

An advanced, full-color guide to identifying and evaluating rubies, sapphires and emeralds including information on treatments, grading systems, geographic sources, lab reports, appraisals, and gem care. This 3rd edition has 173 new photos and two new chapters on geographic sources and appraisals versus lab reports. It updates gem professionals on recent treatments, jewelry styles, grading systems and geographic sources of rubies, sapphires and emeralds. Tips on detecting imitations and synthetic stones are also presented.

"**Enjoyable reading . . . profusely illustrated with color photographs** showing not only the beauty of finished jewelry but close-ups and magnification of details such as finish, flaws and fakes . . . Sophisticated enough for professionals to use . . . highly recommended . . . **Newman's guides are the ones to take along when shopping**."
Library Journal

"**Solid, informative and comprehensive** . . . dissects each aspect of ruby and sapphire value in detail . . . a wealth of grading information . . . a definite thumbs-up!"
C. R. Beesley, President, American Gemological Laboratories, *JCK Magazine*

"**A useful resource for both the experienced gemologist as well as the serious collector** . . . The book simplifies terms and explains concepts like cut, color treatments and lab reports clearly. The photographs, particularly in the sections of judging color, treatments, and clarity, are clear and true to life. All of the charts are clear and easily found and the book is well organized for quick reference. It is a handy, well organized and factually correct compilation of information with photographs that one will find themselves referencing on a regular basis."
Kindra Lovejoy, GG, *The Jewelry Appraiser*

"**The best produced book on gemstones I have yet seen in this price range** (how is it done?). This is the book for anyone who buys, sells or studies gemstones. This style of book (and similar ones by the same author) is the only one I know which introduces actual trade conditions and successfully combines a good deal of gemmology with them . . . **Buy it, read it, keep it**."
Michael O'Donoghue, *Journal of Gemmology*

187 pages, 280 photos, 267 in color, 6" by 9", US$19.95, ISBN 978-0929975412

Available at major bookstores and jewelry supply stores

For more information, see **www.reneenewman.com**

Other Books by RENÉE NEWMAN

Graduate Gemologist (GIA)

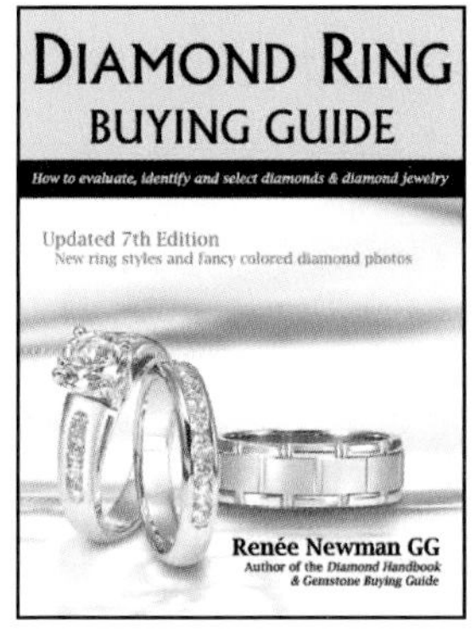

Diamond Ring Buying Guide

How to Evaluate, Identify and Select Diamonds & Diamond Jewelry

"**An entire course on judging diamonds in 156 pages of well-organized information**. The photos are excellent . . . Clear and concise, it serves as a check-list for the purchase and mounting of a diamond . . . another fine update in a series of books that are useful to both the jewelry industry and consumers." *Gems & Gemology*

"**A wealth of information** . . . delves into the intricacies of shape, carat weight, color, clarity, setting style, and cut—happily avoiding all industry jargon and keeping explanations streamlined enough so even the first-time diamond buyer can confidently choose a gem." *Booklist*

"Succinctly written in a step-by-step, outlined format with plenty of photographs to illustrate the salient points; it could help keep a lot of people out of trouble. Essentially, it is a **fact-filled text devoid of a lot of technical mumbo-jumbo.** This is a definite thumbs up!"

C. R. Beesley, President, American Gemological Laboratories

156 pages, 274 color & b/w photos, 7" X 9", ISBN 978-0-929975-40-5, US$18.95

Gem & Jewelry Pocket Guide

Small enough to use while shopping locally or abroad

"**Brilliantly planned, painstakingly researched, and beautifully produced** . . . this handy little book comes closer to covering all of the important bases than any similar guides have managed to do. From good descriptions of the most popular gem materials (plus gold and platinum), to jewelry craftsmanship, treatments, gem sources, appraisals, documentation, and even information about U.S. customs for foreign travelers—it is all here. I heartily endorse this wonderful pocket guide."

John S. White, former Curator of Gems & Minerals at the Smithsonian
Lapidary Journal

"**Short guides don't come better than this**. . . . As always with this author, the presentation is immaculate and each opening displays high-class pictures of gemstones and jewellery." *Journal of Gemmology*

156 pages, 108 color photos, 4½" by 7", ISBN 978-0929975-30-6, US$11.95

Available at major bookstores and jewelry supply stores

For more information, see **www.reneenewman.com**

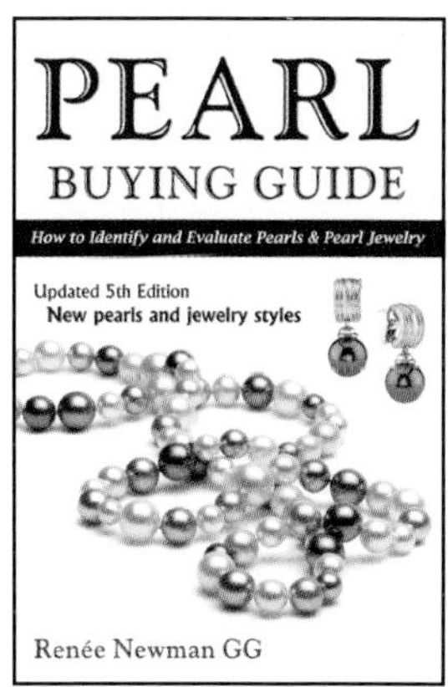

Pearl Buying Guide

How to Evaluate, Identify, Select and Care for Pearls & Pearl Jewelry

"**Copious color photographs** . . . explains how to appraise and distinguish among all varieties of pearls . . . takes potential buyers and collectors through the ins and outs of the pearl world." *Publisher's Weekly*

"**An indispensable guide** to judging [pearl] characteristics, distinguishing genuine from imitation, and making wise choices . . . useful to all types of readers, from the professional jeweler to the average patron . . . **highly recommended.**" *Library Journal*

"A **well written, beautifully illustrated** book designed to help retail customers, jewelry designers, and store buyers make informed buying decisions about the various types of pearls and pearl jewelry. The photos are abundant and well chosen, and the use of a coated stock contributes to the exceptional quality of the reproduction. Consumers also will find this book a source of accurate and easy-to-understand information about a topic that has become increasingly complex."
Gems & Gemology

154 pages, 302 color photos, 6" by 9", ISBN 978-0929975-44-3, US$19.95

Jewelry Handbook

How to Select, Wear & Care for Jewelry

The *Jewelry Handbook* is like a Jewelry 101 course on the fundamentals of jewelry metals, settings, finishes, necklaces, chains, clasps, bracelets, rings, earrings, brooches, pins, clips, manufacturing methods and jewelry selection and care. It outlines the benefits and drawbacks of the various setting styles, mountings, chains, and metals such as gold, silver, platinum, palladium, titanium, stainless steel and tungsten. It also provides information and color photos on gemstones, birthstones, and fineness marks and helps you select versatile, durable jewelry that flatters your features.

"**A great introduction to jewellery** and should be required reading for all in the industry." Dr. Jack Ogden, CEO Gem-A (British Gemmological Association)

"**A user-friendly, beautifully illustrated guide,** allowing for quick reference to specific topics." *The Jewelry Appraiser*

"**Valuable advice for consumers and the trade**, specifically those in retail sales and perhaps even more for jewelry appraisers . . . An easy read and easy to find valuable lists and details." Richard Drucker GG, *Gem Market News*

177 pages, 297 color & 47 b/w photos, 6" x 9", ISBN 978-0-929975-38-2, $19.95 US

Other Books by RENÉE NEWMAN

Exotic Gems Volume 1

This is the first in a series of books that will explore the history, lore, evaluation, geographic sources, and identifying properties of lesser-known gems. *Exotic Gems, Volume 1* has 288 color photos of mounted and loose tanzanite, ammolite, zultanite, rhodochrosite, sunstone, moonstone, labradorite, spectrolite, andesine, amazonite, bytownite, orthoclase and oligoclase. Some of the pictures are close-up shots that show how to make visual judgments about clarity, transparency, color, cut quality and brilliance. A few pictures show how the gems are cut and many others show creative jewelry designs with these stones. *Exotic Gems* also provides tips on caring for the gems, selecting an appraiser and detecting imitations and gem treatments. The healing and metaphysical properties of the gems are also addressed. Written for both consumers and professionals, it's easy to read, well-organized, and packed with fascinating information and photos. If you're interested in colored gemstones, you'll find *Exotic Gems* to be a valuable resource that will help you discover and buy unusual gem varieties you may never have seen before.

154 pages, 288 color photos, 6" x 9", ISBN 978-0-929975-42-9, $19.95

Gemstone Buying Guide

How to Evaluate, Identify and Select
Colored Gems

"Praiseworthy, **a beautiful gem-pictorial reference** and a help to everyone in viewing colored stones as a gemologist or gem dealer would. . . . One of the finest collections of gem photographs I've ever seen . . . If you see the book, you will probably purchase it on the spot."

Anglic Gemcutter

"**A quality Buying Guide** that is recommended for purchase to consumers, gemmologists and students of gemmology—irrespective of their standard of knowledge of gemmology. The information is comprehensive, factual, and well presented. Particularly noteworthy in this book are the quality colour photographs that have been carefully chosen to illustrate the text."

Australian Gemmologist

"**Beautifully produced**. . . . With colour on almost every opening few could resist this book whether or not they were in the gem and jewellery trade."

Journal of Gemmology

156 pages, 281 color photos, 7" X 9", ISBN 978-0929975-34-4, US$19.95

Available at major bookstores and jewelry supply stores
For more information, see **www.reneenewman.com**

Osteoporosis Prevention

" . . . **a complete, practical, and easy-to-read reference for osteoporosis prevention** . . . As the founding president of the Taiwan Osteoporosis Association, I am delighted to recommend this book to you."

Dr. Ko-En Huang, Founding President of TOA

"The author, Renée Newman has abundant experience in translating technical terms into everyday English. She writes this book about osteoporosis prevention from a patient's perspective. These two elements contribute to **an easy-to-read and understandable book for the public. To the medical professions, this is also a very valuable reference**."

Dr. Chyi-Her Lin, Dean of Medical College, Natl Cheng Kung Univ / Taiwan

"I was impressed with the comprehensive nature of *Osteoporosis Prevention* and its use of scientific sources . . . .The fact that the author has struggled with bone loss and can talk from personal experience makes the book more interesting and easy to read. Another good feature is that the book has informative illustrations and tables, which help clarify important points. I congratulate the author for writing **a sound and thorough guide to osteoporosis prevention**."

Ronald Lawrence, MD, PhD
Co-chair of the first Symposium on Osteoporosis of the National Institute on Aging

". . . **clarifies the inaccurate concepts from the Internet**. It contains abundant information and really deserves my recommendation."

Dr. Yung-Kuei Soong, The 6th President of Taiwanese Osteoporosis Association

"The book is written from a patient's experience and her secrets to bone care. This book is **so interesting that I finished reading it the following day** . . . The author translates all the technical terms into everyday English which makes this book so easy to read and understand."

Dr. Sheng-Mou Hou, Ex-minister, Dept. of Health / Taiwan

"**A competent and thoroughly 'reader friendly' approach to preventing osteoporosis**. Inclusive of information on how to: help prevent osteoporosis and broken bones; get enough calcium and other bone nutrients from food; make exercise safe and fun; retain a youthful posture; select a bone density center; get maximum benefit from your bone density exam; understand bone density reports; help seniors maintain their muscles and their bones; and how to be a savvy patient. *Osteoporosis Prevention* should be a part of every community health center and public library Health & Medicine reference collection . . ."

Midwest Book Review

"With great interest, I have read Renée Newman's *Osteoporosis Prevention* which provides complete and practical information about osteoporosis from a patient's perspective. . . . **a must-read reference for osteoporosis prevention**."

Dr. Tzay-Shing Yang, 3rd President of TOA, President of Taiwan Menopause Care Society

You can get free information about osteoporosis prevention, bone density testing and reports at: **www.avoidboneloss.com**

176 pages, 6" X 9", US $15.95, ISBN 978-0929975-37-5

Order Form

TITLE	Price Each	Quantity	Total
Diamond Handbook	$19.95		
Ruby, Sapphire & Emerald Buying Guide	$19.95		
Exotic Gems, Volume I	$19.95		
Gemstone Buying Guide	$19.95		
Pearl Buying Guide	$19.95		
Jewelry Handbook	$19.95		
Diamond Ring Buying Guide	$18.95		
Gem & Jewelry Pocket Guide	$11.95		
Osteoporosis Prevention	$15.95		
Book Total			
SALES TAX for California residents only **(book total x $.0825)**			
SHIPPING: USA: first book $3.50, each additional copy $2.00 Canada & Mexico - airmail: first book $12.00, ea. addl. $5.00 All other foreign countries - airmail: first book $14.50, ea. addl. $7.00			
TOTAL AMOUNT with tax (if applicable) and shipping (Pay foreign orders with an international money order or a check drawn on a U.S. bank.) **TOTAL**			

Available at major book stores or by mail.

Mail check or money order in U.S. funds

To: International Jewelry Publications
P.O. Box 13384
Los Angeles, CA 90013-0384 USA

Ship to:

Name______________________________

Address______________________________

City________________ State or Province________________

Postal or Zip Code__________ Country ________________